Monterey

Omega

ECLAT

THE RED ARROWS

THIRTY YEARS OF BRILLIANCE

All nett proceeds from sales being donated by The Red Arrows Trustees Ltd to The Red Arrows Trust

Published by:
ECLAT INITIATIVES LTD
4a High Street, Acton, London W3 6LJ
tel 0181 896 1470/fax 0181 896 1469

Publisher:
SONIA SEYMOUR-WILLIAMS

Initial Concept:
Squadron Leader Adrian Thurley, Rtd

Editor:
MICHAEL BONELLO
Art Editor:
RICHARD J. CARUANA

Editorial Contributors:
Michael Bonello, Richard J. Caruana, Tim Laming
Additional Contributors:
British Aerospace Defence Ltd, Leslie Coombs, Duncan Simpson, Albert Whitehouse

Project Liaison Director:
Richard Verden
Publishing Consultant:
Brian Rollason
Commercial Director:
Peter Walker LLB (Lond), FFA, MISM
Administration/Research Manager:
Jacqui Young
Marketing:
John Williams, Bertie 'Haggis' Chase

Origination, Print & Product Management:
CARRPRINT Ltd
Coates Mill, Skipton Rd, Barnoldswick, Colne, Lancs BB8 6EN

Origination; from Editors disk, pages created on Apple Macintosh® in Quark XPress®. Images scanned on an Optronics Colorgetter Pro II drum scanner and colour correction/manipulation achieved within Photoshop. Pages imposed in Farrukh Imposition Publisher. Films output on an Optronics 4000XL imagesetter. Colour proofs produced on a Cromalin Eurosprint.

Print & Binding; across four Roland 6043B's with RCI. Thread sewn and covers drawn on Muller Martini bindery equipment.

Paper: R.A. Brands & Co. Ltd,
Swift Valley, Rugby CV21 1QN

Printed on Royal Impression Brilliant - a paper made with Elemental Chlorine Free pulp and from sustainable forests. Environmentally assessed as an ECO-CHECK 4 STAR product.

Front cover photograph courtesy of Albert Whitehouse, British Aerospace, taken over Aberystwyth.

ISBN 09523912 01 Softback
ISBN 09523912 1X Hardback Limited Edition

CLARENCE HOUSE
S.W. 1

As Commandant-in-Chief of the Central Flying School I have taken a particular interest in the achievements of the Red Arrows since their formation in 1965.

In this their 30th Anniversary Season I send them my warmest congratulations in recognition of the superb standard of excellence they have maintained throughout the years.

Elizabeth R

THE BEST DEMAND

THE BEST.
BRITISH AEROSPACE
DEFENCE
WORLD FORCE
BRITISH AEROSPACE DEFENCE LIMITED
PO BOX 87, FARNBOROUGH AEROSPACE CENTRE,
FARNBOROUGH, HANTS GU14 6YU.
TELEPHONE + 0252 373232 FAX + 0252 38 4801.

AIR CHIEF MARSHAL SIR MICHAEL GRAYDON GCB CBE ADC FRAeS RAF

MINISTRY OF DEFENCE
MAIN BUILDING WHITEHALL LONDON SW1A 2HB

Telephone 071-21-86313/86314

CHIEF OF THE AIR STAFF

ROYAL AIR FORCE AEROBATIC TEAM

THE 30TH ANNIVERSARY SEASON

From the public debut at the Biggin Hill Air Fair in May 1965, flying the Folland Gnat, to today's nine British Aerospace Hawks, the pilots of the Royal Air Force Aerobatic Team, the Red Arrows, have set the standards for precision and excellence in formation display flying. The Team has thrilled Air Show crowds around the World at venues as far apart as North America, the former Soviet Union, the Middle and Far East, and in doing so has demonstrated publicly the skill and professionalism which are the hallmarks of the Royal Air Force. This book pays tribute to the pilots, groundcrew and support personnel who over the past 30 years have developed and sustained the reputation of the Red Arrows as the World's foremost Aerobatic Team.

Michael Graydon

Air Chief Marshal Sir Michael Graydon
Chief of the Air Staff

CASw.3064

A formation of 16 Hawks representing the 14 countries which have the aircraft in service was the main attraction at Farnborough International, 1994. The aircraft consisted of 14 Hawks from RAF Valley in a new all-black colour scheme, flown by RAF Instructors, and two of the latest Hawk versions – the 100 and 200 – flown by British Aerospace pilots John Turner and Phil Dye.

The order of the formation reflects the chronological order of the contract signatures. A total of more than 700 Hawks are on order or have been delivered establishing it as the best aircraft in its class. Already 40 Hawks 100 are on order for four customers and the single-seat Hawk 200 has also attracted orders from three customers for 40 aircraft.

1 United Kingdom
2 Finland
3 Kenya
4 Indonesia
5 Zimbabwe
6 Dubai
7 Abu Dhabi
8 Kuwait
9 USA (T-45 Goshawk)
10 Saudi Arabia
11 Switzerland
12 South Korea
13 Oman
14 Malaysia
15 United Kingdom
16 United Kingdom

BRITISH AEROSPACE

BRITISH AEROSPACE
PUBLIC LIMITED COMPANY
Warwick House
P.O. Box 87
Farnborough Aerospace Centre
Farnborough
Hants GU14 6YU
Telephone: (0252) 373232
Facsimile: (0252) 383000
Telex: 859598 BAEFBR G

From: OFFICE OF THE CHIEF EXECUTIVE

Direct Line: (0252) 383944
Facsimile: (0252) 383971

I am very pleased to have been invited to participate on behalf of British Aerospace in this tribute to the Royal Air Force aerobatic display team, the Red Arrows.

Whether military or civil, aerobatic display teams around the world receive the admiration of large crowds who flock to air shows where they can see at first hand the disciplined formation flying of dedicated and highly skilled pilots.

Aside from the public visual presentation of the team, the Red Arrows provides Great Britain with another service, namely living proof that the Royal Air Force produces the finest pilots in the world and operates with the finest trainer aircraft, the British Aerospace Hawk. The Hawk has earned considerable respect as a reliable and rugged aircraft, with its extensive flight envelope enabling the Red Arrows to utilise its capabilities to the maximum while enthralling the crowds. More importantly for British industry, the team have become ambassadors for the United Kingdom's sales export drive. We believe that sales of the Hawk around the world have escalated because of the exceptional flying displays by the 'Arrows'.

On behalf of British Aerospace and the thousands of employees in the UK industry whose dedication has made the Hawk the success it is today, I wish the Red Arrows the brightest of futures.

Dick Evans
Chief Executive
British Aerospace plc

Patron: Her Majesty The Queen
Grand Master: H.R.H. The Prince Philip, Duke of Edinburgh, K.G., K.T.

The Guild of Air Pilots and Air Navigators

(a Livery Company of the City of London)

Cobham House
291 Gray's Inn Road, WC1X 8QF
Telephone: 071-837 3323
Fax No: 071-833 3190

I am honoured, as Master of the Guild of Air Pilots and Air Navigators of the City of London, to be invited to write the Preface for this commemorative book. There is no doubt that The Red Arrows are the leading Formation Aerobatic Team in the world and we have several ex-Red Arrow pilots as members of our Company.

In the early years there were many individual aerobatic teams but The Red Arrows are now the one and only official Team for The Royal Air Force.

Over the last 30 years they have established a worldwide reputation for precision and excellence in flying, so much so that they have been adopted by the UK public as their proud symbol of High British Standards and, moreover, the many smaller airforces around the world use The Red Arrows as a benchmark for brilliance in performance.

All these things together give The Red Arrows a unique Ambassadorial role which we hope will continue for many years to come.

Long may The Red Arrows continue to delight us all.

Christopher Hodgkinson

Captain Christopher L Hodgkinson
MASTER
THE GUILD OF AIR PILOTS AND AIR NAVIGATORS

Correspondence to: The Clerk, Group Captain J. W. Tritton, A.F.C., F.B.I.M.
VAT Registration Number: 480 8093 33

ARTHUR GIBSON

CONTENTS

PERSONAL MESSAGE
From: Air Commodore P.M. STEAN,
Air Officer Commanding Air Cadets
and Commandant Air Training Corps

THE AIR TRAINING CORPS is a national voluntary youth organisation with some 46,000 young men and women who dream of reaching the heights of excellence that the Royal Air Force Aerobatic Team exemplify. The Corps encourages its cadets to take flight — to realise their own potential, to accept and even welcome challenge and always to aspire to the stars.

We, in the Corps, are particularly proud to be associated with this marvellous book and to have the honour of distributing it to as wide an audience as possible. For three decades, cadets have been inspired by the professionalism, skill and breathtaking artistry of the Red Arrows. Many, fired by that brilliant image, have gone on to seek a career in the Royal Air Force — some even to eventually join that elite team — indeed, this year eight out of the nine pilots are former cadets.

The Air Training Corps salutes the Red Arrows in this their 30th year and wishes them much success in the future. Long may they serve as the inspiration to all, and long may the ATC encourage those young men and women to reach for the stars.

RICK BREWELL

ACKNOWLEDGEMENTS

In appreciation of the invaluable support received in the production of this book, the Publisher thanks the many companies and individuals who have made this tribute possible.

In particular, our special thanks to Eric Ward for his inestimable assistance and guidance. To Air Commodores Simon Bostock, Commandant of the Central Flying School and his predecessor Gordon MacRobbie, Director of Public Relations, RAF, for their support. Also, particular thanks to Wing Commanders Royal Air Force Aerobatic Team, Terry Yarrow and his predecessor David Hamilton. Likewise, Warrant Officer John Howard, adjutant to the team.

To British Aerospace for their cooperation, guidance and support and particularly to Barry Woods-Turner who so well coordinated our joint efforts. To those who gave their precious time and efforts in many ways, David Bainbridge, David Boyce, Eira Gibson, John Oaten, Duncan Simpson, Michael Stroud, Albert Whitehouse, Air Vice-Marshal H. Bird-Wilson, John Williams, Rick Brewell, Bill Hunt, Stephen Evans, Joe Grima, Anthony Calleja, Nick Dumphy, Pat Shott, Brian Rollason and last, but most certainly not least, Richard Verden.

To our editor Michael Bonello for his perseverence and dedication, Carrprint for controlling and coordinating the print and production, and Brands Paper for their help.

Sonia Seymour-Williams

This sculpture in a bronze finish on a marble stand showing the Synchro Pair with, symbolically on the underside of the wings, outlines of the other variety of Hawk — the bird in flight — is by Anthony Calleja. It was presented to the Red Arrows on the occasion of their thirtieth anniversary by Mr Joe Grima, Head of the School for Arts and Crafts, Targa Gap, Mosta, Malta and Sonia Seymour-Williams, Managing Director of Eclat Initiatives Ltd

Headquarters Central Flying School
Royal Air Force
Scampton
Lincolnshire
LN1 2TR

Tel: Lincoln (0522) 730421 Ext 7375
GPTN: 95781 Ext 7375
Fax Ext 7561

CFS/2661/RAFAT

INTRODUCTION BY COMMANDANT CENTRAL FLYING SCHOOL
AIR COMMODORE S N BOSTOCK MSc FIMgt RAF

It was with great delight that, as Commandant of the Central Flying school, I accepted the task of introducing this biography of the Red Arrows. The book has been produced to commemorate the Team's thirtieth anniversary, but it does not merely celebrate three decades of Red Arrows existence. Throughout those thirty years the pilots and groundcrew of the Team have been called upon to demonstrate a standard of excellence to which all branches and trades within the Royal Air Force aspire. Their performance has been constantly in the public eye, and the Red Arrows have thus been the 'shop window' of the Royal Air Force. Moreover, during their many displays abroad, they have been ambassadors, both for their Service and for the United Kingdom. Their consistent exhibition of the highest professionalism, in keeping with their motto ('Eclat' meaning brilliance), has captivated foreign audiences, and the benefit to both the Royal Air force and the United Kingdom has been incalculable. Thus this book celebrates far more than the Team's history, and it is fitting, therefore, that the Red Arrows' thirtieth birthday be celebrated by all who appreciate and aspire to excellence.

In addition to my responsibility for the Red Arrows, I am also the Chairman of the Red Arrows Trust, and I am delighted that the profits from this book will go to the Trust for onward distribution to our many deserving causes. I am also gratified that the Air Training Corps and RAF sections of the Combined Cadet Force will be playing an active part in the book's distribution. These organizations encourage in young people an interest in aviation and a knowledge of the Royal Air Force which they take into adult life. Many become loyal supporters and some join our ranks; indeed, the majority of the present day Red Arrows trained with either the Air Training Corps or Combined Cadet Force.

A quick glance at the list of organizations who have supported the production of this book will indicate the extent of the financial and practical support that has made its publication possible. Without this backing, we could not have achieved such high quality and excellent value. To these supporters I offer heartfelt thanks on behalf of the Red Arrows and the Red Arrows Trust. I must also mention Sonia Seymour-Williams who has dedicated so much of her time in producing the book; I feel sure you will agree with me that her efforts have been richly rewarded. Finally, and most important, I am indebted to Her Majesty Queen Elizabeth The Queen Mother, Commandant-in-Chief of the Central Flying School. Her keen interest and support have been unstinting over many years, and Her Majesty has graciously supported this publication through her foreword which precedes my own.

I am sure that this biography will provide fascinating reading for all those who have even the faintest interest in formation aerobatic flying or military aviation. It is also a unique reference document on the Team since its birth. I commend it to you. Good reading!

Simon Bostock
Air Commodore
Commandant, Central Flying School

BREITLING
1884
OLD NAVITIMER II
Development of the flyers' chronograph launched in 1952: it is now water-resistant to 30 metres. Its slide rule, a real computer allowing flight preparation, also enables the conversion of currencies, miles to km, etc. Great legibility, during both night and day. Selfwinding mechanical movement. With leather strap or Pilot metal bracelet.
INSTRUMENTS FOR PROFESSIONALS
BREITLING CONGRATULATE THE RED ARROWS ON 30 YEARS OF PERFECT TIMING.
AVAILABLE FROM SELECTED JEWELLERS THROUGHOUT GREAT BRITAIN AND IRELAND.
FOR YOUR NEAREST STOCKIST TELEPHONE 071 637 5167.

ARTHUR GIBSON

Chapter One: ECLAT – BRILLIANCE IN TEAMWORK

ARTHUR GIBSON

The Sky is a pale iridescent blue,
The crowd is hushed as if they knew
They would soon see beauty they'd never forget
Nine flashes of red and the scream of the jet —
Then the smoky plumes fanning across the sky,
A man-made rainbow which fades like a sigh
As the pilots come back in a diamond shape,
Climbing upwards in attempted escape
From this earthbound mundane ground.
But swiftly the pattern has just unwound,
To planes dividing arrowshaped without sound,
Until they loop and become a scarlet swan
Which gracefully rolls and soars up and on,
But descends in spiralling ribbons of death —
Scarlet planes, pastel smoke, whilst we hold our breath
Until they stretch towards the horizon
Taking the rising ribbons we keep our eyes on
Until sight and sound of these we lack.
Then from all directions the nine shriek back
And climb westwards into an arrowhead,
Returning delta-shaped dissolving into a diving hand
Whose fingers circle before they gently land.

And the crowd is left quiet with all fantasy fled.

Mary Lawrence, 1968 — From the Squadron Album

The cold, icy winds which sweep across the Lincolnshire plains in December are not for the weak in spirit; but the sudden sight of bright, scarlet-painted aircraft beautifully manoeuvring around the sky quickly brings back warmth to anyone's heart. This is Red Arrows country, a piece of English sky where the team works up between one display season and another. It is here, far away from the display circuit, that one can really get to know the Royal Air Force's Aerobatic Team (RAFAT) and its members, as they really are.

R. J. CARUANA

RAF Scampton, where the team is stationed as part of the Central Flying School (CFS), is about 4 to 5 miles from Lincoln. As a base it looks just like any other RAF station and the Red Arrows operate as a normal RAF squadron with the exception that they attract more visitors than usual. Scampton, however, is a legend in the annals of RAF history, the portraits in the Officers' Mess Hall providing ample testimony. These include one of Her Majesty Queen Elizabeth, the Queen Mother, who in her role of Commandant-in-Chief of the Central Flying School is also that of the Red Arrows. Another important portrait is that of Guy Gibson; Wing Commander GD Gibson, VC, DSO, DFC was the legendary Leader of 617 Squadron, famous for the 'Dam Busters' raid at Mohne and Eder on the night of 16/17 May, 1943. In one of the Ante-Rooms there are paintings of immortal aircraft such as the Hampden, Wellington, Valiant and Vulcan, all residents of Scampton during their active careers.

Home of the Reds

The 'Reds' have a special administration building attached to Hangar 4 on the eastern side of the airfield. Just outside their main door, as a gate guardian, is a superbly preserved Folland Gnat, the aircraft which the team flew for the first 15 years of its existence. The ground floor of the building is reserved for the maintenance crews' offices while pilots and administration are on the first floor.

R. J. CARUANA

Also through the ground floor one can enter the hangar where major servicing is carried out during winter . Three at a time, the Hawks are stripped down and checked thoroughly for anything that might need replacing. Engines, ejector seats, rudders, electronic gear and canopies are strewn around the hangar floor — it looks very much like a full-scale construction kit just coming out of its box! All the other aircraft are stored in this hangar when not flying; they are towed out every morning to the flight-line, and back inside under cover at the end of the day's flying. Due to this servicing the team is at times three aircraft short and replacement Hawks are drawn from Flight Training Schools (FTS) squadrons. During this period these air-

Above: The portraits of HM Queen Elizabeth, the Queen Mother, Commandant-in-Chief of the Central Flying School and Guy Gibson in the Scampton Officers' Mess foyer
Right: The preserved Gnat at RAF Scampton

R. J. CARUANA

craft retain their training colour scheme although simulations of the team and CFS crests are carried in the correct positions, as these form reference alignment points during formation flying.

On the first floor one finds the Red Arrows proper, starting from the briefing room, the pilots' coffee bar, the 'Quiet Room' (where pilots spend time at their paperwork), offices for the Manager, Leader, Squadron Adjutant, Community Relations Officer (CRO) and a Conference Room. Very noticeable is the way duty is handled; the Red Arrows are very much another RAF Squadron, and they function as such.

Training and Performance

Traditional awareness of British Armed Forces has always been an important aspect of life even in the RAF, the most junior of the three services. Since its inception, the RAF has always optimised the use of its resources, in both material and human forms. Pilot and aircraft potential had to be utilised to the full as reflected in the way man and machine were integrated through decades of experience, in times of war and peace. This has helped in the development of a prowess in aerobatic and formation flying that brings out the best in pilot skills and operational values.

The Central Flying School was founded on May 12, 1912 at Upavon, on Salisbury Plain, and today it is the oldest military flying establishment in the world. Its main role was identified as that of providing the RAF with Qualified Flying Instructors (QFI). Here, too, scientific methods of training were pursued in parallel with advances in the design and performance of military aircraft.

In 1917 a School of Special Flying (SSF) had been formed at Gosport, outside the aegis of the CFS. Under the direction of Col Robert R. Smith-Barry, a graduate of the first CFS course of 1912, the SSF evolved a new system of flying instruction using dual control aircraft. Thanks largely to Smith-Barry's initiative, the School departed from the then prevailing norms by which pilots were restricted in reaching their full potential due to prevailing limitations in instructional techniques. Some such limitations barred pilots from undertaking certain aerobatic manoeuvres, but fliers at the SSF were taught how to get out of dangerous situations successfully.

Probably no other single factor contributed in this pursuit of aerobatic flying excellence as did the Hendon displays between the two World Wars. This excellence was also the fruit of extensive organisation by the CFS – however polished performances were not intended solely as a means of crowd entertainment. Such training, leading to these public displays, instilled a firm sense of flying discipline, and one which pilots performed with great pride.

With the Second World War looming on the horizon there also came a change in the organisation of training establishments. In 1946 the CFS was reformed at Little Rissington, reverting to its former function as the sole establishment turning out flying instructors. During the war years giant steps had been achieved in aeroplane design and performance — from the Gladiator biplane with which some squadrons were still equipped at the beginning of the war the RAF was now converting most of its fighter squadrons to the first operational British jet, the Gloster Meteor. The CFS rose to the occasion and continued where it had left off in 1938, regaining its unsurpassed reputation for training.

Reviving Display Skills

Ministry of Defence

It was Fighter Command, however, which presented to the post-war public the first RAF jet aerobatic team in 1947, when the Odiham Fighter Wing flew air displays with six de Havilland Vampires, aptly named, if unofficially, The Vampires. Other Vampire teams followed, from N° 54 Squadron in 1948 and N° 1 and 72 squadrons in 1950. Also in 1950, N° 600 Squadron put into the air the first Gloster Meteor team, N° 64 following suit in 1952. The CFS may not have been the forerunner of jet display teams, but it was the first to have one with an official name — The Meteorites — equipped with four Meteors T.7. Formed in 1950, it revived the CFS's pre-war speciality of the leader flying inverted in most of the manoeuvres.

The introduction of the Hawker Hunter into Fighter Command brought about a new, exciting flavour in jet-aircraft display flying. The Hunter F.1 soon proved to be an ideal aerobatic aircraft, debuting in the display circuit when N° 54 Squadron formed a four-ship team in 1955. It was named The Black Knights a year later when the pilots started wearing black flying suits. In 1956 N° 43 performed as The Fighting Cocks while that same year N° 111 flew displays with an unnamed four-aircraft team.

It now became the practice to select each year an operational squadron from within the RAF as its official aerobatic team. In 1957 N° 111's Black Arrows (photo above) were to prove a very fortunate choice. This team left its mark with its stunning – and still unbeaten – 22-aircraft loop at the 1958 SBAC Show at Farnborough. Painted gloss black overall, the Hunters F.6 and T.7 of the Black Arrows epitomised RAF precision formation flying, such as had not been witnessed since the biplane era. However, this time the Hunters were flying at about four times the speed of their predecessors! It was also the first team to wear a special display colour scheme – black overall – remaining the official RAF representative until the squadron re-equipped with Lightnings F.1 at the beginning of 1961.

Meanwhile the CFS's aerobatic teams were eclipsed by the Hunter's dazzling popularity. For the 1957 season Flt Lt J.H. Kingsbury led a four-ship formation of scarcely exciting piston-engined Percival Provosts named The Sparrows. The following year the team re-equipped with more presentable aircraft, the jet-engined Jet Provost T.1, and passed under the leadership of Flt Lt N.H. Griffin. In 1959 a two-aircraft formation displayed under the name of The Redskins. Both teams, however, retained the normal training aircraft scheme of the day. The Jet Provost proved to be a good aerobatic aircraft and the availability of the T.3 in 1960 enabled The Pelicans to be formed with four aircraft and to provide a creditable display.

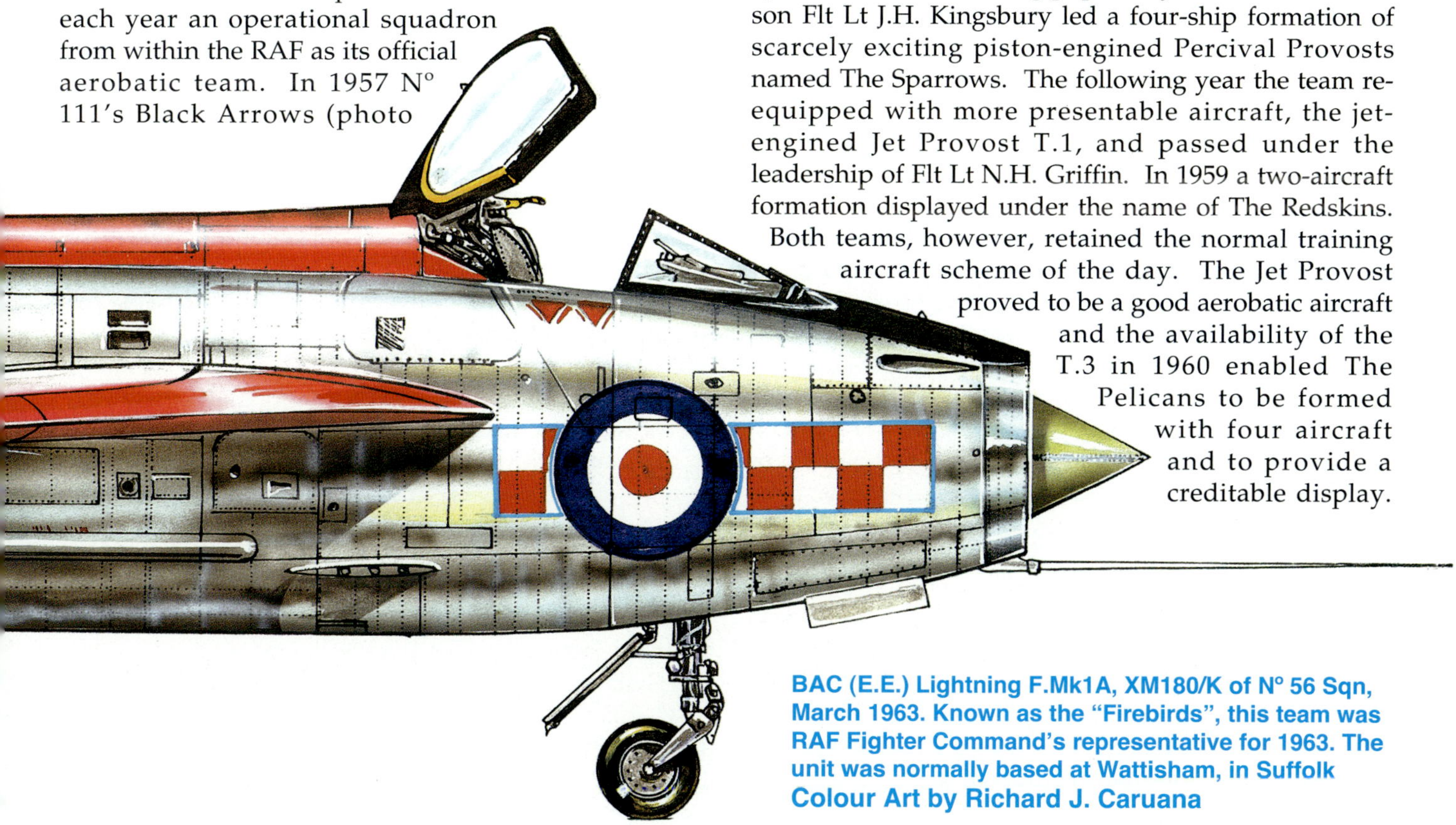

BAC (E.E.) Lightning F.Mk1A, XM180/K of N° 56 Sqn, March 1963. Known as the "Firebirds", this team was RAF Fighter Command's representative for 1963. The unit was normally based at Wattisham, in Suffolk
Colour Art by Richard J. Caruana

In 1962 the team, led by Flt Lt Ian Bashall, received the Jet Provost T.4. Renamed The Red Pelicans (its aircraft now increased to six) they were painted an overall day-glo red scheme for the 1963 season.

Within the RAF fighter squadrons, The Black Arrows were followed in 1961 by another Hunter team — The Blue Diamonds — of N° 92 Squadron, naturally painted gloss blue overall with red and yellow chequered wingtips. That same year the English Electric Lightning F.1 was introduced into the display circuit by N° 74 Squadron which formed The Tigers, sporting black dorsal spines and fins. By that time N° 56 had also re-equipped with the Lightning F.1, and in 1963 its Firebirds, with red spines and fins, replaced The Tigers as the RAF's official team. Frontline aircraft were now becoming more complex and expensive to maintain or replace. The Lightning was not only the heaviest fighter being thrown around the sky but also the thirstiest aircraft to form part of an RAF aerobatic team. After the Firebirds 1963 season ended, it was officially decided that the high cost of operating frontline aircraft, which were by then becoming fewer as the RAF became more compact, precluded their use for aerobatic display. In future all teams were to be drawn from training units.

Above: The "Red Pelicans" of the Central Flying School
Right: Five Folland Gnats T.1 formed the "Yellowjacks" under the leadership of Flt Lt Lee Jones. Note the leader's aircraft carries an all-black fin

From Small Beginnings...

Thus N° 4 FTS at RAF Valley formed a team with five of their new diminutive Folland Gnats T.1 named The Yellowjacks, painted in overall trainer yellow, which was the standard scheme promulgated for the type in RAF service. The Yellowjacks and The Red Pelicans performed at the 1964 SBAC Show at Farnborough. Led by Flt Lt Lee Jones, an ex-Black Arrows pilot, The Yellowjacks set off for a season of impeccable performances at various airshows. The aesthetic difference between the straight-winged, sedate Jet Provost and the sleek Gnat was highly appreciated by the public. The Gnat's swept-wings probably evoked nostalgia of the Hunter's glorious display days.

The decision to adopt the Gnat for the RAF official team was, therefore, a most happy one. Moreover, the team was to be run on the lines of a full-time operational squadron, dedicated wholly to aerobatic flying at air displays and other occasions. This must have helped in the positive projection of the RAF's image to a tax-paying public disillusioned by a period of major defence cuts and particularly harsh criticism. Flt Lt Lee Jones was assigned the task of forming the new team which, with seven (plus one reserve) arrow-shaped, red Gnats, was to be known as The Red Arrows.

The Gnat was originally designed and built by Folland Aircraft Co, which was later absorbed into Hawker Siddeley Aviation Ltd. It entered service in February 1962 as the RAF's standard advanced trainer but possessing a fighter-like performance (a single-seat fighter version was built for the Indian and Finnish Air Forces) enabling trainee pilots to easily bridge the gap between the basic jet trainers and the high performance operational aircraft of Fighter and Bomber Commands. A high rate of climb, 40,000 ft (12,192 m) in 7.5 minutes, a level speed of Mach 0.9 (and the ability to reach Mach 1.15 in a shallow dive) made possible by the excellent thrust/weight ratio of its Bristol Siddeley Orpheus 101 turbojet combined with superb manoeuvrability made it the ideal aerobatic aircraft.

Lee Jones put together a formidable team of experienced instructors for the Red Arrows first season. He himself had flown a variety of operational fighter aircraft, ranging from night-fighter Mosquitoes through Meteors, Sabres to Hunters. His experience with the Black Arrows and Yellowjacks made him the natural choice as team leader.

Jones's number 2 in the first Red Arrows team was Flt Lt Bryan A. Nice, an ex-Red Pelicans member. Number 3 was New Zealander Flt Lt Ray G. Hanna, ex-member of the College of Air Warfare's Meteor aerobatic team of 1962. Flt Lt Gerald L. Ranscombe, another ex-Yellowjacks, was number 4, while number 5 was Flt Lt Peter G. Hay, also ex-Yellowjacks. Flt Lt Bill Loverseed, from the previous RAF College Meteor display team, was number 6, and number 7 was Flt Lt Henry J.D. Prince, ex-reserve pilot of The Yellowjacks. Red Arrows reserve pilot, Flt Lt Eric C.F. Tilsley of Red Pelicans fame, completed the flying team.

Their first season (1965) consisted of 25 venues and 40 displays, mostly in Britain but also included several visits to France, including that year's Le Bourget Salon, and Belgium. A pattern for the display was devised whereby each performance commenced with a fly-past

MICHAEL STROUD

JOHN MIZZI

The Gnats in their original all-red scheme, before the introduction of the red/white/blue fin colours. They are seen at Malta in October, 1966

of the seven aircraft followed by several minutes of constantly-changing formation patterns – Rhombus, Arrow, Swan, Cutlass, Big T, Vixen and Kings Cross – the change in formation generally taking place at the top of a loop while the aircraft were inverted.

For the second part of the display the team split into two groups, one of five aircraft and the other of two, each group performing synchronised manoeuvres designed to demonstrate the versatility of the Gnat and the skill of the pilots. Here the Synchro Pair was born, when two Gnats flew in opposite directions round a horizontal circle and crossed in front of the crowd at a combined speed of 700 mph (1,127 km/hr) in a routine which was coined as the "Roulette". Ten aircraft were put at the disposal of the team for this first year: XR540, XR991-6, XR986-7 and XS111. They were painted post-office red overall, with roundels in six positions and swept-back fin flashes above which was painted the CFS crest on a white disc. Each aircraft's serial, in roundel blue, appeared on the rear fuselage and beneath the wings.

Some First Hand Experience

Flt Lt Lee Jones, just after taking command of the first Red Arrows team expressed himself as follows: "Flying an aeroplane is an occupation demanding a considerable amount of skill and co-ordination. As the flying becomes faster and higher the aircraft become more complex, so also do the required skills become more demanding. Because modern service aircraft perform their allotted tasks at great height and far away from the public, people may well ask 'Where do they go?' and 'What do they do?'. One aspect of flying is, however, always in the public eye — the art of formation flying and formation aerobatics. The Royal Air Force has not neglected this fact. Fortunately this type of flying is not an end in itself and the modern service pilot, especially the fighter pilot, must be proficient in the art of flying in formation, and formation aerobatics is a logical progression of his skill. He gains not only the enjoyment of aerobatics but also the confidence and ability to fly his aircraft in any position and close to the limits of his, and its, performance.

"You first achieve formation by aligning your aircraft with the leader and as long as he flies smoothly, a basic formation is achieved. The formatting pilot concentrates his reactions and energies into following the slightest movement and, as it were, making his aircraft an extension of the leader's. The formation is then gradually built up, each succeeding outside aircraft position requiring more concentration, to accept without question the enlarged movements up and down the line.

"Now the leader, flying as smoothly as he can, begins an aerobatic manoeuvre and literally flies the whole team as one. It feels rather like flying a large cumbersome aircraft through fighter-type manoeuvres. Regardless of their position in space the formatting pilots hang on. Unlike a car, an aircraft can move around its lateral axis, ie, nose up and down, as well as about its longitudinal axis, ie, rolling. So the entire

R.J. CARUANA

VICTOR PISANI

process demands the highest degree of concentration and co-ordination. Gradually the pilots accept that from take-off to landing they are controlling just a part of a large formation which is completely controlled by the leader in whom they have complete faith. They must also have complete trust in one another - there is little margin for error.

"The criteria of a good show are manifold. Did the public see everything easily without straining their necks, without looking into the sun or waiting impatiently during gaps in the performance? Did we impress them with a professional skill and rock-steady flying? Did we, above all, present a show that flowed smoothly and safely — like an airborne ballet? If we did all these things, we succeeded. But if we missed any one of them, we failed. This is precision formation aerobatics."

Promoted to Squadron Leader, Ray Hanna took command of the Red Arrows the following year during which the team started performing at most venues with nine aircraft drawn from the same ten already available in 1965. For the 1966 season Hanna had to prepare the team for more than twice the number of performances (85) which included some important dates including a display in front of HRH the Duke of Edinburgh at Little Rissington and participation at the SBAC show. Another 'royal command performance' was before King Hussein on October 20, at Amman, Jordan.

For that year's season the Gnats wore a slight variation in markings when a Union Jack outlined in white was appropriately painted above the fin flash in lieu of the CFS crest, the latter being moved to the nose just below the windscreen. In October 1966 the Red Arrows made their first visit to Malta when the Team stopped there on its way to a training camp in Cyprus. The unscheduled nature of its transit stay did not prevent the Team from performing a show over the Island. Probably nowhere such as at Malta could the Gnat Synchro Pair be seen crossing each other below eye level, as thousands of spectators lined the high bastions on either side of Marsamxetto Harbour.

For the 1967 season the entire fin was painted in flashes of red, white and blue, with a Union Jack superimposed in the white segment. Still under Hanna's command, the team's stamina was put to the test during the Paris Air Show where they performed every day between June 1 and 4, notwithstanding the fact that the team had been reduced to seven aircraft. The following year the Gnats acquired a very stylish white flash on the forward fuselage which extended from nose to the engine air intake. Being the 50th anniversary of the RAF, the season's climax was a display before HM Queen Elizabeth II at the Royal Review of the RAF at Abingdon.

Ray Hanna commented as follows during the 1968 season: "We fly at between 300 and 350 knots.

VICTOR PISANI

Top: The Argosy in the background was used to transport the squadron's equipment when displaying away from base
Above: The squadron crest as painted on the Landrover which the team had at their disposal
Right: Ray Hanna opening the cockpit of his Gnat on his return to Kemble in April 1968 after a sortie with the team

Separation distances vary with the formation flown, from 10 ft (3 m) down to 4 ft (1.2 m). The leader literally flies the whole team like one large aircraft and the others hang on to him. One of the hardest techniques to acquire is the ability to accept a rapid movement of the aircraft alongside you without reacting so violently yourself that big 'oscillations' are transmitted through the entire formation.

"By the time we start public shows, everybody (in the team) knows what he has to do and when to do it. They don't need lots of orders from me. I just key them in, as it were. We have a fixed interval between the two parts of a command like 'Smoke on — go' or 'Vixen — go' when we're changing formation. I don't need to be told they're doing it. The only acknowledgement I expect is from the two last men when a formation change is completed. All I want then is: Eight...nine..."

That season ended with 98 official displays although the 'magic' century figure must have been easily surpassed if rehearsal displays had to be taken into account. However it was to be another five years before the team officially surpassed the hundred mark during one season.

1969, the season which marked Hanna's last year of command was also the year that pilots' names started to appear in white lettering below the windscreens of the aircraft. The Squadron Leader also carried the appropriate pennant on the nose, just above the zig-zag of the fuselage flash. Up to that time the team had operated as a detachment of CFS, but in 1969 the unit was established permanently as a standard RAF squadron.

World Acclaim

By 1970 the team had become well-known all around the world, having performed some 500 displays throughout Europe and the Middle East. Group Captain Douglas Bader, the legless wonder of WWII fame, had this to say: "The Red Arrows stand alone. They appreciated and have achieved the basic essential in aerobatic demonstration, which is unbroken continuity of manoeuvre from take-off to landing, plus the importance of confining their movements within the aerodrome circuit.

"Aerobatic and formation flying is a military necessity for fighter pilots. Combine the two, add some coloured smoke, and the result is terrific... I could use more superlatives in praising the Red Arrows but let me finish by quoting the highest praise they will ever receive. Last year (1968) the announcer at an international show said as the Gnats started their display, 'Here come the Red Arrows, the best aerobatic team in the world'. And that's a very handsome tribute when you realise it was a French announcer speaking at a French show".

By this time a recruitment practice had to be established. A prerequisite for acceptance was that those who applied had to be Qualified Flying Instructors (QFIs). Volunteers there were aplenty; the selection procedure, however, began to pose a problem. So intake was limited every year to three new pilots who would do a normal tour of duty lasting three years.

Those lucky enough to make it past the selection stage would be posted to RAF Kemble, (where the Red Arrows had moved) during autumn in preparation for the following year's programme. Some initial formation flying practice was undertaken at this stage though the initial period served mostly to integrate the new member into the team. It was usually in January that real training would begin. Up to four sorties a day would be flown, initially with small formations, gradually building up to the full nine-aircraft team. All flying practice was filmed and through a process of constant practice and discussion the new team display would progressively take shape. Aircraft on strength also changed somewhat. The 1970 team machines

ARTHUR GIBSON

ARTHUR GIBSON

The Red Arrows in their Gnats bringing up the rear of the flypast over London to commemorate the Diamond Jubilee of the birth of the Royal Air Force

were XR540, XR545, XR986, XR987, XR991, XR993, XR994, XR996, XS107 and XS111.

On January 20, 1971, four members of the team were killed in a flying accident at Kemble. Although the Red Arrows had been cleared for their flying display the previous December, the loss of four members forced the team to change its planned routine to a seven-ship formation, which was finally cleared on May 11, using Gnats XR996, XS107, XR993, XR987, XS111, XS101, XR991 with XR540 as spare. A very important day marked that year's squadron diary when HM Queen Elizabeth, the Queen Mother, Commandant-in-Chief of the CFS, paid an official visit to Kemble on July 19.

The first public display of the 1972 season took place at Liverpool on April 29. Ray Hanna flew again in the lead position, though this time he was flying his Spitfire rather than the Gnat! That year also marked another milestone in the team's history as it embarked on the first United States tour. This came at a time when the Concorde controversy (which considered the ban of supersonic airline flying over the US) was raging across the Atlantic... so the Red Arrows "Concorde" formation at all US venues must have been seen as some form of sweet revenge! For the display at Dulles, Virginia, the British Ambassador to the US, Lord Craner, British MP E. Griffith (also Under-Secretary of State for the Environment) and Sir John Lapsley, Chief of British Defence in Washington and Lady Lapsley were in the guests' enclosure next to the Vice-President of the USA.

A New Image

A very important person had by this time made his mark working very closely with the team. This was Arthur Gibson FRPS, ace photographer and PR man par excellence who began to give the team a new, professional image. He had been 'official' photographer for years and had designed and produced their publicity leaflets year after year. Among some of his innovations were the design and provision of red flying suits for the team members and year by year photographic coverage which became the envy of every other display team in the world. In 1973 Gibson also designed a new scheme for the Gnat featuring a large section of the Union Jack on the fin, fairing into the white fuselage flash. A full-scale test on a Gnat was made but was never officially adopted.

1973 was memorable for many other events, one of the most important being that of a record crowd of over 650,000 at Lisbon on June 13. That year the Arrows chalked up their first 'century' within one display season, which was performed at Teeside on September 30.

Gnat Swan Song

Towards the end of the "seventies" the Gnat began to show its years. Never an easy aircraft to fly and certainly none the easier to maintain, the day of phasing the type out of service was drawing near. By 1975 the Hawk was already under development and promised to be the most logical and suitable type to take over the RAF's job of public relations within its official aerobatic team. Until such time, the Gnat soldiered on admirably and continued to provide thrills to immense crowds all over the world. The 1000th display on the type was performed at the Military Air Tattoo, Greenham Common, on June 26, 1977. That year also marked the Diamond Jubilee of the RAF and HM Queen Elizabeth II presided over a special display at RAF Finningley where the Reds gave their usual polished performance on July 29.

By 1978, team aircraft had changed considerably mainly due to normal airframe fatigue, though accidents also took their toll. That year's aircraft were: XP514, XP535, XR540, XR572, XR955, XR977, XR987, XR991, XS101 and XS107. A slight change was also

Right: The Red Arrows final change in colour trim was the introduction of the words "Royal Air Force" on the nose in place of the nose flash. Here they are seen at Malta in 1978

Below: The first Hawk to join the Red Arrows, with the Gnats in the background. Sqn Ldr Brian Hoskins proudly holds the aircraft's log book

R.J. CARUANA

observed in the colour scheme: the white nose flash was broken to accommodate the words ROYAL AIR FORCE in white letters, while the CFS badge, still painted on a white shield forward of the engine intakes, appeared also on the fin above the Union Jack. That year's displays included a memorable performance at Malta's RAF Luqa, marking the impending closure of the Malta base after nearly 200 years of British presence.

The RAF's premier aerobatic team flew its 15th successive and final season with the Folland Gnat in 1979, marked by great nostalgia for the type. Sqn Ldr Brian Hoskins (Red One) met the Gnat Orpheus engine designer, Sid Hawkins and was presented with a trophy consisting of highly polished Orpheus compressor blades engraved "The Red Arrows, Coventry, April 1979". That year the team began to travel to Cyprus on detachment before the beginning of the season for an intensive training camp. Away from home base, the ground crews could work in an environment akin to what they would find whenever the team travelled abroad, while the pilots could work up their routine to perfection in splendid weather which usually permitted three or four full training sorties a day. "The time spent in Cyprus every year is just like moving the squadron from Scampton to Akrotiri," explained Chief Tech Kevin Rutter, "but we are working in a different environment, where social life is better and the weather is much warmer. On the whole it's like a bonus before starting the season, notwithstanding the hard work during the week, operating three sorties a day but with weekends off in the sun and sea."

On November 15, a brief ceremony at BAe's plant at Bitteswell marked the handing over of the ninth aircraft, XX266. It was rolled out and formally handed over to Air Commodore Dennis Allison, Commandant CFS, who accepted the log-book on behalf of the aerobatic team. A tenth aircraft was later delivered as a reserve.

Onto The Hawk

While the all-red scheme of the Gnat is retained (though Post Office Red was replaced by Signal Red), the trim differs considerably. The white nose flash, without a zig-zag, extends and broadens towards the rear fuselage, then turns up to form the white area of a

BAe, via MICHAEL STROUD

red/white/blue fin, on which a small Union Jack is centred. The red of the wing under-surfaces is broken by two converging white flashes and other trim in such a way as to form the outline of a large red arrow. Standard red-white-blue roundels are painted on six positions, those on the fuselage, outlined in white, are superimposed on the white flash. The roundel-blue serial number is carried on the rear fuselage only, while the legend "ROYAL AIR FORCE" was added soon after the aircraft entered RAF service. The Team's new badge consisting of the characteristic Diamond Nine was added to the port fuselage side, just ahead of the engine air intake, while the CFS badge is carried in a similar position on the starboard side. Airframes which formed this first Hawk line-up consisted of XX251-253, XX257, XX259, XX260, XX262, XX264 and XX266.

Training for the 1980 season started towards the end of the previous year at the home base though the team was especially anxious to fly out to the annual practice training camp at Cyprus early in March. The first public aerobatic display by the Red Arrows on the Hawk was performed at Episkopi, on March 13, followed by another at Dhekelia the day after in perfect weather. Brian Hoskins commented: "This is just what was needed to confirm our confidence in the new aircraft and work towards the standard which the team has maintained since 1965 when it started. The weather has been all that we hoped for, and the team has been able to fly three or more times a day".

An official UK launch for the new Red Arrows was planned for March 31 but had to be cancelled. Sqn Ldr R. Thilthorpe, Manager, said: "We are tremendously disappointed that we could not get airborne, but it wasn't worth the risk in low cloud, poor visibility, rain and crosswinds." The first season on the new aircraft was marred by a capricious – though, thankfully, not fatal – accident when on May 17, during a display at Brighton Sqn Ldr S. Johnson hit the mast of a yacht, Caramell II. The pilot managed to eject just before the aircraft, XX262, plunged into the sea.

A Better Mount

The Hawk has a number of qualities which make it far superior to the Gnat as an aerobatic aircraft. It can carry more fuel and, with the Adour jet engine's better fuel consumption compared to the Gnat's Orpheus, the Hawk has greater endurance enabling displays to be made 129 km (80 miles) away from base, double the distance of 65 km (40 miles) imposed by the Gnat's restricted range. For the longer journeys to the display base the Gnat had to carry slipper tanks which had to be removed before a display could be flown. The Hawk's greater range does away with this tedious chore, much to the relief of the ground crew. As for the airframe, the Hawk is stressed for +8g and -4g, with a turning performance equalling that of the F-16 Fighting Falcon, which is quite an achievement for what is sup-

BRITISH AEROSPACE AND THE RED ARROWS

The special relationship forged between British Aerospace (BAe), Bitteswell and the RAF aerobatic team was built up over a period of 14 years.

It began in 1968 when Ray Hanna brought the team to Bitteswell (Hawker Siddeley Aviation at that time) after the SBAC Show at Farnborough for a major modification programme to the team's Gnat aircraft. After a display to the employees the ten aircraft were left at the factory and the team flown back to Kemble in an RAF Argosy – another aircraft from the same stable – with the promise that the Gnats would be delivered back to the team in readiness for the 1969 season.

That promise was fulfilled and in subsequent years, during which time the team's aircraft were major-serviced on an annual basis, a bond grew steadily between the workforce and the team. It was always ensured that their Gnat aircraft were returned on time for all the season's displays up to 1979.

Due to this background the MoD/PE decided that Bitteswell (latterly BAe, Kingston Brough Div.) should be tasked to enter New Build aircraft programmes and provide the Hawk aircraft for the Red Arrows and a contract was issued accordingly in 1979 with the aircraft to be delivered for the 1980 season.

To ensure that everything would meet the programme a hangar was dedicated solely for the task. Accordingly, a priority production programme was drawn up to ensure that all the ten aircraft would be delivered to the Team well in advance of the 1980 date in order that the longest training period was available before the that season.

The factory team, supervisory and skilled workers, took on the challenge wholeheartedly and targets set were consistently broken to ensure that the programme would be met. A trial installation aircraft was required in the first instance to the Team's standard – smoke installation pod, special cockpit requirements, etc – which could have set back the dates. In order to ensure time was kept to a minimum the Team's engineering officers were encouraged to visit the factory (as they had in the past with the Gnat aircraft) to follow through the T.I. period and also at any stages of the aircraft build which they would deem to be useful to them when the aircraft entered service. A real team effort between customer and supplier which paid off dividends.

Some problems arose over the period as was inevitable, including the typical English weather situation, sometimes curtailing the flight test programme, but were overcome (notwithstanding some sleepless nights and grey hairs).

However, the first aircraft was ready for delivery to the Team on August 16, 1979. At the initial handing over ceremony I was able to hand over the log book (pristine like the aircraft) to Squadron Leader Brian Hoskins, well on the target our management team had set.

The remaining nine aircraft were delivered to the Team on programme culminating in the formal handover of the ninth aircraft on November 15, 1979 to Air Commodore Allison, Commandant CFS, in the presence of BAe Directors, MoD Directorate and senior officers of Support Command.

It should also be noted that this tight programme was met at a time when the factory was heavily involved on programmes on Vulcan, Buccaneer, Shackleton and Harrier aircraft for the RAF all being required to maintain Strike

posed to be a training aircraft. The Red Arrows, however, rarely exceed +5g with the exception of the Synchro Pair, which do so with full confidence in their Hawks.

The Royal Air Force Aerobatic Team (RAFAT) Hawks differ in minor respects from other RAF aircraft of this type. Apart from using the ARC164 UHF standby UHF radio for clearer reception during displays, they have additional panels for quicker access to the hydraulic system. More powerful disc brakes were fitted before these became standard equipment on all other Hawks. Their Adour engine, although uprated before this became a standard modification throughout the RAF, still has a minor modification to its fuel system which enables faster throttle response. The underbelly Aden cannon pod is replaced by a container (converted from the Aden pod itself) holding tanks for diesel and blue and red dye. Plumbing from the pod carries the contents of these tanks to the rear fuselage where pipes project downwards into the jet efflux. These produce the red and blue smoke emitted for effect while plain diesel, similarly injected into the efflux, produces the white smoke. Three switches on the control column activate emissions from the three tanks. In case of war the Red Arrows aircraft – which in their T Mk 1A version are Sidewinder-capable – can be quickly resprayed in camouflage colours, their gunsights installed and their control column switches returned to their original role of weapons release.

Owing to the nature of the work to which they are employed, Red Arrows Hawks have special maintenance cycles. Primary servicing is carried out at 150 hours' intervals, with minor overhauls at 300 hours and majors at 1,200 hours. Most of the major servicing is carried out in winter while the team is slowly building up its display. Three at a time, the aircraft are stripped down and Hawks from CFS or other RAF units replace those undergoing servicing. Both First Line and Second Line groundcrew agree that the Hawk is a wonderful aircraft to work on with very few snags being encountered during the display season.

The spare (tenth) aircraft is rotated wisely to permit a more equitable wear on the other Hawks while it helps to relieve those scheduled for servicing during the winter season. Special attention is given to those aircraft which fly at the back of the formation as they are subject to more fatigue than those at the front, having to pull more g to stay in position. Also for the purpose of evening out fatigue life, aircraft positions in the formation are periodically changed.

In 1981 the team embarked on a very important Middle East Tour which helped secure Hawk orders for BAe from Abu Dhabi for the United Arab Emirates (Abu Dhabi, Amman, Dubai, Fujairah, Ras al Khaimah, Sharjah and Umm). Over 400 separate sorties were flown, with twenty-seven 9-ship practices/displays. The team also flew the longest ferry flights on internal fuel only, including one of 1000 miles with over 15%

Command commitments plus other new Hawk deliveries to Support Command.

Following the Red Arrows aircraft deliveries Bitteswell took over the remaining contract commitments for the Hawk to the RAF in order to leave our sister factory at Dunsfold in Surrey to concentrate on the ever growing overseas orders for the Hawk. Around one third of the RAF order was delivered from Bitteswell, with the final aircraft to RAF Chivenor in 1982.

Due to Government action on defence requirements and cancellation of contracts under discussion, the BAe Board decided that the Bitteswell unit should be closed. In fact, the unit was subsequently run down and the airfield closed in June 1982, with full manufacturing facilities being closed in December, 1982.

As a gesture to the workforce the closure of the airfield was preceded by an air display, at their request, by Squadrons of the RAF, including the Red Arrows, who had been connected with the factory over the years.

Via ALBERT WHITEHOUSE

From a personal point of view I have many happy memories of the years working with the Red Arrows, making many very good friends.

I suppose the proudest memory of those times came during the lunch following the airfield closure air display, when the Red Arrows Team Leader, Squadron Leader John Blackwell, presented me with the Red Arrows tie as an Honorary Member of the Team (in the presence of my old, alas lamented, friend Arthur Gibson who was already an Honorary Member) in recognition of my involvement with the Team over the years.

When I later moved to Kingston on Thames, as Division Director and General Manager, Kingston/Dunsfold and later Weybridge, it was always my firm intention and wish that the close ties between BAe and the Red Arrows should continue in the future – I am pleased to say this has been maintained ever since my retirement from BAe.

The ultimate accolade personally for me came when the Red Arrows Team, under Sqn Ldr Richard Thomas, dined me out from RAF Scampton following my retirement from BAe.

Albert Whitehouse
Divisional Director and General Manager, Bitteswell 1977-82

DEREK WHITEHOUSE

MARKETING THE ARROWS

I have always been keen on aviation and like most people knew of and admired the skill of the Red Arrows. In 1977 I was Sales and Marketing Director of D. Byford & Co. Ltd, a brand leader in the manufacture of socks and knitwear, with worldwide distribution, employing in excess of two thousand people. I got to know well a particular customer, who bought an abundance of cashmere sweaters and who knew my interest and liking for all things flying. He remarked that I would perhaps like to meet his brother, who at that time had just been selected as a team member of the Red Arrows. The customer in question was Michael Grose and his brother Lloyd was the new member. A meeting was arranged and I duly met the Team under the leadership of Frank Hoare at RAF Kemble in Gloucestershire.

I saw them to be what, of course, they are, the epitomy of excellence in the air, but I have to say, on the ground they were a shambles. I am led to believe that thirty five pounds per team member was allocated for the purchase of non-flying clothing, which when spent, did little for their overall image. I therefore took it upon myself to contact friends in the clothing industry who were only too willing to clothe the Team in the very best of British products, blazers, trousers, shirts, ties, belts, sweaters, socks and leather jackets. My manufacturing friends were only too aware that the only return they would get for their involvement would be one of association with the Red Arrows – this was enough. The position continued for two to three years, when eventually a budget was duly found to supplement their generosity. Such Companies as Berwins, Viyella, Peter England and Smedleys have been involved now for over seventeen years.

Ray Thilthorpe, the then Team Manager, like his predecessors became aware of the commercial exploitation that was going on, particularly by itinerant traders, on occasions even on the high street. The merchandise depicting the Royal Air Force Aerobatic Team (RAFAT) was, it must be said, of poor and inferior quality, which of course did nothing for the image the Red Arrows were endeavouring to portray. The adverse effect this was having had to stop – but how?

Being a friend in camp and a professional marketeer to boot, I had been 'batting' on behalf of the Team on all things commercial. This meant persuading manufacturers to 'back off', which in many cases was regrettable, as the products were ideal and of marketable quality. Ray and I discussed at length the best way forward, the objective of which was (a) have a legal method by which to curtail exploitation, and (b) allow Companies who were desperately keen to put on the market items that would not only be commercially viable, but also reflect well on the Red Arrows.

Following a discussion with my solicitor and accountant, it became apparent that trade marking was the first step, followed by a means by which these could be held and administered. A charitable trust seemed to be the route to take, open for all to see and should royalties accrue, offering a method of distribution. The Red Arrows Charitable Trust was established in 1981, endorsed subsequently by a policy statement from the MoD; the ex officio trustees being Commandant CFS, Wing Commander RAFAT, Team Manager RAFAT, a representative of Command Accounts, together with a civilian solicitor and accountant.

From small and hesitant beginnings we are now fully established with a policy to administer and commercially exercise registered trade marks in forty-two categories.

After seventeen years of close involvement, my original opinion of the Team has, if possible, been enhanced. I think the Red Arrows are magnificent.

Eric Ward
Marketing Adviser

fuel reserve after landing. By that time the Hawk had flown some 8000 miles without any major snags. The display at Amman International Airport was in the presence of HM King Hussein of Jordan, Queen Muna and other dignitaries.

On July 17 the team flew during a flypast on the occasion of the Opening Ceremony of the Humber Bridge by HM Queen Elizabeth II. Another Royal occasion was the Wedding of the Prince of Wales, when the team flew a special display at Caernarvon on July 29. On the lighter side (literally!) was the filming at Kemble of Miss UK contestants with comperes Judith Chalmers and Peter Marshall for Thames TV on August 24, which was transmitted two days later. On September 12, the team performed a flypast at the Royal Tournament.

The ugly spectre of war reared its head in1982 in the distant Falklands which eventually sparked off a full-blown conflict between Britain and Argentina. In recognition of the valour of the men who fought in that war the team performed two flypasts over the frigate HMS Arrow as it sailed into Devonport with 236 survivors from the stricken destroyer Sheffield. Members of the team also met their colleagues of the 'Guinea Pig Club', formed by airmen who since 1941 had to undergo plastic surgery (very much an experimental venture at that time) due to their injuries. This time, however, they met airmen from both WWII and the Falklands. 1982 was to prove the busiest in the Reds' history until then, with a total of 131 displays, under the new leadership of Sqn Ldr J. Blackwell who returned to the team after an absence of seven years.

Moving Home

March of 1983 brought a move from the team's base at Kemble to RAF Scampton, in Lincolnshire. Apart from coping with the transfer of all material and aircraft the team was preparing for a very busy year.

The season started off with an accident involving Hawk XX227 when it hit a power line near the village of Fort Augustus, Loch Ness, during a ferry flight on April 21. The pilot managed to land the aircraft at Lossiemouth but had ordered his rear passenger, Sgt Paul Inman, to eject.

Among the important overseas deployments, the Red Arrows crossed the Atlantic for the first US tour on the Hawk. The ferry flight left Scampton for Kinloss, then on to Keflavik (Iceland), Sondrestrom, Goose Bay, Trenton (Canada) and finally Andrews AFB. This tour was organised on the invitation of Senator Charles Mathias, Chairman of the 1983 Bicentennial Committee. Some 800,000 spectators crammed Andrews AFB for the display. During that tour the team met all three North American display teams, The Thunderbirds (USAF), The Blue Angels (USN) and the Snowbirds (CAF). During three and a half weeks they flew 400 hours and over 11,500 miles. The Hawk stood up well to its reputation for serviceability as all displays were mounted on time without once having to use the spare aircraft.

MARKUS/PHOTO N-G WIDH, T. CASPERSSON

The Gripen Equation.

In a smart aircraft, each individual quality works together to make the whole system worth more than the sum of its parts. Synergy. One plus one equals three.

That´s the Gripen Equation.

Systems integration and true multi-role capability are the keys to the Equation. One Gripen plus one pilot equals a superlative fighter, attack and reconnaissance system.

Small and powerful, JAS 39 Gripen is efficient and flexible, has low life-cycle costs and high growth potential.

Flexibility for optimal use in every situation. An enemy must count on it.

Gripen is the first in the next generation of combat aircraft. It is entering service. Deliveries to the Swedish Air Force have begun.

The Gripen Equation. Where simple addition makes for force multiplication.

JAS 39 GRIPEN. LEADING FROM THE FRONT.

SAAB

SAAB-SCANIA AB · SAAB MILITARY AIRCRAFT
S-581 88 LINKÖPING · SWEDEN
PHONE +46 13 18 00 00 · TELEFAX +46 13 18 18 02

SAAB AIRCRAFT´S ADVANCED AVIATION TECHNOLOGY ALSO PRODUCES THE SAAB 340 AND SAAB 2000, LEADERS IN THE WORLD REGIONAL AIRLINE MARKET.

RICK BREWELL

During 1984 the team was to suffer some accidents which prolonged its training camp at Cyprus. Flt Lt Chris Hirst, flying XX251, escaped miraculously thanks to his 0-0 ejector seat on March 21 at Akrotiri (the day after the team arrived for training). He hit the tail of his Hawk on the ground after he could not recover from a dive. The aircraft was a write-off and the team continued to practice 8 and 7 ship formations until the arrival of replacement pilot Gordon Hannam on March 31. The first 9-ship formation was performed on April 21. On many days some four 9-ship sorties were flown. On May 3 Air Officer Training, Air Vice Marshal Stuart-Paul watched the practice display and gave his approval for the team to perform in public. The team returned to Scampton May 8.

That year's Austrian Grand Prix was graced by a splendid performance on August 19 at Osterreichring. On September 7 Pete Lees had to eject from XX257 during a display at Sidmouth due to engine compressor failure. He was back flying three days later in time for the Farnborough display, but four 8-ship shows had to be performed in the meantime.

Royal Visits

Summer of 1985 is best remembered for the bad weather over most of the UK, including fog in July! Most of that season's programme was hampered but this was more than compensated for by a very special invitation in the form of a royal command performance from the King and Crown Prince of Morocco. The display by the Red Arrows, now under the leadership of Sqn Ldr RM Thomas, was held on the river in front of the city of Morocco and an ornamental dagger encrusted with precious stones was presented to the team by the King as a memento, and is probably the most precious and treasured trophy in the trophy case which one finds as one enters the Reds' building.

HM Queen Elizabeth, the Queen Mother, paid an official visit to the Red Arrows' base that summer while colleagues from the Patrouille de France also paid a visit to Scampton. Exchange visits by display teams are encouraged wherever possible. Sometimes when the Reds go overseas they transit through Rivolto, the home of the Freccie Tricolori, where the crews receive fantastic hospitality. Crews also

RED ARROWS PILOTS SAVED BY G.Q. PARACHUTES AFTER EJECTING FROM THE GNAT & HAWK

Name	Rank	Date	Location	Type/N° of Chute
RUST J.D.	Fl Lt	1969	Kemble	BK Mk 53
DUCKETT R.B.	Fl Lt	1969	Kemble	BK Mk 53
HAZELL D.G.	S/Ldr	1970		BK Mk 53
WHELAN T.	Sgt	1976	Kemble	BK Mk 53
JOHNSON S.	S/Ldr	1980	Brighton	Aeroconical
INMAN P.	Sgt	1983	Fort Augustus	Aeroconical
HIRST C.A.R.	Fl Lt	1984	Cyprus	Aeroconical
LEES P.	Fl Lt	1984	Sidmouth	Aeroconical
FINDLAY D.	Fl Lt	1986	Scampton	Aeroconical
MILLER T.	S/Ldr	1987	Welton	Aeroconical
NEWBURY M.	Fl Lt	1987	Welton	Aeroconical
COLLINS P.	S/Ldr	1988	Scampton	Aeroconical

exchange notes — not so much about the aircraft, since they use different ones, but they do debate the finer aspects such as the best methods of generating smoke.

The official 2000th display of the team was chalked up on May 30, 1986, at Hurn Airport, Bournemouth (on rechecking display data, however, it was found that the actual 2000th performance was flown during the latter part of 1985 since at the end of that season the team had totalled 2005 displays). The red Hawks of the RAFAT embarked on a Far Eastern Tour, with a special display on July 13 before Sayyid Fahr Taimam al Said, Deputy Prime Minister of Oman. A trip to Australia was also planned for that year but after getting as far as Singapore for various reasons the team had to turn back.

Hawk XX297 was lost over the home base on November 11, due to engine surge. Flying a practice display on the airfield at Scampton, the Synchro Pair pulled up into the vertical in-line astern before rolling rapidly through 90° in opposite directions to split and complete the manoeuvre. During a rapid roll at 2500 ft, the pilot of the second aircraft felt a bump which he assumed to be jet wash but shortly afterwards the engine surged. The pilot ejected and the aircraft fell into a field a mile away from base.

A special performance was flown on May 7, 1987, in the presence of the Duchess of York, Sarah Ferguson. Another royal occasion was on May 10, when the Red Arrows performed before the King and Queen of Sweden at Linkoping. A display at Blumberg Flying Club in Germany was considered illegal on environmental grounds and the club who organised the event was fined £17,000 for disregarding a ban on the display.

The 1988 season was to prove disastrous for the Red Arrows. XX241 and XX259 were lost on November 16, 1987 when Red 1 and Red 2 collided over Welton. Sqn Ldr Tim Miller, who had just taken over command of the team, and Flt Lt Spike Newbery were hospitalised. Newbery was replaced by Flt Lt Dom Riley, ex-F-4 pilot and Hawk QFI. Tragedy struck when Flt Lt Neil MacLachlan was killed while practising on January 22 flying XX243. Another aircraft, XX304, was lost on June 24 after a take-off accident. The pilot ejected but the season continued with a 7-ship formation. On August 21 and 22 the Red Arrows performed at Breitscheide Cologne and Wildenrath respectively. These were to be the last shows in Germany as all display flying was banned in that country following the Freccie Tricolori tragedy at Ramstein the following weekend.

Behind the Iron Curtain

The 25th anniversary of the Red Arrows was celebrated in style during 1989 when a world record presence of six aerobatic teams met at Scampton. However it was in 1990 that the team made history when they were invited to visit the USSR. The team flew from Stockholm to Leningrad between June 20-22, and then to Kiev (22-25 June) where the displays were highly restricted due to extremely bad weather. Chief Tech Rutter explained that: "The first place we went into was Leningrad and as soon as we landed with the Hercules after the Hawks the local military men stood around us looking in awe. We were laughing and joking, as usual in high spirits whenever we go somewhere new, and they couldn't understand what we were laughing and joking about. When the initial tension was over we got very friendly and pally. Although there were interpreters, there still were technical

PHIL BOYDEN

ARTHUR GIBSON

The tour to the then USSR (Ukraine) was the first by a NATO unit behind the Iron Curtain. A Soviet Air Force officer is seen familiarising himself with the cockpit of a Hawk (above) while the team are seen on the left flying past the statue of "Mother Russia"

Below: The pyramids in the background form the backdrop for this formation of the Red Arrows during a visit to Cairo

BRITISH AEROSPACE

RICK BREWELL

ARTHUR GIBSON

The Red Arrows in good company: With VulcanXH558 (top), with the famous U-2 Spyplane (above) and with Concorde (left)

The late Nick Grace in his two-seat Spitfire in formation with a Red Arrows Hawk piloted by Tim Miller

language problems, but eventually they understood what we wanted and began to get across as well." Apart from communications problems, some difficulties were encountered with oxygen and nitrogen supplies. The Iron Curtain trip continued with a visit to Budapest (June 25-26).

On May 27 the Dunkirk Evacuation was remembered by a flypast while another over London commemorated the 50th Anniversary of the Battle of Britain on September 15. The Red Arrows left their Golf holding pattern at 11:56:35, joining the 235°T heading towards London. Leading the 169-aircraft assembly were Battle of Britain Memorial Flight (BBMF) Spitfires and Hurricanes which appeared at 550ft/180kt over Buckingham Palace at exactly 12:00:00. The familiar sight of nine Hawks in Big Nine formation swept by at 1000ft/360kt trailing red, white and blue smoke closely followed by the final three aircraft which consisted of the BBMF Lancaster, a Hurricane and Spitfire.

Sqn Ldr Adrian Thurley took over the leadership of the team for the 1991 season. Early the following year one of the few honorary members of the Red Arrows, Arthur Gibson, passed away. Needless to say, a very moving service was held on March 11 at St Clement Danes Central Church of the RAF to commemorate the person who probably more than any other had helped to create the image which the team still enjoys today. On the return leg from the Cyprus training camp the team stopped at Switzerland and met the Patrouille Suisse.

HM Queen Elizabeth, the Queen Mother, Commandant-in-Chief CFS, presented the Queen's Colours to the Central Flying School at RAF Scampton on June 4. Another tour to the East saw the team at a memorable airshow in Czechoslovakia, where one of the team's Hawks flew in a unique formation in company with an L-39, Alphajet, Su-27 and E-25.

Across the Atlantic

Another gruelling tour of America was prepared for the team during 1993 by the Team Manager, Les Garside-Beattie. In his own words: "The transfer of a whole squadron in flight through Greenland and Iceland was an area of concern itself. There were few diversions on the way and once one was well away one was practically committed with no hope of going back.

"On the first leg we encountered a massive headwind; to conserve our fuel we could not climb enough to fly over it so imagine the relief when, on breaking cloud around 200 miles from Greenland we saw land straight in front of us! The weather was so beautiful we ended up sunbathing at -4°, of course it's dry there so you don't feel it that much. On the final run into Canada we had a problem with one of the Hawks, an engine oil pump failure. However the Hawk made it, but needed an engine change.

"By the time we arrived at Denver we were struck

E.J.v.KONINGSVELD

The visits by the Red Arrows across the Atlantic were always memorable occasions.
Below: The team is seen flying over Washington
Left: On September 29, 1993 they performed at Nellis Air Force Base. They are seen taxiing out for the beginning of their display. The nose in the foreground is that of an F-16 of the USAF team "The Thunderbirds"

by the size of this airport — you cannot imagine the scale of this site. The warmth that the team received during their display was shown by a great round of applause at every manoeuvre they performed. That sort of thing followed through wherever we went. We managed to do a show at Houston at very short notice. Unlike US teams we travel from one display site to another even on the same day whereas they fly in and do only one show during the weekend wherever they go. Two days before I had promised them to be there by quarter to six and bang on time we arrived. The display was also broadcast live on a couple of TV channels. It was surprising to arrive at a show on a Sunday morning and find 150,000 people at the airfield already and the interstate highway blocked solid with cars trailing some six miles. When the team taxied by and took off the place went hush; complete silence that you could hear a pin drop! As soon as the team appeared from behind the crowd the place had an electric buzz about it which was indescribable. Two hours after the show when we had to leave for New Orleans you could still feel that the crowd had had that special feeling.

"We had a great number of social occasions but here in America things were different. As anywhere else we met an enormous number of people but everywhere we went they were all different, special in their own way, so we never got bored; they were overjoyed to see the team. At Salinas AFB, California, we were met with lapel badges of 'The British Are Coming'.

"Organising the US trip started 12 months before. Some six weeks were spent planning the display points but then it obviously took longer until approval was forthcoming from every place. But even when we get there I have to organise the day's work for each person on the team, everyone has to know what is happening all the time and that takes a lot of time. In fact I could have done with two more administration people on the trip but we did not have the space for them in our transport arrangements."

Ambassadors to the World

The profound sense of esprit de corps which exists within the Red Arrows rank and file is unsurpassed in any other RAF unit, and this should come as no surprise. Every member of the team knows that his colleagues depend on him, as much as he depends on them. So do the boys on the ground who at times are called to perform small miracles within the time limit between one display and another. The exhilarating displays and the team's magnetic attraction serve as positive and highly successful means of promotion for RAF recruitment. On home ground it is the discerning public that is the best judge of the team's cost effectiveness.

By the end of the 1993 display season the team had flown 2,805 performances and the year 1994, the Red Arrows's 30th year of service, promises to be just as busy as any other. But whether crossing the Channel, the Atlantic or all the way to the Far East the Red Arrows carry with them the onus of acting as the RAF's ambassadors, indeed Britain's too. Their image reflects British skill and technology and judging by their performance in this field they have never been found lacking since the team's formation in 1965.

Their motto Eclat, means 'brilliant', and this is perhaps the word most frequently heard among the watching crowds. Those who have been close enough to appreciate the hard work which goes on behind the scenes between one season and another, and during the most hectic period of the display season itself, can better appreciate how the Red Arrows dare leave nothing to chance if they are to live up to their motto.

R.J.C.

ALAN HOUSE

RED ARROWS

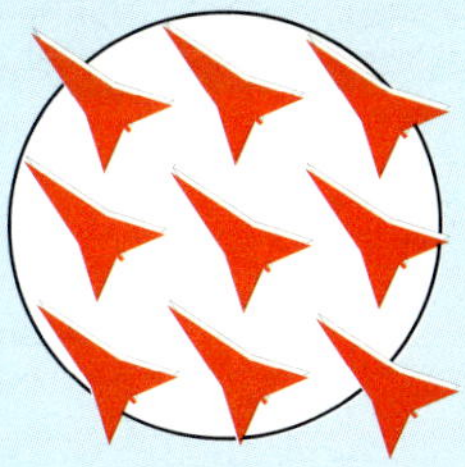

1994 FULL DISPLAY SEQUENCE

NOTE: AIRCRAFT ARE REPRESENTED BY STYLISED ARROWHEADS, SIMILAR TO THOSE USED IN THE SQUADRON CREST.

RED AIRCRAFT DENOTES UPPER SURFACES ARE VISIBLE

BLUE AIRCRAFT DENOTES UNDERSURFACES ARE VISIBLE

BASED ON RED ARROWS PUBLICATION SPT464

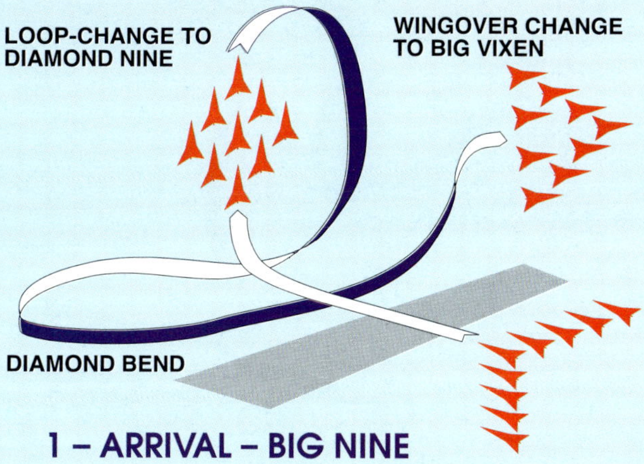

1 – ARRIVAL – BIG NINE

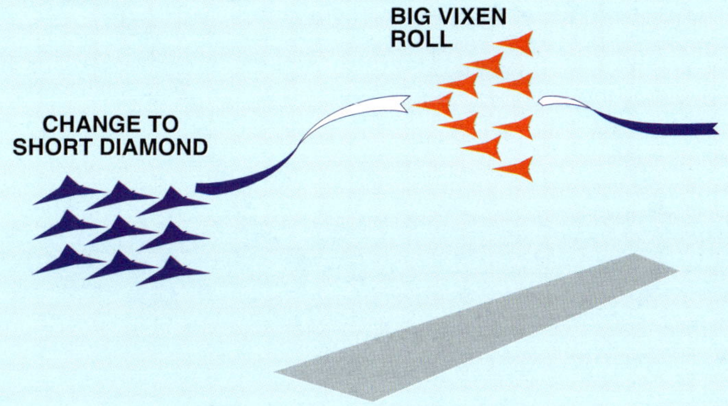

2 – BIG VIXEN ROLL

3 – APOLLO LOOP

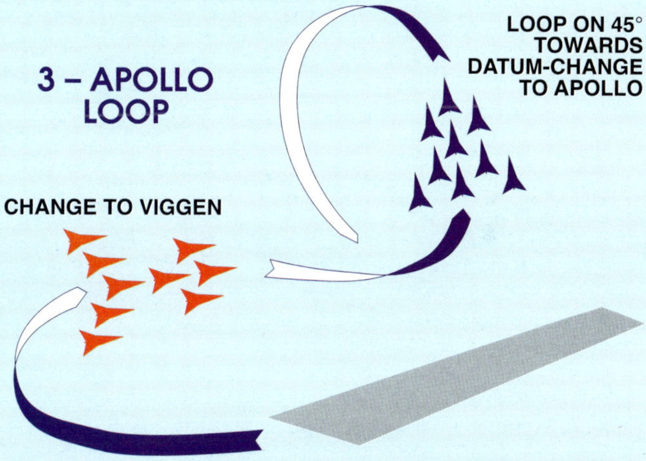

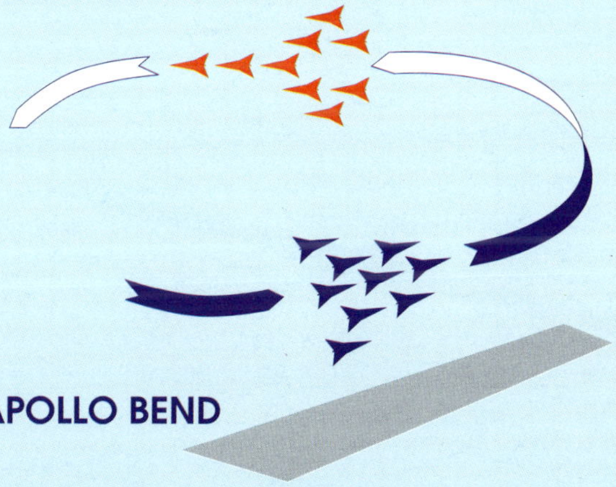

4 – APOLLO BEND

5 – CONCORDE BEND

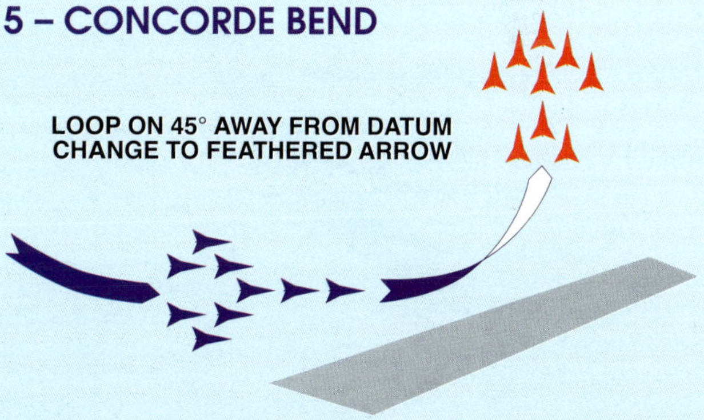

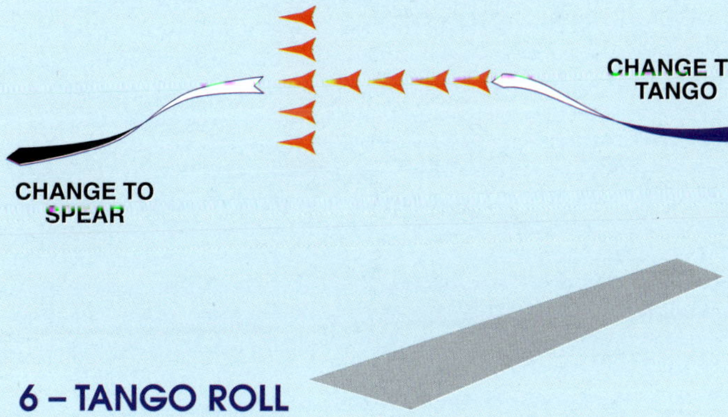

6 – TANGO ROLL

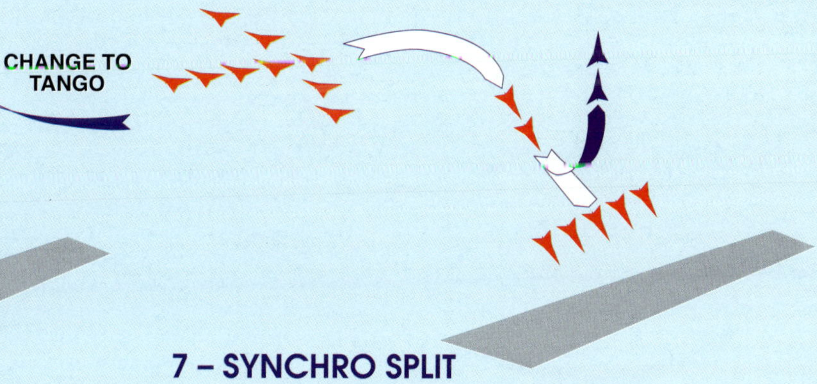

7 – SYNCHRO SPLIT

RED ARROWS

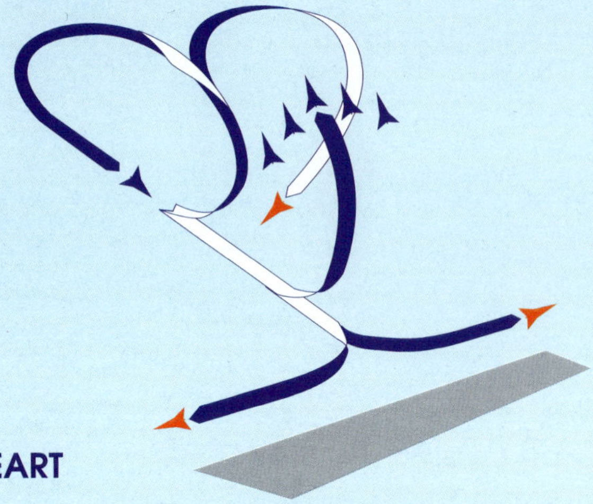

8 - HEART

9 – FAN

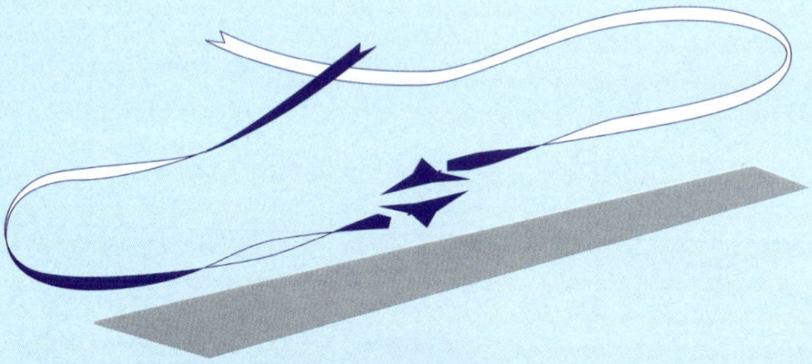

10 – OPPOSITION ROLLS

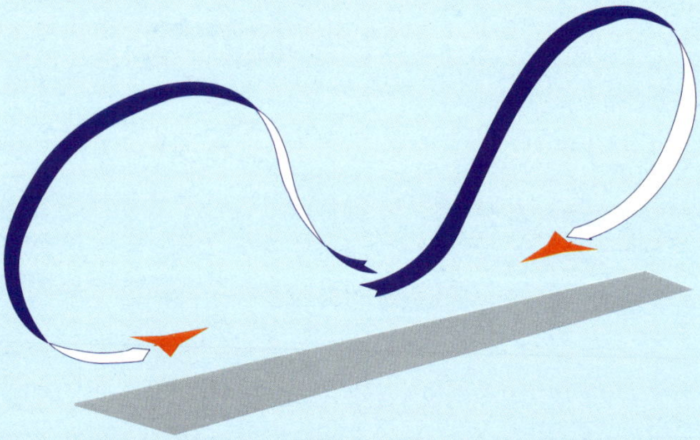

11 – PUSH UP TO OPPOSITION BARREL ROLL

12 – TWIZZLE

13 – CORKSCREW

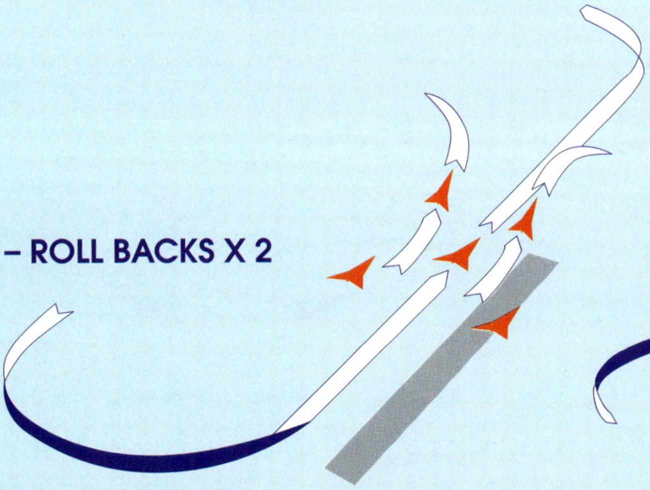

14 – ROLL BACKS X 2

15 – SHOTGUN

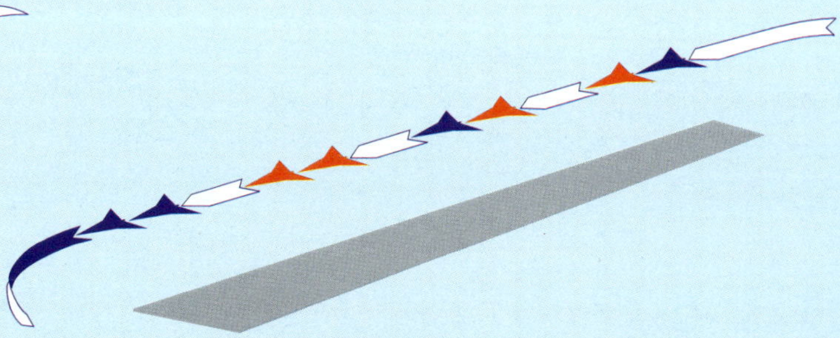

1994 FULL DISPLAY SEQUENCE

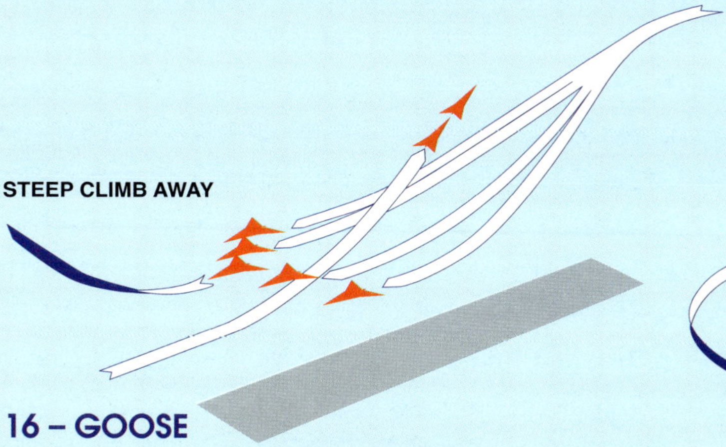

16 – GOOSE

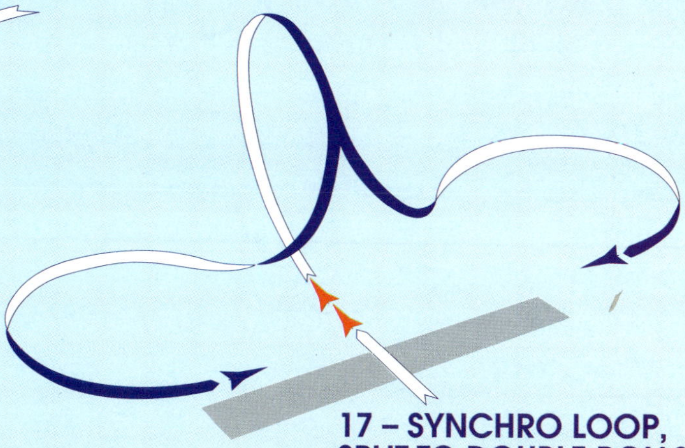

17 – SYNCHRO LOOP, SPLIT TO DOUBLE ROLLS

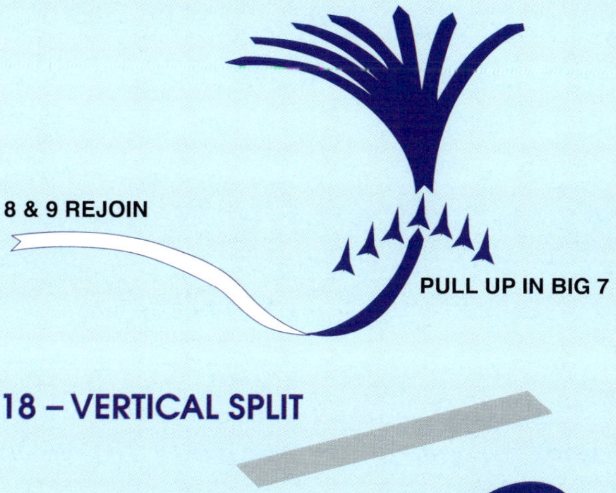

18 – VERTICAL SPLIT

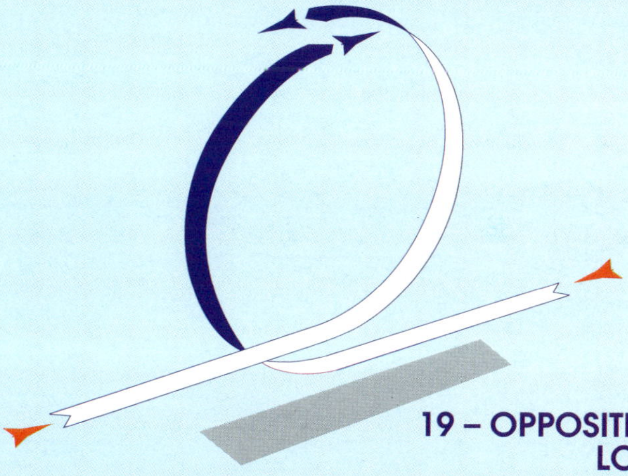

19 – OPPOSITION LOOP

20 – CATERPILLAR

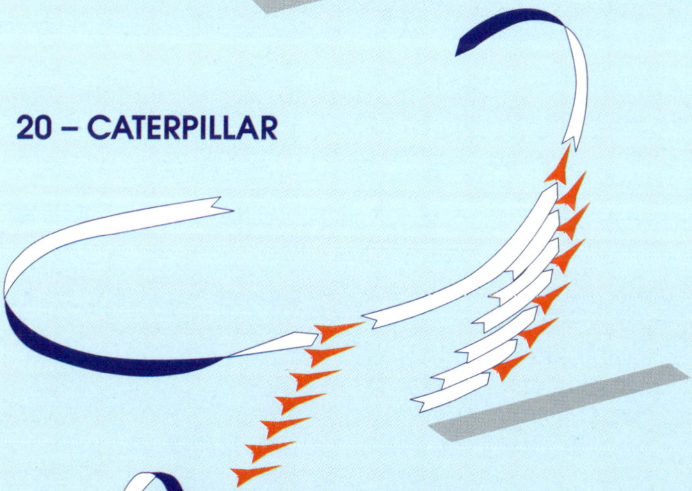

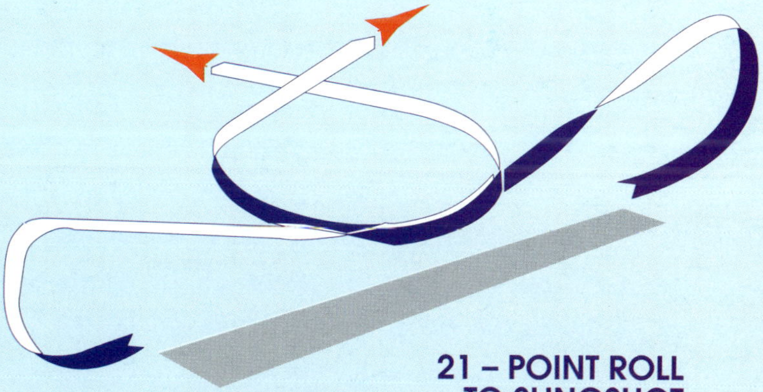

21 – POINT ROLL TO SLINGSHOT

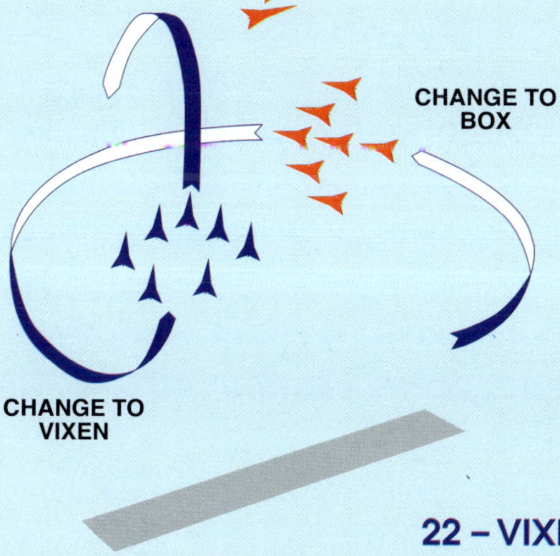

22 – VIXEN LOOP

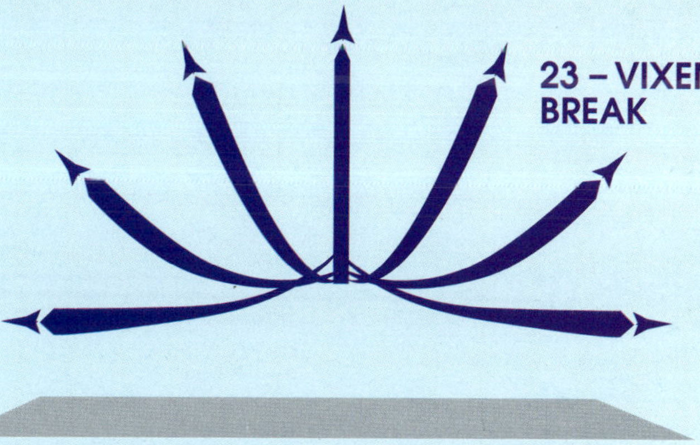

23 – VIXEN BREAK

RED ARROWS DISPLAYS OUTSIDE THE UNITED KINGDOM

AUSTRIA

Osterreichring	8/13/72
Osterreichring	8/19/84
Vienna	8/29/87

BAHRAIN

Bahrain	3/22/81

BANGLA DESH

Dhaka	7/9/86

BELGIUM

Balen-nent	8/29/71
Beauvechain	6/26/66
Beauvechain	6/25/72
Beauvechain	9/6/92
Bierset	6/3/84
Brussels	6/27/65
Florennes	6/21/73
Gosselies	9/10/67
Kieheval	8/21/83
Kiehevel	8/25/74
Kiehevel	8/23/87
Kleine Brogel	7/10/70
Kleine Brogel	9/6/87
Koksijde	8/11/68
Koksijde	8/9/69
Koksijde	7/9/87
Koksijde	7/7/90
Koksijde	7/7/91
Koksijde	7/5/92
Koksijde	7/4/93
Moorselle	6/11/78
Moorselle	8/21/83
Moorselle	8/23/87
Namur	5/23/93
Sanicole	8/5/84
Sanicole	8/4/85
Sanicole	8/11/91
Sanicole	8/1/93
SHAPE	6/14/79
SHAPE	6/10/81
SHAPE	6/8/83
SHAPE	6/5/85
SHAPE	6/18/87
Sonaca	5/15/93
Spa	8/8/65
Spa	8/3/69
Spa	8/8/71
Spa	8/5/73
Spa	6/27/76
St Truiden	6/20/71
St Truiden	9/10/89
Zwartburg	6/6/71
Zwartzberg	6/27/76

BRUNEI

Brunei	7/3/86

CANADA

Bagotville	6/8/72
Bagotville	5/25/83
Goose Bay	5/19/72
Ottowa	10/21/93
Reading	6/6/72
Rockcliffe/Trenton	5/8/83
St Catherines	6/10/72
St Catherines	6/11/72
Trenton	6/10/72
Trenton	5/9/83
Trenton CFB	5/8/93

CYPRUS

Air House	4/30/93
Akrotiri	10/18/66
Akrotiri	10/4/69
Akrotiri	7/6/71
Akrotiri	7/11/72
Akrotiri	9/26/73
Akrotiri	3/11/80
Akrotiri	3/12/80
Akrotiri	3/13/80
Akrotiri	3/10/81
Akrotiri	4/23/86
Akrotiri	4/25/89
Akrotiri	4/24/92
Akrotiri	4/25/92
Akrotiri	5/1/93
Dhekelia	10/22/66
Dhekelia	3/12/80
Dhekelia	3/11/81
Episkopi	10/17/66
Episkopi	10/2/69
Episkopi	7/7/71
Episkopi	7/12/72
Episkopi	9/26/73
Episkopi	3/11/80
Episkopi	3/12/81
Episkopi	4/24/89
Episkopi	4/29/91
Larnaca	5/1/93
Limassol	3/8/81
Limassol	4/30/91
Limassol	4/28/92
Limassol	5/4/93
Nicosia	10/22/66
Nicosia	10/4/69
Paphos	4/30/91
Paphos	4/25/92
Paphos	5/4/93

CZECHOSLOVAKIA

Bratislava	9/4/92
Bratislava	9/5/92

DENMARK

Aalborg	6/17/73
Aalborg	9/13/75
Aalborg	4/10/79
Aalborg	6/14/81
Aalborg	6/9/85
Aalborg	6/6/93
Karup	5/9/66
Karup	9/14/75
Karup	6/20/82
Skrydstrup	9/14/75
Vaerlose	9/13/75
Vaerlose	6/17/84
Vaerlose	6/12/88
Werdohl	9/4/83

EGYPT

Alessandria	6/10/73
Bilbeis Cairo	7/17/86

EIRE

Baldonnel	8/16/87

FINLAND

Helsinki	9/26/70
Helsinki	8/26/77
Helsinki	8/23/84
Josensuu	8/22/84
Koupio	8/25/77
Tampere	9/27/70
Tampere	8/21/84
Turku	9/26/70

FRANCE

Avignon	7/24/66
Beauvais	5/15/66
Besancon	6/13/65
Biarritz	8/31/68
Bourges	7/4/65
Calais	7/21/68
Cannes	9/14/69
Cannes	7/20/70
Chateauroux	6/10/66
Clermont Ferrand	5/9/65
Clermont Ferrand	6/7/70
Dijon	5/20/82
Dunkirk	5/27/90
Le Havre	5/7/67
Lille	6/25/78
Lyon	6/29/67
Lyon	6/11/78
Nice	9/14/69
Nice	7/19/70
Paris	6/20/65
Paris	6/1/67
Paris	6/4/69
Paris	5/30/73
Paris	6/2/73
Perignan	10/6/74
Reims	5/25/69
Reims	6/13/76
Roanne	9/24/78
Salon	4/28/73
Salon	7/6/78
St Pierre	10/1/76
Strasbourg	7/20/69
Tarbles	9/4/65
Tarbles	9/5/65
Toulouse	7/10/65
Toulouse	6/16/68
Toulouse	6/27/71
Toulouse	9/27/87
Troyes	5/18/67
Valence	5/23/65

GERMANY

Allendorf	8/31/86
Auf den Dumpel	8/19/73
Auf den Dumpel	9/8/68
Auf den Dumpel	8/31/69
Auf den Dumpel	9/6/70
Auf den Dumpel	9/12/71
Auf den Dumpel	9/22/74
Auf den Dumpel	9/19/76
Auf den Dumpel	9/11/77
Auf den Dumpel	9/2/79
Auf den Dumpel	9/21/80
Auf den Dumpel	9/20/81
Auf den Dumpel	9/26/82
Auf den Dumpel	9/18/83
Auf den Dumpel	8/31/86
Augsburg	9/8/85
Baden	5/5/73
Baden Soellingen	4/8/76
Baden Soellingen	4/27/78
Blumberg	9/15/85
Blumberg	9/20/87
Breitscheide Cologne	7/31/66
Breitscheide Cologne	7/29/79
Breitscheide Cologne	6/29/80
Breitscheide Cologne	6/23/82
Breitscheide Cologne	8/21/88
Bremgarten	1/7/94
Bruggen	7/6/68
Bruggen	8/2/69
Bruggen	8/9/71
Bruggen	4/20/72
Bruggen	7/28/72
Bruggen	4/13/73
Bruggen	9/22/76
Bruggen	8/30/80
Bruggen	9/3/83
Buechal	8/3/69
Cologne/Butzweilerhof	9/19/76
Cologne/Butzweilerhof	9/24/72
Damme	8/31/80
Damme	8/22/81
Damme	9/4/83
Geilenkirchen	8/7/65
Gutersloh	5/10/66
Gutersloh	5/27/67
Gutersloh	8/16/69
Gutersloh	7/29/72
Gutersloh	7/6/75
Gutersloh	4/20/77
Gutersloh	8/31/79
Gutersloh	9/5/83
Gutersloh	6/12/87
Gutersloh	6/16/88
Hahn	7/29/79
Hangelar	8/31/69
Hannover	5/3/78
Hannover	4/25/80
Hannover	5/22/82

Hannover	5/25/84
Hannover	6/13/86
Hilzengen	9/21/80
Hilzengen	9/19/82
Hilzingen	9/21/86
Hockenheim	7/29/79
Hockenhein	8/10/80
Holzminden	8/17/69
Ingoldstadt	7/21/74
Jever	6/23/82
Kamplintfort	8/17/69
Kamplintfort	8/8/71
Krefeld	8/19/73
Laarbruch	8/6/65
Laarbruch	8/18/69
Laarbruch	8/9/71
Laarbruch	9/1/73
Laarbruch	9/22/76
Laarbruch	8/23/77
Laarbruch	5/8/81
Laarbruch	9/25/82
Lahr	10/6/72
Landsberg	9/20/87
Linkenheim	9/6/81
Linkenheim	9/21/86
Lutzellinder	8/31/86
Mahl-Loemuhle	9/2/73
Marle le Mohle	8/21/77
Marle le Mohle	8/23/81
Marle le Mohle	9/4/83
Michelstadt	6/24/84
Munchen-Gladbach	9/1/85
Munchen-Gladbach	9/3/83
Munchen-Gladbach	8/30/87
Munster	5/27/85
Munster Telgte	9/3/72
Munster Telgte	8/21/77
Munster Telgte	8/31/80
Munster Telgte	9/26/82
Neheim Husten	6/12/76
Niederrhein	8/6/67
Norvenich	6/13/69
Nurburgring	8/3/69
Paderborn	9/26/76
Paderborn	8/20/77
Ramstein	8/26/73
Ramstein	4/14/73
Ramstein	9/22/74
Ramstein	7/31/77
Ramstein	7/30/78
Ramstein	6/20/80
Ramstein	7/13/80
Ramstein	8/2/81
Ramstein	8/7/83
Ramstein	5/24/84
Ramstein	6/23/85
Ramstein	8/10/86
Ramstein	8/2/87
Regensberg	9/19/82
Regensberg	9/2/84
Rheindahlen	8/7/65
Roermond	5/21/82
Rothenburg	5/23/82
Rothenburg	9/2/84
Rothenburg	6/22/80
Schameder	5/27/84
Scharnhorst	9/6/87
Schleswig	8/2/70
Schwenningen	9/24/72
Sembach	6/22/80
Sennelager	6/17/85
Sennelager	6/13/86
Sennelager	6/13/86
Sennelager	6/8/87
Sennelager	6/17/88
Siegerland	9/6/81
Spangdahlem	6/18/78
Werdohl	9/6/70
Werdohl	9/8/68
Werdohl	9/12/71
Werdohl	8/23/81
Wershofen	9/11/77
Wershofen	9/18/83
Wershofen	9/2/79
Wiesbaden	7/31/66
Wiesbaden	5/19/68
Wildenrath	8/9/65
Wildenrath	8/1/66
Wildenrath	6/29/67
Wildenrath	6/15/69
Wildenrath	7/5/70
Wildenrath	4/21/72
Wildenrath	7/6/75
Wildenrath	6/2/78
Wildenrath	9/1/79
Wildenrath	9/5/81
Wildenrath	9/25/82
Wildenrath	9/3/83
Wildenrath	8/22/88
Wildenrath	7/6/68
Wildenrath	4/14/73
Zweibrucken	8/20/83

GIBRALTAR

Gibraltar	9/21/85
Gibraltar	9/27/86
Gibraltar	10/1/88
Gibraltar	9/30/89
Gibraltar	9/28/91
Gibraltar	9/26/92

HUNGARY

Budapest Ferihegy	6/25/90

ICELAND

Keflavik	8/22/70
Reykjavik	8/27/70

INDIA

Hindan	7/10/86

INDONESIA

Kemayoran	6/28/86
Kemayoran	6/26/86

ITALY

Aviano	6/29/80
Bari	5/26/68
Florence	10/1/78
Lucca	5/21/88
Naples	7/17/72
Pescara	7/10/66
Pescara	7/9/67
Pescara	7/6/69
Pratica di Mare	9/22/73
Ravenna	8/22/65
Ravenna	8/27/67
Ravenna	8/24/69
Ravenna	8/20/72
Rimini	8/9/86
Rivolto	9/29/90
Salagareda	5/17/87
Turin	6/11/66
Turin	6/12/70
Turin	9/25/83
Venice	8/1/82
Vergiate (Milan)	5/1/70

JAPAN

Tokyo	3/29/81

JORDAN

Amman	10/20/66
Amman	7/16/86
Mafraq	3/28/81
Mafraq	7/16/86
Totoi	7/16/86

LIBYA

El Adem	10/16/66

LUXEMBOURG

Wiltz	7/12/87

MALAYSIA

Penang	7/5/86

MALTA

Luqa	10/15/66
Luqa	5/27/68
Luqa	9/27/78
Ta' Qali	10/7/69
Ta' Qali	10/3/70
Valletta	10/15/66
Valletta	5/28/68
Valletta	10/7/69
Valletta	10/3/70
Valletta	9/29/78
Valletta	8/12/92

MONACO

Monaco	9/12/69
Monaco	5/10/70

MOROCCO

Rabat	9/23/85

NETHERLANDS

Eindhoven	7/5/84
Eyguieres	4/29/73
Gilze Rijen	7/4/84
Rotterdam	10/2/65
Rotterdam	5/5/85
Scheveningen	6/11/83
Scheveningen	5/16/87
Soesterberg	4/25/70
Twenthe	7/31/70

NORWAY

Deelen	6/30/73
Deelen	7/11/83
Gardermoen	5/8/66
Kristiansand	6/3/89
Kristiansand	6/4/89
Oslo	5/8/66
Rygge	6/15/75
Stavangar	5/30/87

OMAN

Seeb	7/13/86

PAKISTAN

Masroor	7/12/86

PORTUGAL

Estoril	4/21/85
Lisbon	6/13/73

SINGAPORE

Singapore	7/1/86

SPAIN

Rota	5/21/92
Seville	5/21/92
Zaragoza	9/19/88

SWEDEN

Gothenburg	5/16/76
Gothenburg	8/25/84
Gothenburg	8/31/91
Gothenburg	9/1/91
Jonkoping	9/1/91
Linkoping	5/10/87
Vasteras	6/16/90
Vaxjo	5/31/92

SWITZERLAND

Bex	8/31/85
Bex	9/1/85
Constance	7/29/72
Constance	7/29/78
Geneva	8/9/80
Geneva	8/10/80
Lake Constance	7/31/76
Payerne	9/6/91
Payerne	9/7/91
Yverdon	8/20/88
Yverdon	8/11/90

THAILAND

Bangkok	7/7/86

TURKEY

Ankara	7/19/86
Ankara	5/6/93

UNITED ARAB EMIRATES

Abu Dhabi	3/21/81
Dubai	3/21/81
Sharjah	3/21/81

USA

Andrews AFB	5/13/83
Andrews AFB	10/19/93
Annapolis	5/23/83
Charleston	5/15/83
Cherry Point	5/15/83
Corpus Christi	5/21/83
Denver	9/24/93
Dulles	5/26/72
Dulles	5/31/72
Dulles	6/3/72
Eglin	5/18/83
Forth Worth	10/9/93
Houston	10/17/93
Kingsville	5/20/83
Moody	5/22/83
Nellis AFB	9/28/93
New Orleans	10/15/93
Oceana	5/11/83
Patuxent	5/10/83
Pensacola	5/17/83
Salinas	10/2/93
Sheppard AFB	10/6/93
Tyndall	5/16/83

USSR (Ukraine)

Chaika	6/23/90
Chaika	6/24/90

N.B.: Date is Month/Day/Year

Our Congratulations to
The Red Arrows
on 30 Years of Brilliance
From your Friends at Karsten Manufacturing Corporation
& Karsten U.K. Ltd. - Makers of PING Golf Equipment
Karsten Solheim
President and Chief Executive Officer
MARK NORTHOVER
PING
KELVIN TRUSS
PING
1994 Red Arrows
©Copyright Karsten Manufacturing Corporation 1994
Karsten U.K. Ltd. , Corringham Road, Gainsborough, Lincs. DN21 1XZ

ARTHUR GIBSON

Chapter Two – THE MEN BEHIND THE MARQUE

RED ONE

Squadron Leader John Rands currently enjoys the distinction of being 'Red One', the Team Leader and Commanding Officer of the Royal Air Force Aerobatic Team. John first joined the RAF in 1978, and completed his initial officer training at Henlow in Bedfordshire. He was then posted to Linton-on-Ouse near York, where he completed his basic flying training on the Jet Provost. He then moved to Valley on the island of Anglesey, where his training continued on the Hawk, moving to Chivenor in 1980 to begin tactical weapons training.

During the following year, John completed his Hawk training, and transferred to Binbrook in Lincolnshire, where he joined the Lightning Training Flight prior to beginning a five-year association with the legendary Lightning interceptor, primarily with N° 5 Squadron; "I did the Lightning Weapons Instructor course right at the end of my stay, and I never actually consumated my Qualified Weapons Instructor ticket, and never actually instructed anyone in the twin-seaters. I left in eighty-six and came to Scampton for the first time, and spent three years with the Red Arrows and for the latter two years I was with the Synchro Pair. I left in eighty-nine, crossing over from air defence to offensive support, and I was posted to the Harrier Conversion Unit at Wittering, where I spent ten months with 233 OCU which is now N° 20 Reserve Squadron. I flew the Harrier GR3 and T4, and then the GR5, after which I went to N° 3 Squadron at Gutersloh where I was a Flight Commander. We later moved the Squadron down to Laarbruch, and I enjoyed Germany very much: it was a great tour, and the Harrier GR5 was a fantastic aeroplane. I then came back to the Red Arrows towards the end of ninety-three".

John is keen to emphasise how much he enjoyed flying the Harrier, even though he transferred to the offensive support (ground attack) role after having flown the supersonic Lightning; "I don't have any regrets about leaving the air defence world. The change-over certainly wasn't thrust upon me, it was very much my own decision and at the time I just didn't particularly want to go and fly the Tornado F2, which was then coming into service. I didn't want to go two-seat which was a personal decision, very difficult to back-up with good facts or reasons, it was just my own feeling. I did desperately want to go and fly the Harrier and I had lots of friends who were flying Harriers. They had told me about field operations and all the other aspects of Harrier flying. Deep-down though, I did have a certain amount of trepidation about changing roles. Okay, I knew about air defence and although the basics would be the same, I knew it would take me quite a while to learn how to operate all of the new kit. To actually change roles is quite a big leap, and quite a few people didn't think it was such a good idea. I was twenty-nine at the time, which isn't very old, but it's fairly late to be introduced to a new aeroplane and a new role, and on top of that I was also a Flight Commander so there was quite a lot going on".

Certainly, John's experience is fairly unusual, at least by present-day standards. The Royal Air Force is naturally keen to avoid unnecessary expenditure, and money is now a driving factor. Air defence pilots rarely change to offensive support flying, or vice-versa and, for many reasons, very few pilots would want to change roles in this way; "It's interesting how you see yourself, and when I was with the Lightning force we certainly regarded ourselves as the last of a breed. The Lightning was great fun, but after I'd been there about eighteen months, I began to realise how the aeroplane had never really been developed. The radar was only good up to a certain point and the weapons system was very old. By this time, most of the mud-moving community were equipped with Sidewinder missiles for self-defence, which was a much better missile than we used on the Lightning. So we were completely out-classed when compared to aircraft such as the F-15 and F-16. It was a very challenging machine to fly, but by the time it was taken out of service it was certainly time for it to go. The Lightning had been great, but the thought of conversion onto the Tornado F2, then back out over the North Sea and so on, after having done that kind of thing for five years, just didn't seem like a good idea. I'd done it, and I decided it would be better to go and do the low-level role, and I knew that would be much more of a challenge".

John continues: "The Harrier is a very capable aeroplane and I did more combat flying in the Harrier than I ever did in the Lightning. We never had that much fatigue life to play with on the Lightnings, and until they gave us a very firm retirement date, we had to keep on stretching-out the airframe fatigue, so you could just go out and tear the wings off. With the Harrier however, we had a brand-new aeroplane, and even without over-fatiguing the Harrier we could spend maybe forty-five minutes flying combat above Gutersloh, just using internal fuel. With the Lightning F3, ten or fifteen minutes would be our maximum time for a combat sortie".

So what made John Rands leave Harriers and return to the Red Arrows? John explains; "deep-down, a part of me really wanted to come back to the team. I knew the flying would be very different and part of me wanted to come back, but I'm not the kind of person who leaps at something immediately. I was fortunate in that I had the recommendation and the backing so, when I left the team after my first three years, I knew I stood a very good chance of coming back. I knew of three other guys who were in a position to come back, who fitted the criteria of having served before, having stayed in the RAF, having been promoted and so on, and roughly two years ago I found out that they were looking at me for possible selection. I was at Gutersloh, and for about three months I was like the proverbial cat on a hot tin roof until the decision came through. All I'd done was to say on my own report that I'd like to come back. I wasn't called for interview nor was anybody else; it was decided on the strength of the reports. It's quite interesting the way in which there are so many hoops you have to go through to get on the team the first time, whereas things are very different if you come back as leader. It is quite a prestigious post, lots of guys wants to do it too.

"It's a very different kind of challenge. Every day people are relying on you. The physical side of things is very enjoyable too, and you have to climb into an aeroplane three times each day which can get very tiring. Likewise the mental side is a challenge too, having to put the show together and so on, but you get a great deal of support from the people you work with. It is a challenge, and we seem to have lost that kind of attitude from public life. Competition is a good thing, and our guys are out there all the time, trying to make the display as good as possible, and they make me work hard too, just to keep up with them. I can't afford to relax at all, and that's great. Having been here before, I really did wonder if I could do the job. I didn't really doubt my own capabilities, but the job just appeared to be so difficult. In the back of my mind I knew that the team and the display sequence would come together and I knew that I was capable of doing it, but it's a very hard learning curve, making sure that everything I do is right. I was away for about four years in which time I'd flown different aircraft and done many different things. Some of my previous team experience did come back, but it takes time for all the little things to fit back into place. Things like making radio calls at the right time and so on".

Despite John's enthusiasm, there's no doubt that the pre-season training is very, very hard work as he explains; "Some days you go out and fly a sequence, and you think you've taken a step back, but we did get the show together and even with four new guys and having started a month late, we've got the show together. We haven't broken any bad weather restrictions, but if there's a chance to fly, we will fly. We designate a diversion airfield, we get the fuel on-board and we'll go up and take a look at the conditions, and that's the best way to be. It's not that we're gung-ho, it just means that whenever possible the Reds will fly. If the crosswinds are on the limit, we will fly but have a diversion airfield as standby. If visibility isn't too good we can get airborne and get above it. Sometimes in the winter season you can get up to one or two thousand feet and be above the weather in clear air, just glancing at the airfield through the odd gap, and maybe making an instrument approach back into the airfield".

The flexible way in which the Red Arrows train and display, is a sharp contrast to many other national aerobatic teams which restrict their flying to near-perfect weather conditions. The decision on whether to fly or stay on the ground is made well in advance of the scheduled display time. John's philosophy is different; "our display is flexible and we can change between a flat, rolling or full display format. Nobody knows what the weather will be like until you get to the display site and especially in Britain the conditions change in a matter of minutes. So on a nice day we fly the full show, but we can change the sequence if the conditions deteriorate, or on a bad-weather day I might suddenly see a gap in the weather and I can call a change in display sequence, going into the full looping format. If I have sufficient cloud base, then as long as I can work safely underneath then that's okay. The worst days are the hazy ones when I have to make that decision whether to split-off the Synchro Pair, or simply end the display at that point. I have to determine whether the pilots will be able to separate and then safely find each other again in the prevailing visibility conditions. It's my decision. I know the sequences and the team members know them too. They will also get a feel for the conditions and be thinking-ahead, anticipating my next move. They have the ability to utilise their spare mental capacity in this way and that's why they're here. Not everybody could do the job and most of them have to work very hard. They're certainly from the top of the pile, well-respected senior Flight Lieutenants with exceptional flying ability and mental capacity".

Weather conditions are naturally a major factor in the team's decision-making process. On particularly changeable days, John (colloquially known as 'the Boss') may send Red Nine to take a look, returning with a first-hand report on the cloud base heights, and visibility, as seen from the Hawk's cockpit. The Team Leader must be able to think ahead, and constantly monitor the ever-changing weather, deciding when the sequence can change between formats. This is just one small aspect of John's demanding job.

Another vital skill John had to learn quickly, was how to lead the whole nine-aircraft formation through

RAF SCAMPTON

each manoeuvre. Although John had flown hundreds of sorties during his previous tour with the team, taking the 'front seat' is completely different; "At the end of last season when I joined the team, the experienced guys went on leave and gave me some time to lead the new guys through some basic looping and rolling manoeuvres, giving them some confidence, but also giving me a chance to modify the way I flew too. I have to give the guys a predictable ride and I have to be very careful. For example, if I over-pulled at the top of a loop and made it just a little bit too tight, some of the other guys would have a very hard time and on a very hot day they could just run out of sufficient power to keep up".

Away from the flying training and demonstrations, the Team Leader also has to deal with the team's public image; "I have a huge amount of support but I think that by this stage in my Air Force career, I have sufficient confidence to go out there and deal with the public fairly easily. We have lots of visitors here and we do the public relations job very well. The number of people who come through our doors and the number of people who see the team here is quite surprising. We do put in a great deal of effort and we try to get out and meet people. In some ways we're in a kind of show-business and at the end of a long day, after maybe three displays, and you're trying to get from your aeroplane to the accommodation to have a shower, a beer and just relax, there might be fifty-thousand people between you and your destination, so you're just not going to make it. Once you stop to sign an autograph you're stuck there! But that's the job, and the effort we put in pays dividends".

Of course, the Red Arrows could change their public relations philosophy to reflect the approach adopted by America's teams. The number of displays could be reduced in exchange for a larger amount of time spent on the ground, face-to-face with the public. John Rands believes that the Red Arrows have got the balance just right; "It's interesting the way in which the Americans go about their business, but our attitudes are completely different. Our job is flying. We could do a ceremonial start to the display and march out to the aircraft, closing our canopies in formation, stuff like that, but it's not the way Brits do things. We brief, climb into our aeroplanes, go and do the show, and then de-brief. No matter where we are, we will de-brief carefully, using video recordings to look at the formations, positioning, timing, the whole thing, constantly trying to improve things. I'm not above constructive advice either, and the guys will tell me if there are things which I can improve. I'm part of the team too".

Unfortunately, even a world-famous 'institution' such as the Red Arrows is not immune to the attentions of the defence expenditure watchdogs. Although the team's value to the RAF is reviewed every year, the ever-increasing pressure on finances has led to media speculation that the Red Arrows may face a very uncertain future; "if you go back a few years to when the Berlin Wall was still there and the Cold War very much alive, then defence was perceived as being very necessary, and the Red Arrows were just seen as part of that overall military stance. Things have changed now. I think the Peace Dividend doesn't exist; there is no such thing. The former USSR hasn't lost its military capability, it is still there and although the RAF has run-down in Germany, we're committed in other areas around the world. I can understand people saying that the Red Arrows are a waste of money. But for me, I think there is still an important place for the Red Arrows in the Royal Air Force, and within the UK as a whole. In terms of cost I think we're worth it. We're a small and fairly efficient squadron and we give back more than we take. I refuse to walk around with a long face when we have a real job to do. Money has a great impact on our lives at present. We show the Air Force for what it is. The Air Force is all about excellence. Our training and our people are, I believe, still the best in the world and it's taken us thirty years to reach this stage and okay, we're going through lean times, but I believe we're worth it. But once we're gone, that's it, I can never imagine the Red Arrows ever coming back".

It has also been suggested that the Red Arrows could be replaced by a 'part time' aerobatic team, drawn from an operational squadron. John doubts whether this would be a practical proposition; "I don't think it's realistic. Our front-line squadrons are stretched to their limits, the guys on the squadrons are working incredibly hard and their aircraft are committed to operational tasks so that there is no slack in the system to do the kind of things that the Red Arrows do. It takes us six months of intensive training to bring guys up to scratch and get the show out on the road. It would also be too expensive; a Tornado would be so much more expensive to run than a Hawk and would also be much less reliable. The Hawk is the ideal aeroplane for the aerobatic job. There's nothing we can do to change the current financial climate and people lose their jobs every day, so we can't expect to be treated any differently. Thankfully, the people who make the decisions regarding our future are very much on our side".

When John leaves the Red Arrows for the second time, where will he go? John naturally doesn't know for sure, but he has some ideas in mind; "most former Team Leaders leave the Air Force. Leading the Red Arrows is not a major career move if you plan to stay in the Air Force. Very few people get a second flying tour as a Squadron Leader and most go onto a ground tour. I've got my second tour but because I'm flying for three years I don't go to the Staff College or do any sort of ground tour and I'll have basically lost three years of my career when I leave. I'll be thirty-seven by that time, and Leading the Red Arrows isn't regarded as being anything special. I'll have another year of service to complete after I leave the team and I'll make my decision then. A great deal could happen before then. The airlines might be recruiting, although I'm not in any great hurry to fly an airliner. I've got quite a few friends who fly airliners and they all found their jobs very challenging, but after a while I think the job loses some of its excitement and you really need to get military flying out of your system first. By the time I'm thirty-eight I might have changed my views as I'm already getting some grey hairs and I'm probably creaking at the joints a little bit already"!

R.J. CARUANA

Debriefing at RAF Scampton – December, 1993. Having waited for some time for the weather to clear, John Rands discusses the sortie with the 'new boys'

RED TWO

New to the Red Arrows for the 1994 display season, Flight Lieutenant Spike Jepson ('Red Two') trained to fly the Jet Provost at Church Fenton in Yorkshire, before continuing his advanced flying training on Hawks at Valley. He then joined a Tactical Weapons Unit at Brawdy (which has now closed) and was posted to N° 233 OCU at Wittering, the Harrier Operational Conversion Unit, now N° 20(R) Squadron. His first operational tour was with N° 1 Squadron at Wittering after which he became a Qualified Weapons Instructor and moved to N° 4 Squadron at Gutersloh in Germany. He then returned to the Harrier OCU at Wittering as an instructor, but after one year he joined the Red Arrows at Scampton in November 1993.

Why join the Red Arrows? Spike explains; "I thought it would be exciting and lots of fun. I'd done a couple of seasons as a Harrier display pilot with N° 4 Squadron and I enjoyed that immensely. I'd seen a fair bit of the display circuit and enjoyed it, so the only way I could really continue displaying was to join the Red Arrows. Of course, if you want to be a display pilot, it's fine to be a solo performer, but the ultimate job is to get into the Red Arrows and join the real professionals, there's no other way to go".

Before joining the team Spike regarded the Red Arrows as a fairly elite unit; "I think everybody looks at the team in that way, but having seen things from the inside I think it needs to be like that. Lots of people knock the Red Arrows when they're on the outside, but I was never that kind of guy. That kind of negative attitude is often generated by envy, pure and simple, but my own view was that I desperately wanted to join the team as I thought it would be great...and it is".

Spike continues; "I know it's a bit of a trite thing to say, but I really did think it would be easier than it really is. When you come here for selection, you go round the formation and sit in the rear seat of each aircraft to see things for yourself. At that stage however, the team are in a fairly advanced stage and they're pretty competent so things look very easy. But when you come here and have to do it yourself from the front seat, you realise that they've worked pretty hard to get to that stage and it takes an awful lot of training to make it look so much easier than it is. As for the physical task itself, the basic formation flying is pretty much the same as with any other squadron, but in terms of mental energy it's the longest and hardest period of concentration that you could ever have in an aeroplane. For about thirty minutes your concentration is phenomenal, just flying precision formation".

In handling terms, the Harrier, which Spike previously flew, is very similar to the Hawk, as he explains; "The two aircraft are much the same. The new generation Harrier is a high performance machine and when I displayed the Harrier I compared notes with the Hawk display pilot, and all of our speeds and altitudes for loops and so on, were very similar. In terms of pitch the aircraft are similar, and the Hawk is slightly slower in terms of roll rate. As for complexity there's just no comparison as the Hawk is a very simple trainer whereas the Harrier is a very high-tech machine. The engine response is the major difference however, and on the Harrier the engine response is instantaneous in order to operate from short strips and so on, whereas the Hawk's engine is unbelievably sluggish by comparison. But like any sort of motor response, you get used to it quickly and adapt to your new conditions. It's not too difficult to get used to the different handling characteristics of the Hawk".

As a former Harrier display pilot, Spike had already had plenty of experience in dealing with the public, long before he joined the Red Arrows; "you get some complete fanatics talking to you sometimes, and they know more about the aeroplane and the Air Force than you do, and it's absolutely remarkable. It can get quite irritating sometimes, but when you get genuine enthusiasts who have come to see displays, it's very refreshing and enjoyable, and to meet people who are genuinely interested in what you're doing is just great. But there are some real bores around and you can get trapped by the odd one, whom you just have to handle as politely as possible. Most though are very nice people who don't get an opportunity to meet those who actually fly the aircraft, so you just accept that as part of the job. They ask you about the aircraft's performance, like how fast can it go, how high, what g you're pulling in the display, where have you come from and so on. But some people come along and they can tell you where your aircraft was built, when it was built, what squadrons it's served with, just like enthusiasm gone mad, and they're not interested in you, they want to talk to the display pilot. So now I'm with the Red Arrows, you have to understand that you're wearing a red suit, and the public are interested in the Red Arrows, not you as a person, you have to remember that, just in case you start to get an inflated ego".

Looking back to when he first applied to join the Red Arrows, Spike recalls his initial interview with the team; "I think most of the questions were fairly predictable. They are always looking for a particular kind of person to join the team, so that is reflected in the kind of things they ask you. For example, you can bet your life that they'll ask you why you want to join the team, and what makes you special, and why you should be selected rather than the next guy on the list. They'll look through your flying records and if they see any sort of hiccups in your career, they'll exploit that and discuss it with you. Basically, what they're looking for is somebody who they can rely on, who can fit-in with the team atmosphere. They couldn't afford to take on a misfit within a nine-man team for three years and they try to eliminate that kind of thing. They can ask some pretty off-the-wall things, but it's a fairly predictable interview".

The Red Arrows pilots select the people who join their team which ensures that the Red Arrows are certain to have the most appropriate people for the job. Because of this arrangement, the team usually have a fair idea of what each pilot is like, socially and professionally, before they even arrive at Scampton for interview. Not surprisingly, a fairly large number of pilots apply to join the Red Arrows, as Spike comments; "proportionally speaking, if you look at the number of pilots who are eligible to apply, and the number who actually do, it's a pretty high figure. But then, the Red Arrows are regarded as a sort of classic British success story like the QE2 and Concorde, so it's hardly surprising. Your friends and family are genuinely proud of your achievement in joining the team, and they accept that for the next three years you probably won't have a summer of your own, being away with the team, but that's part of the job".

Of course, the question of safety is often raised by friends and family, as the general public often perceive the Red Arrows as being a 'daredevil stunt team'. Spike has his own views on this subject; "I think that people do think it's a dangerous job, but all kinds of flying is inherently more dangerous than an office job, but it's an accepted part of life. By the time you're in a position to join the Red Arrows, you've already been with various other units and you'll have known some guys who have been involved in accidents at some stage or other. People do perceive us as a stunt team sometimes, and that's rather sad because we're actually a very professional team. We have a vested interest in not hurting ourselves, and every safety precaution is taken. Every manoeuvre is thought through long and hard and there are various escape manoeuvres for every part of the display. The team has been around for thirty years so most things have been done before and the whole display is a stage-by-stage building block, nothing is thrown-in without careful planning. Safety is always paramount".

But for a former solo Harrier display pilot, what are the attractions of a nine-aircraft display team? Spike explains; "the Red Arrows display is much more demanding. With a solo display in the Harrier for example, you're able to get away with more minor errors, whereas in a tight formation display everybody is relying on you to get it right. In my number two slot, I set up the symmetry of the formation so if I get it wrong then everybody looks wrong, so there's pressure on me to get it right. In a solo display you can cover up minor positioning and manoeuvre errors and nobody would notice. You can only do solo display flying for so long in any case, and I wanted to carry on displaying to the public, and the Red Arrows was the best and most obvious way to do it".

Spike was never an avid aviation enthusiast, but even before leaving school, he always wanted to be a pilot; "my father was in the Air Force so I've lived on RAF bases for most of my life. I was never obsessed with aircraft, but my only thought about a job after leaving school was never anything other than being a pilot. Had things not worked out I seriously don't know what else I would have done as I'd never considered anything else. I wasn't really passionate about joining the RAF, but it was the obvious thing to do. Certainly, I never looked at the Red Arrows when I was a kid and suddenly decided that I wanted to join the Air Force. It was a sort of natural progression".

Looking to the future when Spike leaves the Red Arrows, he is naturally unsure about where his career may lead; "it's very hard to see ahead so far. Providing the Red Arrows are still here to actually leave in three years time, and providing there's still an Air Force to go back to, I guess I'll probably go back to the Harrier and I'd be very happy to re-join the Harrier force. I don't see the Jaguar or Tornado as an option as in comparison to the Harrier, they wouldn't be much of a new challenge. The RAF look at the experience you already have, so you tend to go back to the aircraft you previously flew, but in any case I can't think of a better aeroplane to fly than the Harrier. It's the most demanding aeroplane that the RAF have, so I'll be delighted to go back to it when I leave the Red Arrows".

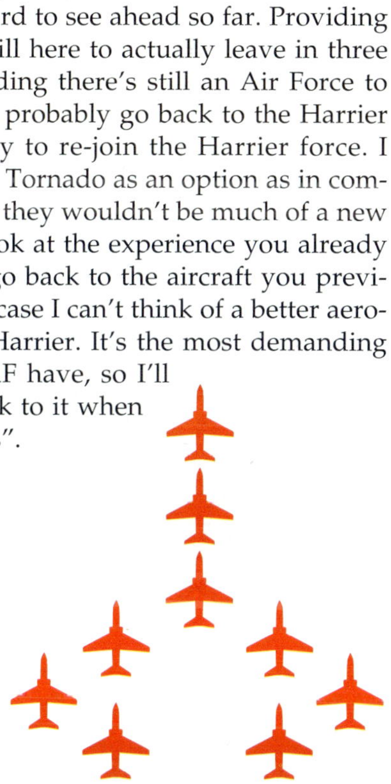

CONCORDE

RED THREE

At the end of every display season most members of the team take two weeks of annual leave, but the skies over RAF Scampton don't fall silent; the training for next year's display season begins immediately as three new pilots begin flying with the Team Leader. They will have already joined the team some weeks previously, and will have occupied the rear seats of the Hawks during some of the displays towards the end of the season, giving them an opportunity to sit back and slowly familiarise themselves with the rather unusual surroundings of their new 'office'.

Flight Lieutenant Mark Zanker joined the team towards the end of the 1993 season, assuming the position of 'Red 3', to the port side of the Leader in the basic 'diamond nine' formation. Prior to joining the Red Arrows, he was a QWI (Qualified Weapons Instructor) with N° 20(R) Squadron, the Harrier Conversion unit at Wittering, near Peterborough. He had previously served with N° 3 Squadron in Germany, and before joining the Harrier force, he was a Jaguar pilot with N° 54 Squadron at Coltishall in Norfolk.

Like every other RAF fast jet pilot, Mark had previously flown the Hawk during the advanced stages of his training. Having learned how to fly, he then learned how to operate an aircraft as a weapons platform, with N° 2 Tactical Weapons Unit at Chivenor, near Barnstaple in Devon (and also spent some time with N° 1 Tactical Weapons Unit at Brawdy, in Dyfed). However, unlike most RAF pilots, Mark didn't follow the normal basic and advanced training syllabus through a BFTS (Basic Flying Training School; either N° 1 FTS or N° 3 FTS) and N° 4 FTS; he was given a rare opportunity to fly and train with the United States Air Force as part of an exchange scheme.

Interestingly, the USAF's training methods are somewhat different to those employed by the RAF, as Mark explains; "there's no doubt that the American system is different, but as to whether it is better or worse, I don't think it made any real difference in the final analysis. The weather factor is different in that it's a case of blue skies pretty much every day, so you're unrestricted in flying terms, but the airspace is very controlled. Whenever you go off flying, it's very different to the UK where you can basically use visual flight rules most of the time. In the States you have to get clearance from civilian Air Traffic Controllers to enter a specific area of controlled airspace, so that part of the flying is fairly regulated. But at that early stage in your training it doesn't really make much difference whether you're flying in the USA or UK to be honest. I also had a full year of continuity which was nice, and I didn't find much of a problem adapting to flying in the UK. Their emphasis is on totally different areas of flying compared to the RAF".

It could certainly be said that the USAF's training is slightly 'unrealistic' in terms of weather conditions. Considering the prevailing conditions in the UK and Europe, it is questionable whether 'blue skies' training is appropriate, but Mark disagrees; "their emphasis is on lots of instrument flying, lots of instrument approaches. When you learn to ride a motorcycle or drive a car, you wouldn't want to start in the middle of London, would you? It's better to start somewhere a little quieter. We did lots of formation flying, which must have been a help I suppose, now that I'm with the Red Arrows".

Mark had always been interested in aviation, but never imagined that he would one day be part of the Royal Air Force Aerobatic Team; "When I was a kid I was very interested in aircraft and my father was a pilot, so I had lots of hands-on experience of aircraft at close quarters. We went to lots of air shows too, and my first priority was to get into the Air Force and become a pilot. When I'd done that, the idea of joining the Red Arrows seemed more achieveable. Before I'd flown in the RAF, the Red Arrows were always an attractive idea to me, the whole public image of the RAF appealed to me. Now that I've flown two types of fast jet, it's a welcome change to do this kind of job. It's very exciting, it's high-profile, and I guess ultimately it's a challenge more than anything else".

To many outside observers, the Red Arrows are often seen as an 'elite unit', distanced from the rest of the Royal Air Force. Mark also regarded the team as something special, as he explains; "I always thought that they were quite an elite unit, probably because I didn't know any of the people who were on the team. By the time I'd finished flying Harriers and started flying Hawks I knew quite a few of the Red Arrows pilots, and they were just mates doing another job, so I then looked at things differently. The team does tend to generate a particular kind of image, usually amongst people who don't have any contact with us. That sort of thing also happened with the Harrier force too, and people used to refer to us as Prima Donnas, doing all kinds of strange flying out of their dispersed sites out in Germany, and really there's no mystery, we're all pilots working for the same company. It's just ignorance really, and there's not much you can do about that, so you just have to get on with your job".

Having joined the Red Arrows, Mark can expect to fly with the team for three years; "people often ask me if the job is how I expected it to be. To be honest, I don't know what I really expected as it's so different to any other sort of flying job. Okay, I had flown the Hawk before but this is a totally different experience with many different demands on my flying skills and mental capacity. I'd flown in the lead aircraft with the Boss, so I'd got a feel for the things that he has to think about and the way the whole display is flown, but you don't get to see most of the action which is going on behind you. When I first flew with the team, all I wanted to do was get down to the back to see more of the action, flying with the synchro guys and so on, to see what it was all about".

Learning to fly as part of a nine-aircraft formation requires a huge amount of skill, and Mark admits that it isn't easy; "it was more difficult than I'd imagined. Maintaining concentration for so long is very difficult, and you can't afford to day-dream even for a couple of seconds. You can't start thinking about what you're having for dinner, or what's on TV, you have to concentrate on the position you're flying, and think what manoeuvre is coming-up next. Most of the things we do are made on a radio call. I sit on the inside of up to three other aeroplanes and in some of the manoeuvres I will turn blind into their position. If they haven't moved, or if I move before the radio call, I'll hit them, so a great deal is done on trust. Concentration is the hardest thing, but it's very physical too, and if you just look at the sweat on the guys when they walk back from their aircraft, you can see that it's very hard work, it's like playing a game of squash"!

Of course, Mark's duties extend beyond display flying. As part of his job he will also be required to meet the public on a daily basis; "I was the Harrier display pilot in Germany for two years, so I visited lots of air displays and met lots of people. In fact, it's one of the most satisfying parts of the job, talking to the public about flying, answering all their questions and so on".

Mark certainly doesn't have any reservations when it comes to meeting the millions of spectators he can expect to see during each display season. All in a day's work for the Royal Air Force's 'Aerial Ambassadors'.

R.J. CARUANA

At home (left) and abroad (below) the Red Arrows are always in close contact with the general public making them 'the Royal Air Force's Aerial Ambassadors'

PETER MOBBS

APOLLO

RED FOUR

Prior to joining the Red Arrows at the end of 1993, Flight Lieutenant Kelvin Truss was a Tornado F3 pilot with N° 56(R) Squadron at Coningsby, after transferring from Leeming, where he had also flown the Tornado F3, with N° 23 Squadron. Before joining the Tornado force, Kelvin was a Qualified Flying Instructor (QFI) at Cranwell, flying Jet Provost basic trainers. The challenge of a tour with the Red Arrows attracted him to the team; "the chance to do something different appealed to me. The job puts new demands on your skills, and the kind of flying skills you have to master are very different to the kind of thing you would do on an operational squadron. It wasn't a long-held ambition, as before then I knew I wasn't in a position to join anyway, but three or four years ago I started to think seriously about the team".

Kelvin recalls his initial contact with the Red Arrows; "I was shortlisted to join the team twice and the first time I came here, my first trip was with the Synchro Pair, and it was pretty exciting, much more than I imagined it would be. The other formation positions are also much more exciting than I imagined too. I did wonder whether the job might become a little routine eventually, just flying close formation all day and every day, but that's certainly not the case. Every sortie is different, despite the fact that you're trying to achieve the same effect each time. On any squadron, you would fly formation, but you would be assuming a stable position at a reasonable distance, just to maintain sight of your leader as you go through cloud and so on. With the Red Arrows we're obviously looking for something much closer and much more precise, and then you have varying Met conditions, and the other pilots are having either a better or worse day than previously, so everything is constantly changing, even though the basic display format might be the same".

Kelvin's early experiences with the team will also extend beyond the demands on his flying skills, as he explains; "when you apply for the team, you understand that dealing with the public will be a major part of the job, so I'm not uncomfortable with the idea. It's fundamental to the team, very much our raison d'être, and I'm very much pro-Air Force, and it gets plenty of bad press, so I'm keen to promote the Royal Air Force if I can. Going to the air shows, being a PR animal, a high-profile guy, is fine, and I'm looking forward to doing it. Even so, it has to be a balance set against the primary job of flying, as a bad display would be pretty bad PR for us too".

With an ever-increasing pressure being applied upon the RAF to make major cuts in expenditure, Kelvin knows that he will not only promote the RAF's role within the United Kingdom's defence strategy, but also 'defend' the position of the Red Arrows, within the Air Force; "in physical terms, we have the hardware out there on the flight line, capable of achieving the same results as any other Hawk, so the Air Force would have them, whether or not we flew them in displays. Likewise, the pilots here on the team will only be with the team for three years, so we'll never be away from the front-line long enough to require any major training to be re-converted back to our operational roles. So in resource terms we're not much of a tax on the system. In overall terms the cost of running the team is incredibly small when compared to other squadrons, so it would be foolish to imagine that if you took away the Red Arrows, there would suddenly be a big block of money to be saved. It just wouldn't work like that. If you talk to anyone in the world of industry, they would tell you that if you're in the business of making cuts in expenditure, the last thing you want to cut is your advertising and public relations. In times like this we need positive PR. The RAF is reducing in size, it's changing roles, and the emphasis is on high-technology and skills, so it's important that we're seen to have centres of excellence, so that people can see that despite all of the cuts, we're still here, and the RAF is still as professional as ever. The vast majority of taxpayers want to be assured that their military services are still able to achieve the things they've always handled in the past".

Coming directly from the Tornado force, Kelvin has already seen how the media can create a great deal of negative publicity for the RAF; "undoubtedly the Tornado Air Defence Variant did have problems when it was first introduced, and it was slow to be brought up to specification. But any complex aircraft will have teething troubles and the way that they're ironed-out is always going to come down to the available budgets, and the people who make the decisions, and maybe things took longer than they could have. But after two

or three years it was brought up to the kind of specification it should have had, for the role it was designed for. But unfortunately, by that time, the role had changed significantly".

Kelvin continues; "because the Tornado F2/3 was such a new aircraft at the time, it took a while for the crews to learn how to fight with it, and now that we're five or so years into regular service, we do have a good level of expertise, and it's pretty good competition for aircraft like the F-16, and a very capable aircraft. It will never be a close-in fighter though, but it was never designed to be that kind of aircraft. It's out in Bosnia now, and the two-seat concept is working well, the night vision goggles work well, and the radar is maintaining good serviceability. Its ability to stay on patrol for a long time is out-stripping the ability of virtually any other aeroplane in the theatre, so much so that some other nation's aircraft are being withdrawn, as the F3 can do the job so well".

Having exchanged the Tornado F3 for a Red Arrows Hawk, Kelvin explains the differences from a pilot's viewpoint; "after flying the Hawk as an advanced trainer, I heard people say that the Tornado handles like a big Hawk, but that isn't strictly the case. The Tornado has fairly carefree handling for sure, but I think the comparison was made by people who had flown the Phantom and Lightning, which really are very different. After flying the Hawk, you find that you don't get as much feel for the controls in the Tornado, because of the computerised fly-by-wire system, and now that I've returned to the Hawk, I'm back to an aircraft in which you have a much greater direct feel for the way the airframe handles. The Hawk is a much more simple aircraft, much more responsive to every minor control input I make, and it's certainly a perfect aircraft for close-formation flying".

Although Kelvin will be with the Red Arrows for some time, he already has some thoughts in mind as to what he'd like to do when he leaves the team; "personally I'd like to fly a single-seat ground attack aircraft, but I think it's unlikely that I'd be able to do that now that I have so much experience on the Tornado F3. The Air Force probably wouldn't think it worth re-training me for the ground attack role, after having gained so much experience on the Tornado F3. So I may well go back to the F3, even though I'd like the challenge of doing something totally new".

After having flown with the Red Arrows for three years, it might be difficult to find any really new challenges. In terms of flying experience, there isn't much to beat what is almost the 'ultimate job' as a Red Arrows pilot. So how did Kelvin's family and friends react, when he learned of his new appointment with the team? Kelvin explains; "my family were delighted, and they were very supportive. My wife realised we'd have to move house, but we've moved fairly regularly over the past few years and she's happy to tag along behind me. She's pleased for me, and it's a close-knit environment here, so she's made friends very quickly. There are always strains placed on families no matter what unit you're with, and even though I'll be away quite often in the display season, it will be for fairly short periods, whereas I'd be away on detachments to Bosnia, Falklands or whatever, if I was on a Tornado F3 squadron, so my wife's likely to actually see more of me, now that I'm with the Red Arrows. My mum asked whether it would be a dangerous job, like any parent would, but in some ways it's less dangerous than flying in an F3, as it's a very carefully planned routine, with everyone following the same profile, and everyone knowing precisely what everyone else is doing, whereas in some of the more fluid air combat scenarios, things aren't quite so certain, so I could always argue that flying with the Red Arrows job is probably safer, if anything. My friends outside the Air Force were very pleased for me too. As for my friends inside the RAF, some guys just wouldn't want to do the job, and they might think it's a job which is a long way from what they feel the real flying is all about. But even when you get all the banter, all the comments you'd expect, in reality, everyone is very pleased for you, and very supportive".

Looking back at his RAF career so far, Kelvin recalls why he joined the RAF; "I always wanted to be in the military. I don't know why for sure, and I guess if you asked some shrink he'd probably say it was because I played with guns when I was a kid, or something like that. But I was always impressed with the military, their professionalism and so on, and I couldn't see anything in the civilian sector which attracted me. I would have probably joined the Army Cadets at that time, but all my school friends joined the Air Cadets, so I just went along with them, and I developed an interest in helicopters, although I always saw flying as a means of delivering weapons, even at that stage. It was always more important to be a military man rather than a pilot, which is why I'd have never become an airline pilot. I was turned-down by the Air Force, and worked for a Building Society and then re-applied. I was turned-down again, so I put in applications to the Marines, RAF Regiment and Parachute Regiment.

"I was accepted by the RAF Regiment, and joined as an airman. Then shortly after completing my training, I received a letter from the officer selection people, saying that I would now be accepted. I assume that they must have entered a new financial year with a new budget, and they had looked back for people who had just failed to be accepted. So I told them that I was already in the RAF Regiment, and they transferred me directly across to officer training and then flying training. But I never sat down and watched Top Gun at the movies and decided to become a pilot, nothing romantic like that. I remember being at Catterick which is very near Leeming. I used to drive past the base, looking at the Jet Provosts which were based there at the time, and after having been turned down for pilot training twice, I often wondered to myself what it would be like to be flying one of the Jet Provosts, even though I knew I'd probably never be able to do it. But a year later I was doing it for real"!

RED FIVE

Flight Lieutenant Benny Ball ('Red Five') joined the Red Arrows during September of 1992, flying the 'Red Three' position to the left of the Team Leader. Before joining the Team, he was a Hawk pilot with N° 79 squadron at Brawdy, as part of the Weapons Instruction Flight, teaching the skills of weapons delivery. Previously he was based at Chivenor with N° 63 Squadron, as a Tactics Instructor. His career has not been devoted entirely to Hawk flying however, as he joined N° 41 Squadron at Coltishall in April 1986 after completing the Jaguar Operational Conversion Unit course at Lossiemouth. Like every other RAF fast jet pilot, he completed his advanced flying training (on Hawks) at Valley, and undertook basic flying training at Church Fenton, one of three Flying Training Schools in operation at the time (now reduced to two).

Benny's interest in the Red Arrows began during his childhood; "I've been going to air shows for years and years, and the Red Arrows were always something special, a boy's dream. But once I actually got into the Air Force I was more interested in the tactical side of flying after flying the Hawk and Jaguar. But you can't go straight to the Red Arrows in any case, and by the time that I became eligible to join the team, I'd already done lots of tactical flying. So I'd gone from what I thought was a demanding job as a single-seat ground attack pilot, on to teaching students tactical weapons flying, then on to teaching instructors, which was yet another challenge, having to instruct your colleagues, which is pretty hard to handle. So the Red Arrows seemed like another obvious challenge".

As for the non-flying tasks associated with the team, Benny enjoys the opportunities to meet people; "it's another kind of experience which I hadn't had before and it was exciting to be out there meeting so many people, being in the public eye. So I felt I was pretty fortunate to have the opportunity. When I went through the selection procedure I sat in the back seat of the aircraft to see what it's like. I'd flown with the Team Leader before, but when I was on the shortlist I got to see the display from other positions and my initial impression was just to see how much movement there is between the aircraft. It was quite amazing to see how much they moved about. When you're at the back of the formation you can see that the guys are working their butts off, whereas from the ground it looks like a really smooth formation. It's also amazing to see how everyone uses the Leader as a reference point rather than the guy next to them, and that's quite an eye-opener. I didn't have second thoughts at that stage, in fact I was raring to go, and by the end of the two weeks I spent flying in the back seats I was wishing they'd finish their display season so I could get in there and have a go myself".

Of course, the task is far from simple, and the winter training season is hard work; "sometimes you might find a manoeuvre doesn't go exactly as you wished and you look at the post-flight video and you can feel really frustrated. But you have to look carefully at the video and not let things get to you, and keep on trying to get it right. Most people could stay roughly in the right formation position, and you'd be able to hang-in there, but you'd be too long or too deep, or maybe you just couldn't keep in the formation at all. But it's more psychological really, as your previous experience of formation flying doesn't include being upside-down with a guy next to you, and you haven't had a guy rolling towards you, things like that, and it is fairly exciting to start with, but you get used to the initial shock and get on with the task of dealing with it. You gradually improve and when you get to Cyprus you finally get the formation into the kind of tight package that you're looking for. Even while you're inside the formation you have a fairly good idea whether things are going right. The video recording is a useful aid, but it only serves to highlight mistakes that you make in the air, which you have to identify and try to resolve next time".

Although each pilot formates on the Team Leader, they will also 'cross-refer' to other aircraft in the formation to get a complete picture; "you can use other aircraft to check that you have the right separation width and you really need at least two other aircraft to say whether you're too close or too far apart. We use some basic reference points for aligning the formations, for example, you look along the leading edges of the wing as one reference. You also line up the flap-jack at the wing trailing edge and together they will give us a good reference. We also use the wing tip, aligning it with the engine intake and the badge just in front of that, and they will give you a good alignment. But this year I've moved position so I have to use different references, like using the pilots' heads, which give me the right impression of whether everyone's in the right place. When you first arrive here you are given the basic reference details, the two I've mentioned are called Arrow and Diamond, but if we want to move those points slightly depends on how we judge them for ourselves. But when I moved out to the number Five position it was left up to me to find my own references, I was basically left to go up there and get myself into position. But it's built-up gradually with four guys, then a few more until we have the full nine-ship formation".

Benny continues; "when you're in the close formations you really can't move the throttle and control column too much, if you're trying to maintain a nice, steady formation. The Leader is basically setting the throttle and you really don't want to make any large control inputs. But if you move to the outside of the formation, on some of the rolls for example, you'll have to use larger control inputs, taking throttle off and then putting it back on, as the roll progresses. But when the throttle is off, when you try to put the power back on again, it takes time to wind-up like any jet engine, even though our Hawks are modified to improve the throttle and engine response time, so sometimes we do use the airbrake, especially on the formation re-joins. The Synchro use airbrakes quite frequently and we all use the airbrake in the formation roll-backs, rather than lose the available thrust".

As Benny explains, the Red Arrows Hawks are suitably modified, to give the Rolls-Royce Turbomeca Adour engines an improved throttle response, lowering the time needed to wind up to full power; "in the winter season we borrow Hawks from Valley while our aircraft are serviced, and they have standard Adour engines. We use these in the Two and Three slots where they don't do quite so much manoeuvring, but the pilots find that they have a real disadvantage. I flew one of the jets recently and after having

"when you're in the close formations you really can't move the throttle and control column too much, if you're trying to maintain a nice, steady formation"

ARTHUR GIBSON

got used to a Red Arrows Hawk, it was quite a surprise. I moved the throttle back once and I learned my lesson, I was waving the formation goodbye"!

Away from the display flying, dealing with the public has been a source of great interest for Benny; "most of the people we meet just want to talk to us, and get autographs, stuff like that, and some people have some very interesting stories to tell us too. If there was one thing I'm asked most of all, it has to be, 'will you sign this mate', that's the thing you get used to hearing. But you get former Air Force people too who tell you about the jobs they did, and we meet a real cross-section of people ranging from the directors of big companies right through to the average guy from the local high street. Some questions can surprise you though, like asking if we use autopilot, which of course we don't have, and when they learn that everything is flown manually they can't believe it, they think that it must be done automatically. In the winter we do lectures too, and we get more general questions about the RAF, although we don't get so many people wanting to talk about disarmament any more. I remember one lecture when some peace campaigners came-in, dressed-up like zombies and they sat down right at the front. I wondered how on earth the lecturer would handle them, but he used them as a primary part of his presentation, he played to them really, and that was an interesting experience, which teaches you something about the way in which potentially difficult situations can be handled".

Lecture questions can often be concerned with local matters however; "for example, if you go to an area where there is plenty of low flying, you get questions about low flying more than anything else. I went to one lecture in the North Weald area where we no longer display because of the congested air traffic situation there, and I was asked lots of questions about that, and one guy was being particularly persistent which was putting me in a difficult situation, but the rest of the audience tended to bat him down, and that often happens, as people are very much on our side. Our job is public relations orientated whereas a typical squadron would be tactics-orientated, so we're geared-up to handling publicity, but we constantly monitor the situation to make sure that the flying is always paramount, as safety is the main consideration. At airshows we always have a set schedule so that we have enough time to get away from the crowds, and do the briefing on the wing of number Five's aircraft, and we always ensure that we have a quiet area where we can get away and get our minds in order before getting airborne. You have to be big and ugly enough to ensure that you get away from the people and concentrate on your flying".

Whether the Red Arrows spend enough time with the public is a question which is regularly asked, but the Red Arrows feel that the balance between display flying and talking directly with the public is just about right. It's certainly different to the concept of the American display teams, who devote complete weekends to just one display venue; "we have to judge what comes first, the PR or the flying. If you're talking to the public, you're dealing with a fairly small group of people, whereas if you're able to go off and maybe do another two displays, we're showing what we can do, in the air, and that has to take priority when we might be displaying to fifty thousand people at another show site. I recently saw how the Thunderbirds operated, and they were quite surprised at the way we worked. We were scheduled to do a show at New Orleans when we were asked if we could fly at Houston. They were expecting us to cancel New Orleans in order to do Houston, but we did both, we saw no problem with that, and we met as much of the public in Houston as we possibly could by getting into Jeeps and driving over to the crowds. We're flexible enough to do that".

Benny continues; "Our display has evolved from the feedback we get from the public, and if guys come here and tell us that they don't like something, we'll try to do something about it. For example, last year we had the formation split to loop at either end of the runway and we thought that would look good. But people came here and said that they weren't too impressed, as they didn't know where to look and so on.

So we considered their comments and we dropped that manoeuvre. You can get very blinkered, as anyone at Scampton sees the display every day, so you need to get somebody from the outside, and see what they think. If somebody points out one particular thing, you might not say anything, but you'll remember what they said, and check if other people think the same way. We can change anything we want, but we want to keep some basic trademarks like the Diamond Nine, and the way we arrive from behind the crowd, but for ninety-four we've changed the way we leave, opting for a Vixen Break instead of the old Parasol Break. Likewise, Red Eight and Red Nine are breaking away from the formation during the display, working with the Synchro for the first time, so we try to introduce new ideas".

Benny is convinced that the Hawk is an ideal aircraft for the Red Arrows; "okay, you could pull the corners tightly in an F-16 or F/A-18, but we display our aircraft to the limits, and we opted to use our advanced trainer to show the public what the Hawk can do. Okay, we could use Tornado F3's, but the display would get bigger, you would get more unserviceability, and the aircraft are hugely more expensive, plus we'd be taking aircraft away from the front-line, and the Air Force has lots of stuff going-on around the world in places like Bosnia, Turkey, the Falklands and so on, and you couldn't afford to take aircraft and manpower away from those tasks. Even with just six Tornado F3's it would take more people to maintain them, whereas the Hawk is simple to maintain, it doesn't go unserviceable very often, and it turns well. Looks nice too".

Benny hopes to re-join the Jaguar community as a Flight Commander if possible, after leaving the Red Arrows, finding a new challenge within the RAF.

RED SIX

Having joined the Red Arrows late in 1991, Flight Lieutenant Rob Last is now the leader of the Synchro Pair, flying 'Red Six' within the main nine-aircraft formations, positioned immediately behind the Boss in the 'diamond nine'. Before joining the Red Arrows, Rob had trained at Cranwell, Valley and Chivenor, before joining the Jaguar Operational Conversion Unit, followed by tours with N° 54 Squadron and N° 41 Squadron at Coltishall.

Joining the Red Arrows had been a long-standing ambition for Rob, as he explains; "it was a schoolboy dream really. I first became interested in the Royal Air Force after seeing the Red Arrows perform at Halton near my home town. I managed to get into the Air Force as a pilot, and for me, I had two ways I wanted to go; one was to get an exchange tour, and the other was to join the Red Arrows. I joined the Air Force to fly, and it's difficult to imagine a better form of flying than being here, flying five days a week, three times each day during the winter season, which is very challenging and enjoyable. In terms of flying hours I probably don't fly any more than I did on the Jaguar squadrons, but as the Red Arrows flights are much shorter and more intense, in overall terms I probably fly less hours in fact". Rob also recalls the day when the Red Arrows flew a practice display at Cranwell; I was on the Basic Flying Training School there, and I'd just started basic formation flying. I remember watching the display and thinking that I could never be able to do things like that. I could barely keep in formation doing a thirty-degree bank turn, never mind loops and rolls. It was very impressive and certainly was inspiring". Most BFTS students would no doubt feel the same way, but as each RAF pilot progresses through advanced and tactical flying, then to an Operational Conversion Unit and on to his first operational squadron, the idea of joining the Red Arrows doesn't seem quite so unrealistic. The pilots will obviously have learned how to handle a high-performance jet with ease by this stage, but they will also occasionally meet Red Arrows pilots, and often realise at this stage that even the world-famous Red Arrows pilots are just 'ordinary guys'.

Rob Last also reached this conclusion; "as time went on, I met guys who I'd trained with who had joined the team, and I remember thinking that I'd performed just as well, so there was no reason why I shouldn't apply to join the Red Arrows too. However, I did find that life here was more difficult than I'd imagined, and most of the guys think the same. In many ways it's a repetitive business, and we do things over and over again until we're really good at it, but that can be very hard work".

In terms of flying skills, the Red Arrows pilots are already well-qualified to fly close formation aerobatics even before they join the team. However, their skills need to be sharpened in order to fly ultra-close within a nine-aircraft formation, whilst performing loops and rolls. Dealing with the public is also a major part of Rob's job; "we all do four or five lectures each winter, going to all kinds of places ranging from schools to Women's Institutes. You get all kinds of questions; they ask whether you've crashed, how fast do you fly, all kinds of stuff. You do get some very odd questions, and you do have to try and give a sensible answer. We don't really get any difficult questions in terms of politics and so on, basically because the people are usually pleased to see us, so they're not going to try and knock us down with criticism. But people want to see us fly most of all, so even though they do like to see and talk to the pilots, we must ensure that this side of the job doesn't intrude too much upon the flying schedule. Ultimately it could be a flight safety problem if the guy's flown maybe four times in one day, as he'd probably be pretty tired by that stage, and in no position to be doing a major publicity job, so we try to fit the public side of things around the flying".

Of course, the Red Arrows pilots do sometimes have to defend themselves when questioned about the cost of a nine-aircraft formation team. As the national defence budget becomes progressively smaller, the distinctly non-operational role the Red Arrows perform can be seen as an additional expense which the country can no longer afford. Rob is keen to express his own view; "in terms of the benefit which the RAF obtains from the Red Arrows, we're very valuable. There's no doubt that many officers and airmen first became interested in joining the RAF after seeing the Red Arrows perform, so we're a great aid to recruitment. On a wider theme, when people see the Red Arrows they're proud to be British, as we show the world just what we

A great team

Motorola Telco is delighted to support the Red Arrows and their fund raising for ChildLine. Motorola Telco is the leading airtime provider for both Cellnet and Vodafone networks. Motorola is the world's largest manufacturer of mobile phones.

MOTOROLA
Tel·co

For more information about Motorola Telco and the provision of cellular telephones contact Mark Terry 0256 790302
Motorola Telco, Midpoint, Alencon Link, Basingstoke, Hants, RG21 1PL

can achieve, and there's no doubt about that. We've also helped to promote sales of the Hawk and other areas of British industry, so the team does have an important function. You could argue that we contribute nothing to the defence of this country, but for the small cost of our operation, we more than justify our existence. We do have a wartime reserve role, and although we don't actively train for this role any longer, it wouldn't take us long to get trained-up again, and the Red Arrows Hawks could be fitted with guns and missiles if necessary".

Having joined the Synchro Pair in 1993 (as 'Red Seven'), Rob became Leader of the Synchro in 1994; "As Synchro Two approaches the end of his year, he knows that he'll be leader of the pair the following year, so he chooses a new Synchro Two from the guys who have been flying their first year with the team. The guys who are eligible for the job have the right to refuse, but everybody wants to do the Synchro Pair, and it's up to the Synchro Lead to pick his number two. During the winter we fly three times each day on our own until around February, when we then join the rest of the team, so the flying is even more demanding than before. Additionally, our manoeuvres are more severe too, we pull up to seven-and-a-half g's and up to negative three-and-a-half, whereas the main formation wouldn't exceed perhaps four g".

The Synchro Pair's element of the complete Red Arrows display is planned by the two Synchro pilots, and although they are free to introduce any manoeuvre which they may consider appropriate, there is obviously a finite number of possible manoeuvres which can be performed. Additionally, the Synchro Pair must fit their display into the overall show format, and so the Team Leader and Synchro Leader carefully plan the various manoeuvres in order to mix the two elements of the display into a smoothly-flowing show.

The Hawk is a particularly suitable aircraft for the Synchro Pair, even though the aircraft does have limitations as Rob explains; "in many ways the Hawk is perfect for what we do, but for example, when we're in a hot and high location, it does run-out of performance, so the show has to be a little slacker. Aircraft like the F-16 and F/A-18 have much more power with a similar turning performance, so we could do much more with aircraft like that, but the Hawk is a great little aeroplane which doesn't place any real limitations on the kind of show we do".

Training for the Synchro Pair begins with 'Red Seven' flying up to fifteen trips on his own, learning to fly aerobatics down to 100 feet. It obviously takes time to become confident at such a low altitude. The Synchro Lead then joins in and the two pilots fly timing runs, performing straight and level opposition passes. 'Red Six' sets up a predictable flight path along the off-crowd edge of Scampton's runway, and 'Red Seven' flies along the on-crowd edge, aiming to comfortably miss the Synchro Lead. Manoeuvring is then slowly built in, together with escape manoeuvres which are planned into the sequence. The cross-over manoeuvres look dangerous, but the safety margin is fairly wide as Rob comments; "it doesn't have to be that close to make it look exciting. Because Red Seven is nearer to the crowd he will fly a little lower than me so that we appear to be level to an observer on the ground. That's what we call a fudge, and as long as that is done properly it looks as if we've merged, whereas we're not that close. We obviously have a vested interest in not hitting each other, and if we get too close I'll say so. We have a set separation distance of one hundred feet which is enough to make the crossovers look dynamic and exciting".

The Synchro Pair's display is often regarded by the public as being particularly thrilling. Of course, there is always a risk with any kind of display flying, but Rob doesn't think that the Synchro Pair's manoeuvres are dangerous; "the whole display has been made as safe as possible and even though there's a danger in any kind of aviation, the head-on manoeuvres look more dangerous, but they're not. We always try to display to a datum point and we always try to aim our crossovers to that point. We then end up maybe three miles apart after we've crossed, so we go behind the crowd, flying at five hundred feet, two hundred and seventy knots, and then we turn in and accelerate to manoeuvre speed. We're trying to fly exactly the same as each other, so that we end up in the middle of the display site, so accurate instrument and pattern flying is the key to a successful synchro display, and a great deal of the hard work is going on out of the crowd's sight".

Away from the demands of display flying, Rob enjoys the brief opportunities to relax; "it doesn't matter how well you get on with people, I still enjoy my week off in the middle of the season. Just to have a break from the people you're living with so much is essential, no matter how good the job is. We pick the team members ourselves, and you have to get on with the guys, and no matter how good his ability to fly, if the guy is a real pain to be around, he'll disrupt the team, so it's vitally important that we all have the right kind of personality".

After having flown with the team for two years, Rob looks to the future, after leaving the Red Arrows; "I think the three-year cycle is correct, as formation display flying is a very repetitive business. Joining the Synchro keeps up your interest, and it's good to have three new guys coming in each year with lots of enthusiasm, tempered by the guys who have been around for two or three years. I'll be very disappointed to leave, but I'd be happy to go back to Jaguars, hopefully after being promoted. Of course I'd love to come back to the Red Arrows as Leader, but I'm certainly not the only guy with that ambition, so I've had a great time with the team and if I get to come back, that would be a real bonus".

BIG VIXEN

RED SEVEN

Having flown in 'Red Two' position for the 1993 display season, Flight Lieutenant Sean Chiddention assumed the 'Red Seven' position for 1994 as the second member of the Synchro Pair. Sean used to live in Biggin Hill during his childhood, and saw the Red Arrows display sometimes twice each year at the nearby RAF station. At that time he didn't have any major interest in aviation, but in later years he joined the Air Training Corps, which gave him an opportunity to spend some time at various RAF stations, encouraging him to later join the RAF.

His first tour was as a flying instructor, and Sean became a Jet Provost display pilot for 1987 and 1988, whilst based at Cranwell. He then joined N° 6 Squadron, flying Jaguars from Coltishall, and prior to the beginning of Operation Desert Storm, he flew Jaguars from Oman and Bahrain. Having displayed the Jet Provost, he felt that joining the Red Arrows would be the ultimate display flying experience; "the nine-ship formation is much more of a spectacle than just one solo aircraft, so it's great to be part of that team. It's the thing to naturally aim for".

Sean, like his colleagues, found his early experiences with the Red Arrows to be particularly demanding; "the one thing which struck me was just how difficult the flying is. If anyone sat in on the formation they would see that it looks difficult, but guys coming from front-line fast jet squadrons, capable of flying a single-seat aeroplane, go to war in it and so on, it's still incredibly difficult to come here and do pure hand, eye and feet co-ordination. It's something that people don't understand, and although we try to make it look easy, it's probably the most demanding flying you could do. There are phases during your early training here when you go off and you do something new, and it works. You think that's great, but then trip-by-trip something will creep in and suddenly things just don't look right and you can't work out why. So on the next trip you come up to that same manoeuvre and you start thinking about how it went wrong last time, but you try to put that out of your mind. Even so, it still goes wrong and it just builds up until you begin to wonder if you'll ever be able to do the job. But then you get a day when everything goes right, and that's fantastic. It's really when we get out to Cyprus, doing fifteen trips each week, that we learn very quickly and everything comes together".

The Red Arrows display sequence features a wide variety of formations and manoeuvres, and although much of the team's flying is peculiar to their own particular role, the basic concept of formation flying is an essential skill learned by every RAF pilot as Sean explains; "formation flying is basically a means of getting several aircraft through cloud. Taking weapons to a target requires several aircraft, and several aircraft can give each other mutual cover, so formation flying is basic to most forms of military flying. Aerobatics have always been a part of Royal Air Force training, as it teaches you to fly the aircraft to the edge of its envelope, using the aircraft to its maximum potential. When you put these two elements together, we're basically showing skills that all RAF pilots have. Okay, if you're a Jaguar pilot you will devote more time to your weapons and tactics skills, whereas a Hercules pilot may spend more time on instrument flying and so on. As Red Arrows pilots we develop our formation aerobatic skills. Every Air Force pilot concentrates on a particular aspect, but we're certainly demonstrating what the Air Force is all about".

Changing from 'Red Two' position to 'Red Seven' was a major step for Sean, with the new challenge of the Synchro Pair manoeuvres. However, even the change in the main formation position requires even more flying practice, as Sean explains; "I was on the right side of the Boss in the main formation last year, and now I'm right at the back. Okay, it's not as completely new as starting from scratch as you're familiar with the environment and you're used to having lots of other aeroplanes around you. But there are new skills to learn in your new position. For example, I couldn't climb into a Hawk and fly number Five's slot tomorrow, and that's the reason why we can't simply replace a pilot if he goes sick. People often ask if we have a spare pilot, but if someone can't fly we would fly eight aircraft. It takes all winter for us to train to fly in our own slot so it would be impossible for somebody to be prepared to just step-in and fly any position in the formation".

Of course, Sean's big challenge for the 1994 winter training season, was to begin Synchro Pair flying; "it is a huge task. I'd done low level aerobatics before in the

Jet Provost, but that was down to five hundred feet, whereas this is down to one hundred. The Jet Provost was a fairly slow aeroplane too whereas the Hawk is pretty fast which is a huge difference, and learning to point your Hawk at another aircraft takes some getting used to. But it's a slow building process and I spent some time flying aerobatics on my own down to fifteen hundred feet base height. After I'd done a few trips at that height I worked down to a thousand feet, then five hundred, then two-fifty and finally down to one hundred feet, with people watching me on the ground to make sure it's safe".

Flying the Synchro manoeuvres requires a mix of precise 'pattern' flying and instrument flying skills; "with something like the big heart manoeuvre, we'll pull-up with me flying formation on the lead, then we go Synchro split and then pull together on our control columns. The way things work, if we both fly in the same manner to the same numbers, the cross-over should be in the middle, but it's up to me to make the fine tuning to make things look right. So we pull over the top and we're on instruments at that stage, flying to the aircraft's maximum performance, with light buffeting at full power, then as we come down the other side, if we're flying at the right angles, I should be able to look up through my canopy to see Rob's smoke, and then it's up to me to fine tune things, watching him. He's flying thirty degrees nose down so there's mutual trust here in that I'm trusting him not to fly me into the ground, and he's trusting me not to hit him. I fly to miss him, making a nice cross at the bottom of the heart shape".

Training almost continually at Scampton can also create problems for the team; "we will recognise every little pond and farmhouse out there, and it is a temptation to rely on familiar landmarks which isn't a good idea, when you're going to be displaying at different venues all year. But we have to train here until we've got the basics right. Once we're all happy, we will then switch to the cross runway, using that as the display datum, the standby line as we call it. That's very disorientating as you see all the familiar features but in completely different places, and that's very difficult to cope with. After that we'll go off to four other airfields and do practice displays. Cyprus provides us with lots of different datum points to work from and we'll use different points on the runway, we've got cliff sites, over the sea, all sorts of different perspectives".

If the team is displaying at a site which has been visited by the Red Arrows before, the team will have information available on the site, plus a report from the Team Leader and Synchro Leader, with notes on features which are specific to the site, together with photographs, maps and so on. The site is also surveyed by the show organisers prior to the show date. Unlike teams such as the Blue Angels and Thunderbirds, the Red Arrows don't overfly the show site prior to the actual display, as the team are happy to rely on an aerial photograph of the site, together with the afore-mentioned information. Unless there are any specific points which need to be known by individual team members, only the Team Leader and Synchro Leader need to have full details of the show site, as the rest of the team will be flying in response to their manoeuvres rather than to ground references.

Sean also handles his share of distinctly non-flying tasks, not least the continual need to answer the mountains of mail which the team receives; "some people just write in asking for stickers and things like that, which is simple enough, and the admin staff can handle it. Sometimes it's children doing school projects and they want information from us. Others write in with ideas for the display, they ask if we've ever thought of trying this, that or the other, and some ideas are good, and others are useless, but you have to write-back and answer these letters. As the season runs on you get letters from people who have seen you display and they want you to sign photographs and so on. You're writing five or six letters every day just to keep on top of that job and if you don't answer them for a few days you tend to get snowed under. When you've seen how little time we have between flights, it's easy to see what a challenge it is to get everything done".

Sean, like some of his colleagues, hopes to return to Jaguar flying when he leaves the Red Arrows; "I joined the Red Arrows after flying a single-seat aeroplane, and it's nice to fly single-seat as you're very much your own boss. You're in charge of that aeroplane. Okay, you need navigators and weapons systems operators for some aircraft, but I like to be single-seat and I like the Jaguar. Coltishall is a great base too, so I'd be happy to go back there".

PHOTOFINISH

RED EIGHT

Flight Lieutenant Barry Cross flies the 'Red Eight' position for the 1994 display season, which will also be his last year with the Red Arrows. Prior to joining the team, Barry was with N° 74 Squadron at Wattisham, flying F-4J's and Phantom FGR2's. After completing his advanced flying training at Valley, he stayed at the same base as an instructor and spent three years teaching students to fly the Hawk, before moving to Wattisham. Barry enjoyed his tour as an instructor, even though he had yet to join an operational squadron for the first time, as he explains; "I'd be a liar if I said that I didn't want to get to an operational squadron, but providing you understand that you haven't got the depth of experience that the other instructors have, you can offer the students the viewpoint that you've just gone through the same course yourself, so you know what they're feeling like. I hope I put a great deal into it, and I'm still on friendly terms with all the guys who were my students, so I must have done something right".

Barry continues; "if you come-across as the big, heavy-handed, I-know-it-all kind of guy, they'll pick that up straight away. They know if you're trying to pull the wool over their eyes, but if the students understand that you have a recent view of how it is to pass the course, then you can teach them the right techniques, and I never experienced any hostility to me, just because I'd gone straight to instructing. I used my three years there to improve my own skills too, and I flew with other instructors and picked up things from them too. After I left Valley I went to the Tactical Weapons Unit at Chivenor, and then I was moved into the F-4 world because the RAF were looking for instructors at the time. The Phantom wasn't my first choice as like most guys I wanted to go single-seat, but as it turned out, I had a great time at Wattisham, and after six months I became a flying instructor with the squadron. The F-4J was a great aeroplane to fly, and although I was sad to see it go, I had eight or nine months with the FGR2's too. The F-4J was a nice aeroplane to fly, as it was much lighter than the FGR2, and the engines were turbojets, which behaved better at height than turbofans. It was great fun".

Had Barry not joined the Red Arrows, he would almost certainly have re-joined the Tactical Weapons Unit at Chivenor as an instructor. However, he applied to join the Red Arrows twice, and his second application was accepted; "that's not unusual, and some people make three or four applications before they join. It's a very satisfying job, and the results are immediate. On a front-line squadron when you go off and drop bombs, you have a good idea of how well the sortie went, but with the Red Arrows you're on display, surrounded by other guys who are very competent, and you're putting yourself on the line. Anybody can fly formation, but we're taking that skill to an extreme degree. When I was a kid, I did watch the Red Arrows at Farnborough, and I did wonder if I could do that kind of a job. So the time came when I realised that I'd reached the stage where I had to have a go. When you're in the Air Force, the Red Arrows always seemed to be something beyond what you're capable of, until you start to see friends in the team and you realise that you could do it too".

The team invites applications from RAF fast-jet pilots, and people who are eligible to apply will visit Scampton and fly with the Team Leader to see what aerobatic formation flying is all about. The applicant then submits a letter to the team, accompanied by comments from his squadron commander and station commander. These 50 or 60 applications are then carefully considered by the nine team members and the Manager. The Royal Air Force is a comparatively small fighting force, and at least one team member will know who the applicant is, which helps to establish who has sufficient experience, and who has the right type of personality. Certainly, the applicant should have made at least one fast-jet operational tour and have had eight or nine years of service in the RAF. Additionally, he should be capable of fitting-in with the team on a social level.

Eight applicants are then invited to Scampton to spend a week or so with the team, seeing the formation display from the back seat of each Hawk, undertaking a flying test, and to attend interviews. Additionally, it is also an opportunity to see whether the applicant will fit-in with the other team members. It's quite an ordeal, as Barry explains; "it's quite nerve-racking, as there's no feedback on how you're doing, deliberately so, and you're with seven guys whom you'll probably know

ARTHUR GIBSON

from training days, all of whom are equally capable, so you're in competition with them, but they're all friends too, so it's difficult to try and be yourself. You go away, and you worry about how you handled things, waiting to hear whether you've been accepted or not. Now that I'm on the team, I can see things from the opposite side of things, and you can see how some people just try too hard. They think they're being really natural when you can see that they're not. You can certainly see that they're nervous and everybody is, and you have to try and see how they really are. We'll go out for a drink, or maybe a curry house, just socialising, and hanging-around in the crew room. At the interviews they will be asked all the obvious questions, and there are no real surprises there. You are sat there in the middle of a room in your Number One uniform, facing three people in flying suits, so you do feel like you're in the spotlight even though you're only in there for about fifteen minutes. It's worth all the trouble of course".

Barry continues; "you also do a flying test, and you go up as a pair, with the Boss. You sit in the back seat with the Deputy Leader and each applicant follows the same profile, flying loops and rolls in formation. The idea is to see how you improve over about twenty minutes. Some people won't be current on the Hawk, so you can't start at the same base level, but it's an opportunity to see how you perform. That's pretty nerve-racking too, as you don't know how you've been judged, even though you know if you've made a real mess of it, and everybody is out there watching you do it over the airfield. When I flew that test I hadn't flown the Hawk for about four years. I must have done reasonably well as I'm on the team now, but I thought I could have done better. You never fly perfectly though, and it was great fun, even though it was a test".

After being accepted into the team, Barry flew 'Red Three' position, with two other new pilots flying 'Red Two' and 'Red Five'. His first two weeks were spent flying four-ship formations, the new pilots learning to formate on the Team Leader during a series of three sorties each day, progressing from a base height of 3,000 feet down to 500 feet. Barry felt that the first couple of weeks went very well, although doubts did eventually begin to creep in; "there comes a stage around Christmas time when you begin to wonder if you can actually do the job, as nothing appears to be going right. It's very, very tiring as, although it's not a physically-demanding job even though there's plenty of g-forces, it's because you're concentrating for thirty minutes. Normally when you're flying it's like driving a car, and you can relax occasionally, whereas here you're concentrating flat out for thirty minutes, three times each day. All of us found that by Christmas we were crashed-out by about nine at night.

"The briefings for each flight are extensive, as are the detailed de-briefings, when the pilots look through the whole sortie on video. The team pilots will offer as much constructive criticism as possible, and now that I've been on the team for a while, I have to realise that it would be pointless to just sit there and destroy the new guy every time he lands. It's pointless unless you can tell him how to correct his mistakes. He knows when he's made a mistake and he'll tell you so, and it's up to the other guys to help him out".

Safety is an all-important consideration, as Barry comments; "for example, nobody will change formation unless the correct radio calls have been given. If the right words don't come out, nobody moves anywhere, as the radio calls mean that the piece of airspace you're about to move into is clear. We also brief very strictly how to get out of the formation if things go wrong. You have to carry out the correct escape manoeuvre, otherwise you'll endanger somebody behind you or beside you, and ultimately that will endanger the spectators on the ground".

During the initial stages of training, the team

employs a building-block approach. If a manoeuvre doesn't work easily, the pilots can simply repeat the exercise again until it is handled successfully. The Team Leader can see fairly clearly how things are going by checking his rear-view mirrors. The gradual increase in expertise enables the formation to be built up gradually, starting with half of the formation, essentially one side of the Diamond Nine flown on separate sorties. To the pilot, it makes no difference if half of the formation is missing, and as confidence and skill improves, the two halves of the formation will be put together. As aircraft are added to the formation, the new pilots have to learn to handle the situation, as Barry explains; "it's quite unusual at first and you feel hemmed-in, which makes you tense-up. That's probably the worst thing that can happen as you start to get more jerky on the controls, just the opposite of what you want. But you get used to it, so you're not immediately hemmed in by other aircraft straightaway, it's gradually built up so that you get used to it".

When the team deploys to Cyprus, the display sequence is essentially established, and the pilots are able to polish their performance before returning to the UK; "you know that at the end of the detachment, the Air Marshal will watch the display, and decide if we're fit to be seen by the public. It's not a frenzy of panic and activity though, as you have the good weather, and a chance to practice over a variety of different sites. The team has been together for a few months, so you have a chance to be away as a team, and it's a sort of natural progression. We do get bad weather out at Akrotiri sometimes which can make the training schedule slip, but you can do everything just as if you're out on the road during the display season. We have the airfield pretty much to ourselves for three or four weeks".

After returning to the UK, the display season begins, and for all of the pilots, especially the 'new guys', the first public displays are quite an ordeal, as Barry recalls; "you're very nervous, concentrating so hard that you could be flying almost anywhere, and you've no time to notice the venue as such. At places like Mildenhall, you park in front of the crowds, you taxi-out past a mile-and-a-half of people, and on the runway you look to the right and there's this huge crowd, which is really nerve-racking. But once you're airborne you're too busy concentrating. If you make a mistake during the display it's pretty public. There will always be good shows and bad shows though, and conditions make a big difference. If the Boss is working hard to position the display in bad weather, then you'll be working hard to keep up with him. Coastal sites are always hard as you haven't got a line as such to work to, and when the weather is bad with low cloud or strong winds, it's hard work. Or maybe one day you're just not on top of things. If you're not fit to fly, you have to say so, but although you could imagine that there is a sort of moral pressure not to back out with a cold, you have to make the decision, as your neck is on the line, and you're not being fair to the other guys on the team if you fly when you're really not fit.

ARTHUR GIBSON

"The best shows are often the ones where you can meet with the public, the weather is good, and everything is relaxed, and you really want to get up there and put on a good show for the people you've been talking to. It's always amusing to see how people aren't particularly interested in talking to you when you're a regular squadron pilot, but when you put-on a red suit, everybody wants to meet you. But you have to remember that it's only for three years, and your celebrity status only lasts until you leave. One good thing is that you can take your red suit off and suddenly you're anonymous, and that makes you understand how people who are really in the public eye must feel. People are very nice though, and you get a chance to really make somebody's day. You sometimes meet disabled kids and so on, and when you go and talk to them you're doing something which is very important to them, and that's great to have made a difference to somebody".

RED NINE

Flight Lieutenant Jerry Bird (flying 'Red Nine' position for the 1994 season) joined the Red Arrows towards the end of 1992. Prior to joining the team, he was a Qualified Weapons Instructor (QWI) with N° 151 Squadron at Chivenor, after having served as a QFI (Qualified Flying Instructor) with N° 4 Flying Training School at Valley. Previously, Jerry had been based at Bruggen, flying Jaguars with N° 31 Squadron. He had almost 3,000 hours of Hawk flying experience, and was delighted to get the opportunity to join the Red Arrows, as he explains; "like everybody says, the job is a real challenge, and you get immediate visible results from your work. People are watching you, so the pressure is always on. They put you up on a pedestal and you have to work hard not to fall off. When I was flying Jaguars, I wasn't particularly interested in joining the Red Arrows, and it didn't seem like an achievable aim at that stage. You don't know any of the pilots and you assume they're all brilliant heroes, so you don't put yourself in the same bracket. It was after I'd been an instructor for some time that I started to get to know people in the team, and realised that it wasn't an impossible dream. It's the best job you could have, as we're all pilots, but here we're concentrating on purely flying, driving the aeroplane if you like, whereas the flying task is only a part of the job when you're in an operational squadron, and weapons delivery is your main objective".

Jerry came to the team with expectations of hard work, and admits that his first year was a real struggle; "at the start you seem to be hanging on by your fingernails most of the time. It's very different to operational flying, and we're much closer together for starters. Everyone in the Air Force can do formation, but here we tighten things up, so there's less room for mistakes. The first time I flew formation here there were four of us, and I remember that I couldn't write or anything after the flight, my arms were so tense. It seemed like I'd carried five tons of aeroplane around with me. It always begins like that, just flying the new guys with the Boss for a week while the rest of the team are on leave. Most of these early flights were done above cloud as the weather was pretty poor at that time, so thankfully very little of it was seen on the ground!

"Even after you've been bashing away at it for a few months, it's still very frustrating and you still can't position the aircraft as precisely as you want to, and you're making little mistakes, and it's very frustrating. You just don't seem to be able to get things together and it can be very demoralising sometimes, for the new guys. Everybody goes through that though. We tend to change positions within the formation each year, although I did two years in the number five slot, so the second year was much more routine. Now I've moved position and the workload is back on again. I'm obviously much more relaxed now with close formation, but I'm doing things that are new to me and sometimes I'm having to work very hard, even after having been with the team for quite a while".

Jerry also enjoys dealing with the non-flying tasks, including plenty of direct contact with the public; "it never really bothered me and I was always happy to talk to people about my job. We get lots of people visiting us at Scampton during the winter and the crewroom is often full of visitors. We get all kinds of questions, and you get all the standard questions like how we train, how close we are to each other, how fast we go and so on. Surprisingly perhaps, I've never really got any really ridiculous questions, and people tend to ask some pretty intelligent questions, and it's a pleasure to talk to the public, whenever we have the time. We try not to carry worries into the air with us, and it can be difficult when we have people to entertain on the ground. It's easy to devote extra time to people and then your briefing starts late and so on, and that would be a big mistake, as you have to give the flying your full concentration".

The team deploys to Cyprus in April, and has an opportunity to 'knit together' for the first time, living and working at the same location; "in our spare time, nobody expects everyone to do everything together at the same time, so if you want to go off on your own and do some windsurfing or whatever, that's fine. But during the year we tend to divide into little groups to do different things in our spare time. It's not like there are little cliques, it's just the way things work out. Some might go off and play golf, some might go running, or whatever, and it's very seldom that we go out together as a bunch unless it's a formally arranged event. So we never really get on each other's nerves, we get enough opportunity to go off on our own to do our own things".

Despite the team's continual training, some parts of the routine are still more challenging to fly than others, as Jerry explains; "there are always parts of the sequences that are more difficult than others, depending on your position within the formations. You have to concentrate that little bit more on those aspects right through the years, as they would be the times when errors can creep in and the slightest inaccuracy would make the manoeuvre look a mess. We flew a manoeuvre called the Caterpillar, with the aircraft peeling away from each other in a kind of loop. In any kind of formation position when you start to move further away from each other, then positioning errors are very difficult to judge in the air even though they're very obvious to an observer on the ground. If you're close to each other you can see if you're a few inches out of position, but if your formation is widely separated, it's hard to judge things. Some of the bigger looping manoeuvres can be difficult too, as if you don't concentrate on pulling up precisely, you tend to mess up everyone who is positioned outside of you".

JOHN OATEN

The Team Leader is responsible for looking at the weather conditions, deciding what format can be flown and at which stages in the display. But for the other pilots in the formation, weather is still a potential problem; "you get used to keeping position when the conditions are very rough, it's a discipline you develop during the winter training season. You trust the people around you to bounce around within a kind of box area, within the confines of a few feet. You don't react to them, and you tell yourself that the guy next to you isn't going to move significantly, and intrude into my airspace. The aeroplane closest to me is moving around an awful lot and he's in a very close formation, but I'll be looking at the leader, just keeping a sort of wary eye on him, just in case things do go wrong and I have to react. During the early stages of training you tend to react to what is happening around you and in a big formation with maybe four people stacked alongside, any kind of movement gets magnified and you get an awful sort of wave action down the line.

"The Team Leader maintains a constant radio commentary during the display, calling every manoeuvre he's making, even though the whole team knows precisely what is going to happen; he still calls the moves so that we can react when he reacts rather than waiting to see him move and then react, which would leave us a little bit late. So we could do the manoeuvres blind in effect without seeing the leader. He'll use his tone of voice to indicate how he's adjusting things and he'll call the smoke-on and smoke-off signals, and other people in the formation will also call smoke changes so that the Boss knows when he's clear to manoeuvre again. Any formation change is called by the Boss, and the aircraft that should move are expected to acknowledge the call so that nobody moves if somebody has had a radio failure. You should know what the Boss is going to do, and you can't blindly follow the routine, just in case the Boss makes the wrong call. But the Boss can change between any one of three sequences and you have to react to his calls, as the difference between the three formats could mean the difference between going in two different directions. Much of the time we wouldn't have much of a clue when a change in format will be called, as we are busy following him around while he will be looking around, maybe for a break in the clouds to pull into a loop. We might have a clue that he's looking for something like that if we see his head moving up and down, but it can be a very last-minute call".

Three pilots in the team are Navigation Officers and on every flight, one officer will be responsible for planning the sortie, preparing the brief and so on; "the nav officer will be on his radio talking to the local air traffic controllers during the display. If it's somewhere that is within an area of controlled airspace, he'll co-ordinate any possible traffic conflicts. If for example, an airliner might come through, either by prior arrangement or by accident, the nav officer will tell the Boss to keep to the flat display while somebody is going over us. The nav officer is working very hard indeed, listening to a busy air traffic frequency, whilst listening to the formation communications and also filling his formation position carefully at the same time. We do brief the controllers to keep transmissions to us as concise as possible though, in order to help things along".

The use of coloured smoke has been a part of Red Arrows tradition ever since the team first began display flying; "each aeroplane's smoke use will be different, and we only carry a minute-and-a-half of it, so we balance the smoke plan to use as much of the available coloured dye as possible. So when the guys use red smoke on one manoeuvre, we might change to blue on the next move, so as to swap around as much as possible, as you can easily run-out of coloured smoke. There is a great deal of mental counting to judge when to switch on and switch off the smoke, and each pilot has to commit his smoke usage to memory. There's no way we could write down anything as we're too busy looking all the time at our formation references".

The Team Leader tries to fly as much of the display at a fixed throttle setting, rather like flying an airliner, rather than leading a formation of nine individual machines. But the pilots positioned to the edges of the formation will have to make fairly large throttle and flying control movements in order to keep the whole formation stable; "you tend to get in tune with your engine and you can start to pre-judge your requirements. You start to know when you'll need power in a few seconds time so you push the throttle forward and the engine is winding-up ready for when you need it. At first, during the early training, you tend to select power just when you want it, and the relatively slow engine response comes too late and you just slip right out of formation. I don't think people realise just how close we are to the aircraft's performance limits much of the time. During many of the manoeuvres we can be hanging on at the back, often with almost full power, so if you make the slightest mistake and you're a little wide, you haven't got the power to catch up and you're up there for everybody to see, and you can't do anything about it".

Some displays tend to be more memorable than others, as Jerry explains; "Mildenhall for example, is a big show, and we park just yards from the public. It's also one of the first shows of the season, and I remember coming back after my first display there, opening the canopy, and hearing this fantastic applause, and you felt like looking around to see why they are clapping, it's very strange, as for much of the time we're very isolated from the air show crowds. Realistically, we can't spend much more time with the public than we already do without cutting down on the number of displays, and I think everyone would prefer us to be actually flying the displays".

When Jerry leaves the Red Arrows, he will have three years to serve with the RAF before having an option to leave, although he isn't sure what job he'd ideally like to do; "I quite fancy doing something completely different, maybe flying bigger aircraft, although most of the Red Arrows pilots tend to go back to the kind of job they were doing before they came to Scampton. So depending on what the job was, I wouldn't mind flying a multi-engine aircraft, although I'm pretty sure that won't happen, and I'll probably end up being an Instructor again".

"each aeroplane's smoke use will be different, and we only carry a minute-and-a-half of it, so we balance the smoke plan to use as much of the available coloured dye as possible"

RICK BREWELL

RICK BREWELL

RED TEN

The Red Arrows Team Manager is responsible for the smooth running of the team, ensuring that everything apart from the flying demonstration is organised properly. He also relieves the workload of the Team Leader, the other team pilots and, to a lesser degree, the Engineering tasks. Squadron Leader Les Garside-Beattie is the current Red Arrows Team Manager, having arrived at Scampton for the 1992 season. He joined the RAF in 1976 as a Technician and later underwent flying training, becoming a Jet Provost QFI (Qualified Flying Instructor) at Linton-on-Ouse. He then spent nine years flying the Harrier, becoming the UK Harrier display pilot, and later becoming the Deputy Commanding Officer of N° 1 Squadron at Wittering.

The overall planning of the Red Arrows display season is one of his main tasks, as he explains; "when an organiser bids for a Red Arrows display, we forward all of the requests to the RAF Participation Committee within the Ministry of Defence. They collect all of the bids together and forward all of the show requests back to me, so in October or November I receive a list of around four hundred displays. From there, we have to make a joint decision as to which venues will be acceptable or not. I know which shows the RAF will want to support more than others, and I can weed out all the shows which are non-starters. We have to look at the size of the show crowd, so things like the International Air Tattoo, Mildenhall and Southend with massive crowds, go to the top of the list. There are other events like the Battle of Britain shows at Finningley and Leuchars which are always number one and number two on our list because that's the time that we get an opportunity to show the public what we're doing with their money. We also place a priority on St.Athan and Cosford. I'm the one guy who sees the size of the crowd at most of these shows, so my input is valuable in deciding whether a show is going to be on our list. In terms of recruiting, the North East has always been a valuable area, so we place an emphasis on that area when we can, and of course there are very few shows in Scotland, so we're encouraged to do shows over there whenever we can, not least because we do lots of low flying in Scotland, so we have to show the public what we're all about".

Many displays are flown in support of the RAF Careers Information Service, as they will try to target specific schools and areas. Like any major industry, the RAF is keen to recruit the best, and the Red Arrows help to encourage recruiting wherever they go. Ultimately, the Manager works out a smaller list of shows which he feels is workable for the next display season. The Team Leader is busy with pre-season flying training at this stage, and the decision on venues is essentially left to the Manager, who returns the short-list to the RAF Participation Committee. Finally, a meeting between the Committee and the entire range of RAF display teams and solo performers takes place, to establish the complete RAF participation programme for the coming year, although few modifications are made to the list submitted by the Red Arrows.

The 1993 season was particularly busy for the Red Arrows, with a large number of displays including a trip to the United States. With a new Team Leader and three new pilots for the 1994 season, the number of shows will be somewhat smaller, in order to allow the team to build their experience and expertise level, and Les will have the unenviable task of deciding which shows will see the Red Arrows, and which will not; "it would be very easy for me to accept displays for almost every day right through summer, but you have to look at the impact on the team. Unless we had a Hercules to support us every day, it wouldn't be possible, and from an engineering standpoint it wouldn't be practical either. It's really logistics rather than finance which dictates the number of displays we do. The most we would ever do in one day is three displays, and to do that we would have to be based in one central location, for example in the ninety-four season we plan to do shows at Leicester, Church Fenton and Pontefract all on one day in July, doing everything directly from Scampton".

Les continues; "another important point is that we might have two major shows on one day, and most big shows have flying displays of maybe eight hours, so it's easy for us to do one show in the morning and the other late in the afternoon. If the show has a smaller flying display of maybe three hours, we couldn't do two shows with transits and refuellings within the show timescales. As for totally new venues, we will do between five and ten each year, but ultimately, the smaller sites are often unsuitable for us to perform. We look at the site on an Ordnance Survey map, and providing the RAF and participation people are happy with it, we'll look at the map to see if a display is prac-

PETER MOBBS

tical. Obviously if it's right in the middle of a built-up area, we couldn't do it, and I remember last year we were asked to display in Scunthorpe, a great local show idea, but we couldn't display over a sports field in the middle of the town. We're allowed to fly at a thousand feet over built-up areas, but if there isn't enough space to fly a totally clear display line, we can't participate. Some show sites are pretty marginal and people look to the experts to decide whether to display, and we're basically the experts so it's up to us".

After looking at a possible venue on a 1:50,000 scale map, the team will then visit the location. Normally the Manager or the Synchro Leader (sometimes Synchro Two) will perform a site survey, followed by a survey by RAF Police and Security personnel who will visit local police units, hospitals, the council and other appropriate groups, ensuring that the event is planned properly and that everybody knows exactly what the Red Arrows will do. New sites will be surveyed in February, ensuring that the team can make a decision on whether a display is practical at the earliest opportunity, giving the show organiser plenty of notice to re-arrange the show, if the Red Arrows do not feel able to perform there.

Even though the team displays at some venues every year, the task of setting-up each individual performance is still far from simple, as Les explains; "there are not many weekends in the year where I can use virtually the same plan as the previous year. We send each show organiser a package of information, and we ask them to illustrate the display datum and display line on a couple of maps. We give them examples of similar sites, and we ask for sensitive areas to be highlighted, such as bird concentrations, waste dumps, farms, hospitals, things like that. We then send them our Operational Procedures Brief, and we ask them to tell us what time we're expected to display. I tell them how I'll be getting to the site, be it by Hawk, Gazelle, Bulldog, car or whatever and I'll ask who is going to meet me there, where the commentary position will be, and so on. Some shows will always want us to close the event, largely to keep the crowds at the site, in order to satisfy traders at the event. But sometimes the local police will not want them to have the Red Arrows close the show, as the last thing they'll want is the whole crowd trying to get out all at the same time. Leuchars is one such place, as they need to ease the effects of people all wanting to leave at the same time". The team will always try to meet the required display time as specified by the show organisers, but the logistics of performing more than one display on any given day will sometimes force the team to negotiate alternative appearance times.

Red Arrows displays are sometimes supported by RAF Hercules transport aircraft, easing the task of moving engineers and equipment to show sites around the country. However, the increasing demands on the RAF transport fleet require the Red Arrows to keep requests for a Hercules to an absolute minimum, and many events are supported by road, effectively sending all of the equipment carried on the Hercules by truck. Of course, this drastically increases the transportation timescale, which will dictate the number of shows which can be performed. Certainly, the Hercules support aircraft isn't used as often as in previous years, but it is still vital for some events where equipment needs to be moved rapidly between show sites. The Manager can also request a Bulldog in order to reach small show sites where his Hawk cannot be used, or a Gazelle helicopter to gain access to small gardens, beaches or other confined locations. The Manager has to be on-site at every display, as although Les is the Red Arrows show commentator, he is primarily the team safety officer, acting as a pair of eyes on the ground for the Team Leader.

Finance is an important aspect of the team's appearances too, as every show organiser is required to pay a display fee as Les explains; "civilian show organisers will pay a fixed fee of just under five thousand pounds for the Red Arrows to appear. That includes insurance and because it's a fixed fee we can tell people that in January, so they can budget well in advance. Of course, that fee covers virtually nothing in terms of the overall cost, but it enables the Ministry of Defence to recover the costs of what we call additional expense. What that means is that if we did all our shows here at Scampton there wouldn't be any additional expense. It's the extra cost of moving our display to another venue, things like travel, accommodation, landing fees, and insurance to cover things like if a panel fell on someone's property or, in a worst case, a mid-air collision. The show organiser effectively buys-into the MOD's insurance policy".

Interestingly, the Red Arrows are prohibited from making simple fly-past appearances at air shows. The reason for this is because show organisers tend to advertise a 'Red Arrows appearance', and don't specify whether the appearance will be a flypast or full show, which is naturally unfair to spectators. Consequently, in order to avoid some potentially bad publicity, the team only makes publicised appearances when a full display is scheduled. However, Les is keen to point out that the Red Arrows do still make flypasts; "we still make as many flypast appearances as we possibly can within the show guidelines. If somebody asks us to overfly their church fete for example, we'll look at a map, check the route between the main show venues, and if we don't have to deviate more than about ten miles from our transit route, we'll do it as long as the timing matches with our schedule. It doesn't cost anything and we'll probably fit in up to forty such flypasts each year, but we don't advertise them, not least because it would be an administrative nightmare to fit in many more requests".

Having fixed the basic outline of each display venue, the Manager and Team Adjutant fix accommodation, having already established whether any given show will be supported by Hercules, road, or with the 'circus', the team Engineers flying in the Hawk's rear seats. After timings and every other detail has been fixed, the Manager issues a 'WHAM' one week before each show. The 'WHAM' ('What's Happening, Manager'?) is a detailed document specifying who goes where and when; "if the document says we are due to display at seventeen hundred, that is the time they'll overfly in Big Nine, so they'll be rolling on the runway at sixteen-fifty-seven and they'll want the runway at sixteen-fifty-five...all that sort of information is specified, together with things like where we're staying, with telephone and fax numbers, the kind of PR support we're taking, if we have local tasks to perform, aircraft parking details, briefing facilities, all the relevant stuff, so each display venue creates a large amount of information which needs to be fixed in advance".

While the team displays, the pilots are surrounded by an area of Temporary Restricted Airspace, a six-mile area extending up to 8,000 feet, which is cleared of any other aircraft, and any aircraft entering that airspace would be liable to prosecution under the Air Navigation Act. Some areas of the United Kingdom are particularly congested in terms of air traffic, which has created additional problems for the Red Arrows. Biggin Hill for example, is situated under an approach to Gatwick Airport, and conditions sometimes dictate that the Red Arrows are forced to perform a Flat display, even in good weather conditions, because of the surrounding air traffic, but the team enjoys good co-operation with air traffic control authorities; "the nice thing is that we've built up a good relationship so that the air traffic people know we're flexible and we know that they will do everything they can to let us do a Full Show up to six thousand feet. One of the navigation guys will be talking to the air traffic people during the display, and during the show we may get clearance to go Full. Then, as another airliner approaches the airspace, we'll lose the height clearance again, so they don't give us a blanket refusal, we try to do the best we can in the prevailing conditions". The flexible nature of the display can cause problems for Les, while he provides the spectators with a commentary; "I have an earpiece, so I listen to what the Boss is saying and when he calls to change between the display formats, I know what the next manoeuvre will be. I memorise the commentary from an outline script,

The highlight of the 1993 display season was the US Tour. On September 26, the Red Arrows gave a memorable display at Denver, Colorado

RICK BREWELL

and I have to try and fit my comments with the display, but conditions can change the way I do things. The wind direction can affect the time at which the crowd can only hear the aircraft, so I have to work my commentary around that. Likewise an aircraft might be seen in the restricted airspace area, so I'll have to advise the Boss about that, which means I have to break into whatever I'm saying to the spectators. Flight safety is my main concern even while I'm doing the commentary.

"We try to tailor our show to what the audience expects, and what the display organiser wants. It's very different to the way they do things in America, where the Blue Angels or Thunderbirds will be the centrepiece of maybe three days of activity at a show site, so they might bring the star pupil from a local school to meet the team. They'll stay at one show site for three or four days, visiting hospitals, schools and so on. That's the way they do things. They also insist that everything stops while they're performing which is great if you're at the place where it's happening, but if you're stuck ten rows back, or somewhere else on the airfield, that's not going to be much of a show for maybe thirty minutes or more. It's not what the British public would want to see, as they go to a show to see aerial entertainment. That's not to say that I'm in favour of maybe ten hours of jet noise either! I don't think we're likely to change our approach significantly".

Les is also well aware of the financial restraints which are placed upon the team; "the classic example is our publicity material. Some things carry manufacturers' logos, and that's allowed us to produce a quality item to give to the general public, and before people like British Aerospace came on board, the publicity material had to be paid for by the military. We're not going to become the 'Coca-Cola Red Arrows' even though we'd suit the colours, as we have a clean image to protect, and the British Public wouldn't like it either. There aren't so many Harriers, Jaguars and Tornados available for displays, and aircraft like the Buccaneer, Phantom and Lightning have gone, so the RAF's public appearances are slowly reducing. So there's possibly a case to ensure that the Red Arrows participation continues at the current level, so we can display the RAF to the nation, and show the public what they're getting for their money".

FEATHERED ARROW

RED ARROWS TEAM MEMBERS 1965–94

1965

Leader	Flt Lt L Jones
Red 2	Flt Lt BA Nice
Red 3	Flt Lt RG Hanna
Red 4	Flt Lt GL Ranscombe
Red 5	Fg Off PG Hay
Red 6	Flt Lt REW Loverseed
Red 7	Flt Lt HJD Prince
Red 8	Flt Lt ECF Tilsley
Manager	Sqn Ldr RAE Storer
Engineers	Fg Off Harrow
	Fg Off Whitby

1966

Leader	Sqn Ldr RG Hanna
Red 2	Flt Lt DA Bell
Red 3	Flt Lt RW Langworthy
Red 4	Flt Lt PR Evans
Red 5	Flt Lt R Booth
Red 6	Flt Lt HJD Prince
Red 7	Flt Lt TJG Nelson
Red 8	Flt Lt FJ Hoare
Red 9	Flt Lt G McGregor
Manager	Sqn Ldr RA Storer
Engineers	Fg Off Harrow
	Fg Off Whitby

1967

Leader	Sqn Ldr RG Hanna
Red 2	Flt Lt DA Bell
Red 3	Flt Lt FJ Hoare
Red 4	Flt Lt PR Evans
Red 5	Flt Lt R Booth
Red 6	Flt Lt HJD Prince
Red 7	Flt Lt EE Jones
Manager	Flt Lt LG Williams
Engineer	Fg Off D Whitby
Adjutant	Flt Lt R Dench

1968

Leader	Sqn Ldr RG Hanna
Red 2	Flt Lt DA Bell
Red 3	Flt Lt DA Smith
Red 4	Flt Lt PR Evans
Red 5	Flt Lt FJ Hoare
Red 6	Flt Lt R Booth
Red 7	Flt Lt JT Kingsley
Red 8	Flt Lt ICH Dick
Red 9	Flt Lt RB Duckett
Manager	Sqn Ldr LG Williams
Engineer	Fg Off D Whitby
Adjutant	Flt Lt R Dench

1969

Leader	Sqn Ldr RG Hanna
Red 2	Flt Lt PR Evans
Red 3	Flt Lt DA Smith
Red 4	Flt Lt RB Duckett
Red 5	Flt Lt ER Perreux
Red 6	Flt Lt JT Kingsely
Red 7	Flt Lt ICH Dick
Red 8	Flt Lt JD Rust
Red 9	Sqn Ldr RP Dunn
Manager	Flt Lt P Mackintosh
Engineer	Fg Off GE White
Adjutant	Flt Lt R Dench

1970

Leader	Sqn Ldr D Hazell
Red 2	Flt Lt ER Peereux
Red 3	Flt Lt DA Smith
Red 4	Flt Lt JD Rust
Red 5	Flt Lt J Haddock
Red 6	Flt Lt ICH Dick
Red 7	Flt Lt RB Duckett
Red 8	Flt Lt DSB Marr
Red 9	Flt Lt REW Loverseed
Manager	Flt Lt P Mackintosh
Engineer	Flt Lt GE White
Adjutant	WO L Ludlow

1971

Leader	Sqn Ldr REW Loverseed
Red 2	Sqn Ldr DBS Marr
Red 3	Flt Lt AC East
Red 4	Flt Lt WB Aspinall
Red 5	Flt Lt PJJ Day
Red 6	Flt Lt CF Roberts
Red 7	Flt Lt RE Somerville
Manager	Flt Lt KJ Tait
Engineer	Flt Lt GE White
Adjutant	WO L Ludlow

1972

Leader	Sqn Ldr ICH Dick
Red 2	Flt Lt WB Aspinall
Red 3	Flt Lt AC East
Red 4	Flt Lt RE Somerville
Red 5	Flt Lt KJ Tait
Red 6	Flt Lt PJJ Day
Red 7	Flt Lt D Binnie
Red 8	Flt Lt EEG Gridley
Red 9	Flt Lt CF Roberts
Manager	Flt Lt B Donnelly
Engineer	Flt Lt I Brackenbury
Adjutant	WO S Wild

1973

Leader	Sqn Ldr ICH Dick
Red 2	Sqn Ldr WB Aspinall
Red 3	Flt Lt B Donnelly
Red 4	Flt Lt EEG Gridley
Red 5	Flt Lt KJ Tait
Red 6	Flt Lt D Binnie
Red 7	Sqn Ldr RE Somerville
Red 8	Flt Lt DJ Sheen
Red 9	Flt Lt PJJ Day
Manager	Flt Lt RM Joy
Engineer	Flt Lt I Brackenbury
Adjutant	WO HED Rundstorm

1974

Leader	Sqn Ldr ICH Dick
Red 2	Flt Lt KJ Tait
Red 3	Flt Lt B Donnelly
Red 4	Flt Lt EEG Gridley
Red 5	Flt Lt CM Phillips
Red 6	Flt Lt D Binnie
Red 7	Sqn Ldr RE Somerville
Red 8	Flt Lt DJ Sheen
Red 9	Flt Lt R Eccles
Manager	Flt Lt RM Joy
Engineer	Flt Lt I Brackenbury
Adjutant	WO HED Rundstorm

1975

Leader	Sqn Ldr RB Duckett
Red 2	Flt Lt MJ Phillips
Red 3	Flt Lt B Donnelly
Red 4	Flt Lt R Eccles
Red 5	Flt Lt J Blackwell
Red 6	Flt Lt DJ Sheen
Red 7	Flt Lt BR Hoskins
Red 8	Flt Lt M Cornwell
Red 9	Flt Lt RS Barber
Manager	Sqn Ldr AL Wall
Engineer	Flt Lt A Hunt
Adjutant	WO HED Rundstorm

1976

Leader	Sqn Ldr RB Duckett
Red 2	Flt Lt MJ Phillips
Red 3	Flt Lt R Eccles
Red 4	Flt Lt DR Carvell
Red 5	Flt Lt RS Barber
Red 6	Sqn Ldr BR Hoskins
Red 7	Flt Lt M Cornwell
Red 8	Flt Lt MT Curley
Red 9	Flt Lt NS Champness
Manager	Sqn Ldr AL Wall
Engineer	Flt Lt A Hunt
Adjutant	WO HG Thorne

1977

Leader	Sqn Ldr FJ Hoare
Red 2	Flt Lt DR Carvell
Red 3	Flt Lt RS Barber
Red 4	Flt Lt MJ Phillips
Red 5	Flt Lt NS Champness
Red 6	Flt Lt M Cornwell
Red 7	Flt Lt MT Curley
Red 8	Flt Lt RM Thomas
Red 9	Flt Lt MB Stoner
Manager	Flt Lt MB Whitehouse
Engineer	Flt Lt A Hunt
Adjutant	WO HG Thorne

1978

Leader	Sqn Ldr FJ Hoare
Red 2	Flt Lt DR Carvell
Red 3	Flt Lt MB Stoner
Red 4	Flt Lt MJ Phillips
Red 5	Flt Lt LA Grose
Red 6	Flt Lt MT Curley
Red 7	Flt Lt RM Thomas
Red 8	Flt Lt SR Johnson
Red 9	Flt Lt BC Scott
Manager	Sqn Ldr MB Whitehouse
Engineer	Flt Lt RA Lewis
Adjutant	WO HG Thorne

1979

Leader	Sqn Ldr BR Hoskins
Red 2	Flt Lt MT Curley
Red 3	Flt Lt BC Scott
Red 4	Flt Lt MD Howell
Red 5	Flt Lt MB Stoner
Red 6	Flt Lt RM Thomas
Red 7	Sqn Ldr SR Johnson
Red 8	Flt Lt NJ Wharton
Red 9	Flt Lt W Ward
Manager	Sqn Ldr R Thilthorpe
Engineer	Flt Lt RA Lewis
Adjutant	WO HG Thorne

1980

Leader	Sqn Ldr BR Hoskins
Red 2	Flt Lt MD Howell
Red 3	Flt Lt W Ward
Red 4	Flt Lt NJ Wharton
Red 5	Flt Lt BC Scott
Red 6	Flt Lt RM Thomas
Red 7	Sqn Ldr SR Johnson
Red 8	Flt Lt BS Walters
Red 9	Flt Lt TR Watts
Manager	Sqn Ldr R Thilthorpe
Engineer	Flt Lt RA Lewis
Adjutant	WO HG Thorne

1981

Leader	Sqn Ldr BR Hoskins
Red 2	Flt Lt BS Walters
Red 3	Flt Lt W Ward
Red 4	Flt Lt MH DeCourcier
Red 5	Flt Lt NJ Wharton
Red 6	Sqn Ldr SR Johnson
Red 7	Flt Lt TR Watts
Red 8	Flt Lt IJ Huzzard
Red 9	Flt Lt JR Myers
Manager	Sqn Ldr R Thilthorpe
Engineer	Flt Lt GM Nisbet
Adjutant	WO HG Thorne

1982

Leader	Sqn Ldr J Blackwell
Red 2	Flt Lt BS Walters
Red 3	Flt Lt JR Myers
Red 4	Flt Lt IJ Huzzard
Red 5	Flt Lt W Ward
Red 6	Flt Lt TR Watts
Red 7	Flt Lt MH DeCourcier
Red 8	Flt Lt TWL Miller
Red 9	Flt Lt PA Tolman
Manager	Sqn Ldr R Thilthorpe
Engineer	Flt Lt GM Nisbet
Adjutant	WO HG Thorne

1983

Leader	Sqn Ldr J Blackwell
Red 2	Sqn Ldr IJ Huzzard
Red 3	Flt Lt JR Myers
Red 4	Flt Lt TWL Miller
Red 5	Flt Lt EH Ball
Red 6	Flt Lt MH DeCourcier
Red 7	Flt Lt PA Tolman
Red 8	Flt Lt SH Bedford
Red 9	Flt Lt CAR Hirst
Manager	Sqn Ldr JE Steenson
Engineer	Flt Lt MEJ Render
Adjutant	WO HG Thorne

1984

Leader	Sqn Ldr J Blackwell
Red 2	Flt Lt SH Bedford
Red 3	Flt Lt GI Hannam
Red 4	Sqn Ldr TWL MIller
Red 5	Sqn Ldr EH Ball
Red 6	Flt Lt PA Tolman
Red 7	Flt Lt AR Boyens
Red 8	Flt Lt PD Lees
Red 9	Flt Lt AK Lunnon-Wood
Manager	Sqn Ldr JE Steenson
Engineer	Flt Lt MEJ Render
Adjutant	WO DHA Chubb

1985

Leader	Sqn Ldr RM Thomas
Red 2	Flt Lt PD Lees
Red 3	Sqn Ldr EH Ball
Red 4	Flt Lt SH Bedford
Red 5	Sqn Ldr GI Hannam
Red 6	Flt Lt AR Boyens
Red 7	Flt Lt AK Lunnon-Wood
Red 8	Flt Lt CDR McIlroy
Red 9	Sqn Ldr AB Chubb
Manager	Sqn Ldr HR Ploszek
Engineer	Flt Lt MEJ Render
Adjutant	WO DHA Chubb

1986

Leader	Sqn Ldr RM Thomas
Red 2	Flt Lt PD Lees
Red 3	Sqn Ldr AB Chubb
Red 4	Flt Lt PJ Collins
Red 5	Sqd Ldr GI Hannam
Red 6	Flt Lt AK Lunnon-Wood
Red 7	Flt Lt CDR McIlroy
Red 8	Flt Lt DW Findlay
Red 9	Flt Lt AP Thurley
Manager	Sqn Ldr HR Ploszek
Engineer	Flt Lt S Chantry
Adjutant	WO DHA Chubb

1987

Leader	Sqn Ldr RM Thomas
Red 2	Sqn Ldr PJ Collins
Red 3	Flt Lt MA Carter
Red 4	Flt Lt MJ Newbery
Red 5	Sqn Ldr AB Chubb
Red 6	Flt Lt CDR McIlroy
Red 7	Flt Lt AP Thurley
Red 8	Flt Lt JE Rands
Red 9	Flt Lt GM Bancroft-Wilson
Manager	Sqd Ldr HR Ploszek
Engineer	Flt Lt JS Chantry
Adjutant	WO MRJ Fleckney

1988

Leader	Sqd Ldr TWL Miller
Red 2	Flt Lt GM Bancroft-Wilson
Red 3	Flt Lt DC Riley
Red 4	Sqn Ldr PJ Collins
Red 5	Flt Lt SWM Johnson
Red 6	Sqn Ldr AP Thurley
Red 7	Flt Lt JE Rands
Red 8	Sqn Ldr JW Glover
Red 9	Flt Lt MA Carter
Manager	Sqn Ldr HR Ploszek
Engineer	Flt Lt JD Williams
Adjutant	WO MRJ Fleckney

1989

Leader	Sqn Ldr TWL Miller
Red 2	Flt Lt AW Hoy
Red 3	Flt Lt MJ Cliff
Red 4	Flt Lt GM Bancroft-Wilson
Red 5	Flt Lt DC Riley
Red 6	Flt Lt JE Rands
Red 7	Flt Lt SWM Johnson
Red 8	Sqn Ldr JW Glover
Red 9	Flt Lt JM Newton
Manager	Sqn Ldr AJ Stewart
Engineer	Flt Lt JD Williams
Adjutant	WO MRJ Fleckney

1990

Leader	Sqd Ldr TWL Miller
Red 2	Flt Lt A Smith
Red 3	Flt Lt PCH Rogers
Red 4	Flt Lt AW Hoy
Red 5	Sqn Ldr DC Riley
Red 6	Flt Lt SWM Johnson
Red 7	Flt Lt JM Newton
Red 8	Flt Lt DA Wyatt
Red 9	Flt Lt MJ Cliff
Manager	Sqn Ldr AJ Stewart
Engineer	Flt Lt CR Bushell
Adjutant	WO MRJ Fleckney

1991

Leader	Sqn Ldr A Thurley
Red 2	Flt Lt GP Howes
Red 3	Flt Lt NC Rogers
Red 4	Flt Lt A Smith
Red 5	Flt Lt SC Meade
Red 6	Flt Lt JM Newton
Red 7	Flt Lt DA Wyatt
Red 8	Flt Lt AW Hoy
Red 9	Flt Lt MJ Cliff
Manager	Sqn Ldr AJ Stewart
Engineer	Flt Lt CR Bushell
Adjutant	WO MRJ Fleckney

1992

Leader	Sqn Ldr A Thurley
Red 2	Flt Lt R Last
Red 3	Flt Lt B Cross
Red 4	Flt Lt GP Howes
Red 5	Flt Lt J Bird
Red 6	Flt Lt DA Wyatt
Red 7	Flt Lt SC Meade
Red 8	Flt Lt A Smith
Red 9	Flt Lt NC Rogers
Manager	Sqn Ldr L Garside-Beattie
Engineer	Flt Lt S Miller
Adjutant	WO MRJ Fleckney

1993

Leader	Sqn Ldr A Thurley
Red 2	Flt Lt S Chiddention
Red 3	Flt Lt B Ball
Red 4	Flt Lt B Cross
Red 5	Flt Lt J Bird
Red 6	Flt Lt SC Meade
Red 7	Flt Lt R Last
Red 8	Flt Lt G Howes
Red 9	Flt Lt N Rogers
Manager	Sqn Ldr L Garside-Beattie
Engineer	Flt Lt S Miller
Adjutant	WO MRJ Fleckney

1994

Leader	Sqn Ldr JE Rands
Red 2	Flt Lt CD Jepson
Red 3	Flt Lt M Zanker
Red 4	Flt Lt KP Truss
Red 5	Flt Lt B Ball
Red 6	Flt Lt R Last
Red 7	Flt Lt S Chiddention
Red 8	Flt Lt B Cross
Red 9	Flt Lt J Bird
Manager	Sqn Ldr L Garside-Beattie
Engineer	Flt Lt M Northover
Adjutant	WO J Howard

Congratulations to the Red Arrows for hitting the target with total precision for 30 years
As the world's leading specialists in aviation support services, Serco-IAL Limited would like to offer their congratulations to the Red Arrows, the world's leading aerobatics team, and hope that the next 30 years will be equally exciting.
SERCO
SERCO-IAL LIMITED, SERCO HOUSE, HAYES ROAD, SOUTHALL, MIDDLESEX UB2 5NJ TEL : 081-843 2411 FAX : 081-843 3901

Chapter Three – THE UNSUNG HEROES

RICK BREWELL

PETR MOBBS

As the crowds look up at the sky and marvel at the beautiful formations being flown by nine sleek, red aircraft, few, if any, ever spare a thought for the backroom boys whose responsibility it is to ensure that those very aeroplanes up there in the sky are performing at peak efficiency.

The Red Arrows squadron organisation is somewhat different from that found in a normal operational squadron. This is natural when one considers the different aims and needs of each. The ten Red Arrows aeroplanes must not only be serviceable for the whole twelve months of the year but they must always be in perfect condition. The fact that the Red Arrows travel around the UK and overseas for six months of the year means that they have to be either supported via road or air all of the time. All this places a great deal of stress not only on the engineering staff but also on the administrative staff, the Mechanical Transport Section and the myriad other personnel whose team effort is perhaps not as appreciated as it should be – a veritable host of unsung heroes. To describe every single diverse job would be almost impossible without taking up more space than is available but the people who were interviewed make up a broad cross section of 'the backroom boys'.

The Squadron Engineers are divided into two sections, First Line and Second Line. On the First Line engineering side are the travelling ground crew, ten of whom have the opportunity to fly with the pilots to

XX264
FLT LT NC ROGERS
CPL D W BECKETT
ROYAL AIR FORCE

and from shows during the display season occupying the back seats of the aircraft. The ten flying ground crew are traditionally known as the 'circus' and it is not an easy outfit to get into.

Flt Lt Mark Northover (left) is Eng. One. He is top dog of the backroom boys. He is on his first season with the team and looks forward to 1994 with trepidation and excitement. "My background is that after University and Engineering Officer training I was posted to RAF St Athan on an Airframe Instructural Repair Squadron as a flight commander. After two years there, I went to Germany as a junior engineering officer with 3 Sqn where after some time I applied for the job of Eng. One with the Red Arrows. After an interview and the normal selection process I got the Arrows job and was posted to RAF Scampton. I do not have any previous Hawk experience, that's not a prerequisite for the job, but it is a requirement to have done a previous fast jet junior Engineering Officer job which I did on Harriers in Germany. The Hawk is simple enough for one not to have had previous experience. Compared to some of the front line aircraft we have in the air force today, the Hawk is a relatively simple beast and it doesn't take that long to pick it up. But one definite prerequisite is to have had previous man management experience in a fast jet squadron."

A normal sequence of events with engineers would be that as an individual is posted into the squadron he goes into Second Line engineering which is at its busiest period throughout the winter when the aircraft go into detailed maintenance. Second Line is considerably deeper and more complex than First Line engineering which consists of day-to-day handling, refuelling and rectifying minor faults. Second Line is where the aircraft gets put into the hangar, probably gets jacked up and stays there for two or three weeks for routine maintenance.

In engineering and maintenance, job continuity is essential. Normal procedure is that people are posted into Second Line and usually spend one or two years getting to know not only the aircraft but also the way it operates. Then, every subsequent year, as people are posted naturally and so long as progress is maintained there will be vacancies for three or four to move up to First Line. The next step will be for them to serve for a year on First Line as road support and then if they reach the required standard of excellence, they move into a 'circus' seat where perhaps they will do a year or two as circus members.

"We really have to be careful who we select for the back seats. It is really my job to select and it is done about December each year, in preparation for the display season. What I do is select two or three from each trade so that we have basic trade coverage in the 'circus'. That means that we will have two or three airframe technicians, a propulsion technician, a couple of avionics technicians and an electrician so that we have some engineering cover whatever the problem might be. Hopefully we have the know-how within those ten back seat occupants to come up with a solution to any problem that might arise", comments Eng. One.

The relationship between the pilots and the back seat boys is a good one though Mark Northover is somewhat caught up in the middle. As an officer he

R.J. CARUANA

Second Line engineering is at its busiest period throughout the winter when the aircraft go into detailed maintenance

obviously has allegiance to the pilots, his fellow officers, but being Eng. One also necessitates allegiance to his troops. "I have to try and smooth the ground between the two factions and it doesn't require much input from me 99% of the time. The engineers realise that the pilots work very hard when they're actually flying and it's really not all glamour as it might seem to be. Our bit comes in as soon as the aircraft reaches the ground and we have to get on with it. There is no resentment that the pilots get out of the aircraft and go home because that's when our job actually starts. Fortunately, the Hawk is a very reliable aircraft and there are very few occasions when we have to work two or three hours beyond landing time. So there is always some time for us to get on with a bit of socialising".

Undoubtedly the Red Arrows aircraft are the most serviced in the RAF. Certainly nothing is left to chance, everything is checked and then double-checked by an extra pair of eyes. One must bear in mind that this is no ordinary squadron. On several occasions the pilots are only on the ground for half an hour before they are off on another display. "It is very important that we do our job efficiently and that is why we have a lot of people looking over other people's shoulders. This is not normally done in an operational squadron as the interval between sorties is much greater. When you come to a situation like the Battle of Britain weekend in September, where every airshow from the North of Scotland to the south coast of England wants the Red Arrows, the aircraft could be at Manston on the south coast and two hours later they could be displaying over RAF Leuchars in Scotland. Two hours after that, they could be displaying somewhere else, so obviously in this type of situation the time spent on the ground is very limited. The ground crew must be completely reliable and there must be a great deal of supervision to ensure that the job is done efficiently and correctly", concluded Eng. One.

Working in the engineering section of the Red Arrows is unlike anything you will find in normal RAF stations. Chief Technician Stroud is an electrician by trade and one of two Second Line shift controllers on the maintenance side. He is in charge of manpower and responsible for ensuring that everything is done properly and on time. His shift consists of between fifteen and twenty people. During the display season his shift will be on call to rectify any faults that may occur on the Hawks and during the winter his team is responsible for general maintenance as well as servicing the aircraft that are still flying for continuation training. Obviously whilst some Hawks are stripped in the hangar the unit has to borrow other aircraft to ensure that at least ten are in flying condition. The shifts are always 'on base' unless there is a situation like the six week deployment for the US tour when some Second Line personnel will travel abroad with the team. Yet even in this situation the Red Arrows hangar facility at Scampton is always manned 24 hours a day. At any time during the display season, in the

R.J. CARUANA

eventuality of having to replace an aircraft even on a Saturday afternoon, the base is always ready to receive the incoming unserviceable aircraft and fly out the replacement. Chief Stroud is naturally very happy that the Hawk is a very reliable aircraft, though he feels "they are now getting a little bit tired; we're getting little things going wrong that were OK before but, having said that, there is still a lot of years left in them".

Stroud maintains that the Second Line work pattern is not ideally suited to the married man. The shifts work on a twelve-day on, two-days off pattern which means that they have to work every other weekend. During the display season at least three people from Second Line will travel with First Line and as can be expected, there are always volunteers to get overseas. Chief Stroud, who has vast experience on the Hawk, has been with the Red Arrows before (1969-73) when they were flying the Gnat. "It's a little bit different now than it was. Then it was like a flying club, I wouldn't say it's more professional now but it has really tightened up. It's more a class act than it was before", maintains Stroud.

All the engineering personnel who have worked on Gnats before agree that the Hawk is definitely a much more reliable aircraft. Chief Stroud thinks that it may not look as good but it is definitely much cleaner. "The Gnat was a very dirty aircraft to work on and engineering-wise it was a nightmare. At least when they designed the Hawk they thought of the engineers, so we can do a lot with this that we couldn't do with the Gnat". On the Hawk, there are very few jobs that would take the team more than a day and a half to

CONGRATULATIONS
RED ARROWS
KIWI
PARADE GLOSS
PREMIUM SHOE POLISH
BLACK
ON 30 YEARS OF BRILLIANCE

ARTHUR GIBSON

complete. On the rare occasion of an engine change, Chief Stroud says that "if I got the aircraft early in the afternoon, I could have it ready for air test the following morning". And here lies the difference between the Red Arrows and a normal RAF squadron. The Red Arrows have eleven aircraft and during the display season all eleven must be serviceable. In a squadron, this situation would never arise. From a total of twelve aircraft there would only be a need to have enough aircraft serviceable to fulfil the flying commitment.

Life is full of surprises in the Engineering Section. "Sometimes if I need a spare part and it's only available from RAF Valley, I could send one of my boys out at 3am to get it. The boys come in and never know what they might be doing during their shift. I've done it myself. I once had to ring the wife up to tell her that I wouldn't be back for tea as I was up at RAF Leuchars. The boys think it's great; they've all got bags packed and that's the beauty of the job. It's totally out of the ordinary and you never know where you're going to end up from one day to the next. This place never sleeps. If an aircraft develops a fault and can be flown down, we always have a replacement but whatever the fault, it will be rectified as soon as it arrives. If it can't be flown, we have to go and get it", says Stroud.

During the season, Corporal Ashley Doo, who is an airframe technician, "has to work very hard". His particular job today is wheels and brakes but last year he was part of the 'circus' doing the turnarounds and the after-flights for the aircraft to make sure that they remained serviceable. At night he would have to put right any snag that might have arisen during the day, most times these are relatively few but on rare occasions there have been enough to keep him up half the night. Doo came to the Red Arrows in a very roundabout way. "In 1983 I got posted to RAF Valley and in

those days they used to borrow Airframe Technicians to do winter servicing on Arrows aircraft. I applied for the Arrows then and I was put on a waiting list. In the meanwhile I was posted to RAF Abingdon doing major repairs and then one day in 1989, there I was doing a horrible job and someone came up to me and told me I was posted to the Red Arrows. I've been here ever since". Cpl Doo hopes to stay with the Red Arrows for a long time. Unlike the pilots who only do a three-year tour, technicians can stay on for a long period. Doo had always wanted to fly but as an engineer this would have been almost impossible. So his request to be posted to the Red Arrows was partly prompted by the fact that if he was selected for the 'circus', his wish would come true. It did.

Communications, radar and flight systems are looked after by the avionics trade. As Avionics Trade Manager, Sergeant Rick Brown is loaded with responsibility. He maintains that the Hawk is such a basic aircraft that his team does not really get too much work. As a training aircraft, it must be simple for the pilots "otherwise they'd have to get the ground crew to fly it", claimed Brown with a twinkle in his eye! He spent six years on First Line and travelled around a good deal. He describes his First Line tour as good fun "although my wife didn't appreciate it very much". Sgt Brown is one who has never wanted to be a pilot, although he admits that before he joined up he did consider the possibility. "In any case it would have been impossible to fly in a Hawk because I'm too big. My legs are the wrong length, I'd leave them behind on the coaming if I had to eject!" He has, however, flown in a Lightning and a Phantom although he spent most of his six-year First Line tour in the back of a Hercules. Most of his lads enjoy flying and apart from the nine lucky 'circus' members, many others even from Second Line, get the occasional flight on air tests or if there is any continuation training taking place. Sergeant Brown is happy with RAF policy that allows technicians to stay at one posting for as long as possible. He has been with the Red Arrows since 1986 and at the moment there is no sign of him moving. With only five years service to do, he is firmly settled off the base where he has bought his own house and put down his roots.

I asked Corporal Glenn Parker whether he got much work as an electrician. His reply is worth repeating: "when I joined up the officer told me that the easiest job in the Air Force was an electrician. I said, 'right, I'll have that, thank you very much'. But I didn't realise that he was lying through his teeth. Everybody

BRITISH AEROSPACE

Loading up the Hercules for a distant deployment is a precision job and no inch of space can be wasted

PHOTOS THIS PAGE: PETER MOBBS

is busy here but electrician-wise, we're mega-busy". Hydraulics and engine control all predominantly use some form of electrical control on the Hawk and when there is an engine fault the engineer will invariably ask for electrical assistance, meaning that the electricians are not only responsible for their dedicated kit but they are also drafted in to help other trades as well. Parker has worked on all sorts of aircraft and although he has only been in the RAF for twelve years he has even worked on Vampires. This was when he was working with the famous Vintage Pair. At the time he considered this period of his career as almost a nightmare particularly when he remembers the enormous problems encountered as a result of lack of spares and old fashioned wiring. However in retrospect he realises that all in all he enjoyed his tour though he would have been happier to have had some experienced technician to work alongside him.

When not needed on the electricians team, another job of Corporal Parker's is to help out with the Souvenir Stall that follows the Red Arrows around at displays during the season. All profits from sales of

souvenirs go to the Red Arrows Trust, which in turn distributes them to charity. The stall is usually set up early in the morning and, at first, things are rather slow. But as soon as the Arrows display ends, the sales staff get what they call a 'frenzy' and the stall is crowded four deep with people wanting to buy anything that is available. "This goes on non-stop for about forty minutes and at the end of it all you thank God that the Arrows only give one display at a time, otherwise we'd be inundated", said Parker.

There are, of course, no weapons in the Hawks so it was strange to discover that the squadron possesses no less than six weapons experts. Corporal Ian Wright is one of three

PETER MOBBS

weapons experts on First Line and he was quick to explain the situation. "We are responsible for anything to do with explosives. The ejection seats and the escape systems, fire extinguishers, etc, are explosively operated on the aircraft and the emergency undercarriage and flaps system have a certain amount of explosive involved as well. On First Line we have very little to do but in Second Line we get involved in the annual servicing programme". Like many others, Wright has secondary duties to keep him gainfully occupied – last year he was a loader for both the Hercules and road transport. Unlike many others, Corporal Wright did not volunteer for the job. He was posted to RAF Leuchars on a Phantom squadron which was disbanded and after ten years working on Jaguars and Phantoms he was posted to the Red Arrows. "It's a nice change," he says, "it's like serving in two different Air Forces".

Another essential job done by the backroom boys is that of the Mechanical Transport Section, better known as MT. During winter it mainly consists of refuelling the serviceable aircraft after training flights, but as Corporal John Howells observed, his section's duties are quite unlike any other MT section in the RAF. Engines have to be taken down to RAF St Athan in Wales when they are due for a major overhaul, diesel has to be provided for the Hawks' smoke pods and transport has to be provided when displays are close enough to be road-supported. When they are not, it is the responsibility of MT section to load up the Hercules with all the kit that might be needed. Corporal Howells has only one grouse – he does not have

H.E. & INFLITE

SALUTE THE UNPARALLELED ACHIEVEMENTS OF

THE RED ARROWS

In modern, newly developed facilities at London Stansted Airport, H.E. and Inflite provide the aircraft user with a complete spectrum of Aviation Services. We maintain, refurbish, convert, hangar and handle your aircraft as well as care for your passengers and crews in superbly appointed lounge and crew facilities. In depth support comes from our design and manufacturing organisations which serve with distinction the Aerospace and Defence industries.

H.E. and Inflite Limited, Stansted Airport, Essex CM24 1QU
Tel: 0279 680990/680736 Fax: 0279 681005/680104

Established 1750

COALPORT

For information on any of our *Collectors Gallery Plates* please contact:
Consumer Service, Josiah Wedgwood & Sons Limited, Barlaston, Stoke-on-Trent, ST12 9ES. Tel: (0782) 204141

R.J. CARUANA

enough drivers in his section. Because of some new equipment that has recently been added, in particular the new dye rig which takes up more space, he has had to reshuffle the load about on his low-loader in such a way that road support has to use an extra vehicle "so when we go out we can have four drivers on the road and as there are only five of us, if one of us is off sick we could find ourselves in a situation where there would be nobody here to meet the aircraft when they get back". Howells hopes to be getting

PETER MOBBS

PETER MOBBS

Top: Part of the MT Section's duties include the towing of the Hawks out of the hangar in the morning and back inside at the end of the day's training
Centre: Refuelling the Hawks on the flightline
Left: The support provided by a suitably decorated Land Rover is essential to tow the equipment which the 'Circus' carries wherever it goes

X294

ALL PHOTOS THIS PAGE: PETER MOBBS

BILL WALKER

SAC Peter Mobbs operating the 'indispensable' video camera

an extra driver before the season starts though he feels that MT is a dying trade and that it will be civilianised before too long.

SAC Peter Mobbs is the squadron photographer whose primary task is video, although he does 'still' work as well for brochures and publicity. Each training flight and display has to be recorded on video and this is used for debriefing purposes. The displays may look perfect to the uninitiated but for the team there is always some little thing that needs to be polished up before the next show. Mobbs does all his filming from the datum point which marks the display centre. He starts his video camera as soon as the aircraft are on the runway and then follows them throughout the display recording all the radio communications between the pilots which gives an accurate time span of what is happening. The camera is left on even when it cannot see the aircraft in order to ensure that there is perfect continuity. Mobbs travels with the team wherever it goes and when he is not photographing he forms part of the four-man loading team for the road support vehicles. He goes wherever the Team Manager goes and whilst the former is giving his commentary, Mobbs is filming the display. "We really have the best job", he says. "We get to meet the public. Whilst the pilots are up there doing all the work we're getting the nice bit down on the ground".

Undoubtedly those working on propulsion matters are regarded as being extremely important people. On Second Line, Sergeant Craig Rouse is Propulsion Manager and he proudly proclaims that not much ever goes wrong with the Adour 151/02 engine that powers the Hawk. His biggest problems are normally associated with birdstrikes. These can, and often do, cause problems in the air for the pilot. Yet Rouse maintains

E.J.v.KONINGSVELD

Polishing up the Hawk before a photo session at Denver, Colorado, in September, 1993

PETER MOBBS

that the Adour is very good when dealing with small birds though when operating over the sea, gulls can cause a considerable amount of damage. For the past two years there has been no occasion where an engine has had to be changed because of a birdstrike though Sergeant Rouse is proud of the record that his team can do it in six hours. "During the display season we don't take a spare engine on the road with us, so it's really a matter of logistics should we ever need a change. On long overseas deployments like the annual Cyprus visit we normally take a spare with us. When we went to the United States we took one as well and this was providential as in fact we had to change an engine in Goose Bay, Canada". It is interesting to note that the squadron Hawks are standard issue and the only modification that Red Arrows aircraft have is one to give them quicker acceleration.

Working in all kinds of weather conditions is part of the First Line Team's duty

PETER MOBBS

During an actual display the Red Arrows aircraft do not utilise any radar, although the Hawks are equipped with Identification Friend or Foe (IFF) and Tactical Airborne Navigation (TACAN) systems. If Corporal Jonathan Cost was to concentrate on his own trade as Radar Technician he would have almost nothing to do. "Maybe one fault per week," he explains, "but the RAF is now amalgamating the three electronics trades – air radar, communications and flight systems – to become one: avionics. When that happens there will be quite a bit of work because most of the work is concentrated on communications". At present and until he attends an assimilation training course he is only locally cross-trained and can only work on jobs specific to the Hawk. Attending the course at RAF Cosford will mean that he will be entitled to work on all three specialisations on any aircraft. Sgt Cost is one of the newest arrivals at Scampton and has set himself a specific target – to get a job in the circus. He holds a Private Pilot's Licence (PPL) and has always wanted to fly in the RAF; having been rejected for flying duties five times he looks forward to flying in the back seat of a Hawk.

No Red Arrows display would be complete, nor would it be so effective, without smoke. Those pretty patterns in the sky are the responsibility of the team that has, without doubt, the most uncomfortable First Line job on the squadron. Sergeant Percy Smith and his black-suited gang of five provide the smoke. This they do by putting diesel and dye into the tank under the aircraft's centreline for the smoke generation system. This fits in place of the normal gun pod on the Hawk T Mk1A and carries fifty gallons of diesel, ten gallons of each colour and is pressurised by the aircraft's fuel system which pushes it

"No Red Arrows display would be complete, nor would it be so effective, without smoke. Those pretty patterns in the sky are the responsibility of the team that has, without doubt, the most uncomfortable First Line job on the squadron"

PETER MOBBS

PETER MOBBS

through a set of pipes down to the back end. It comes out at the tail through three smoke pipes where it is atomised by the heat of the jet efflux. Smith and his team are always busy; "the main problem in the job is that the dye is horrible stuff to work with and it's therefore the dirtiest job on the team," he says. Yet dirty or not, the job has to be done after every display and, like everything else connected with the Red Arrows it has to be done well.

PETER MOBBS

To complete up to 100 displays in a season requires meticulous planning and coordination. It is the responsibility of the Squadron Adjutant, Warrant Officer John Howard, and his support team (facing page) to arrange all the necessary administrative and logistics requirements for every display. This includes organising accommodation, overnight guarding, ensuring fuel, diesel and dye are available, reserving the necessary UK airspace around each display and diplomatic clearances for overseas transits. In addition the Adjutant arranges Hercules support when necessary and the Team Managers' Bulldog and Gazelle requirements. He also calculates display and transit timings for each day and liaises with operating bases and show organisers to permit the team to perform at up to three venues in any one day. Finally, the administrative staff distribute a programme so that all concerned are aware of the Team's movements.

As you can imagine, organising so many displays can be both time consuming and, at times, extremely frustrating. This is particularly so when all the preparation for a particular display is close to completion and then the display, for whatever reason, is subsequently cancelled. The result is that all the hard work has to be undone, which can be equally time consuming, before new arrangments are made to accommodate a replacement display. Another major aspect to the Adjutant's job is answering both the telephone enquiries and correspondence from members of the public and show organisers, which constantly inundate the administrative staff. Indeed should anyone visit the Adjutant in his office, there is every likelihood that he has a telephone stuck in his ear! Of course in between display paperwork and answering the telephone, the Adjutant has to look after the needs of ten pilots and 70 engineers!

With the Red Arrows the majority of the 'unsung heroes' are hardly ever seen and definitely never heard. Yet the whole unit works cohesively as a team. Everybody will agree that working on the squadron is different, exciting and unlike anything else encountered in the RAF. The Red Arrows are not just a team of nine aircraft doing fascinating things in the air. It is a team of dedicated and skilled professionals who collectively provide the country with a superb aerobatic performance and an excellent public relations vehicle in the best traditions of the Royal Air Force.

M.B.

PETER MOBBS

PETER MOBBS

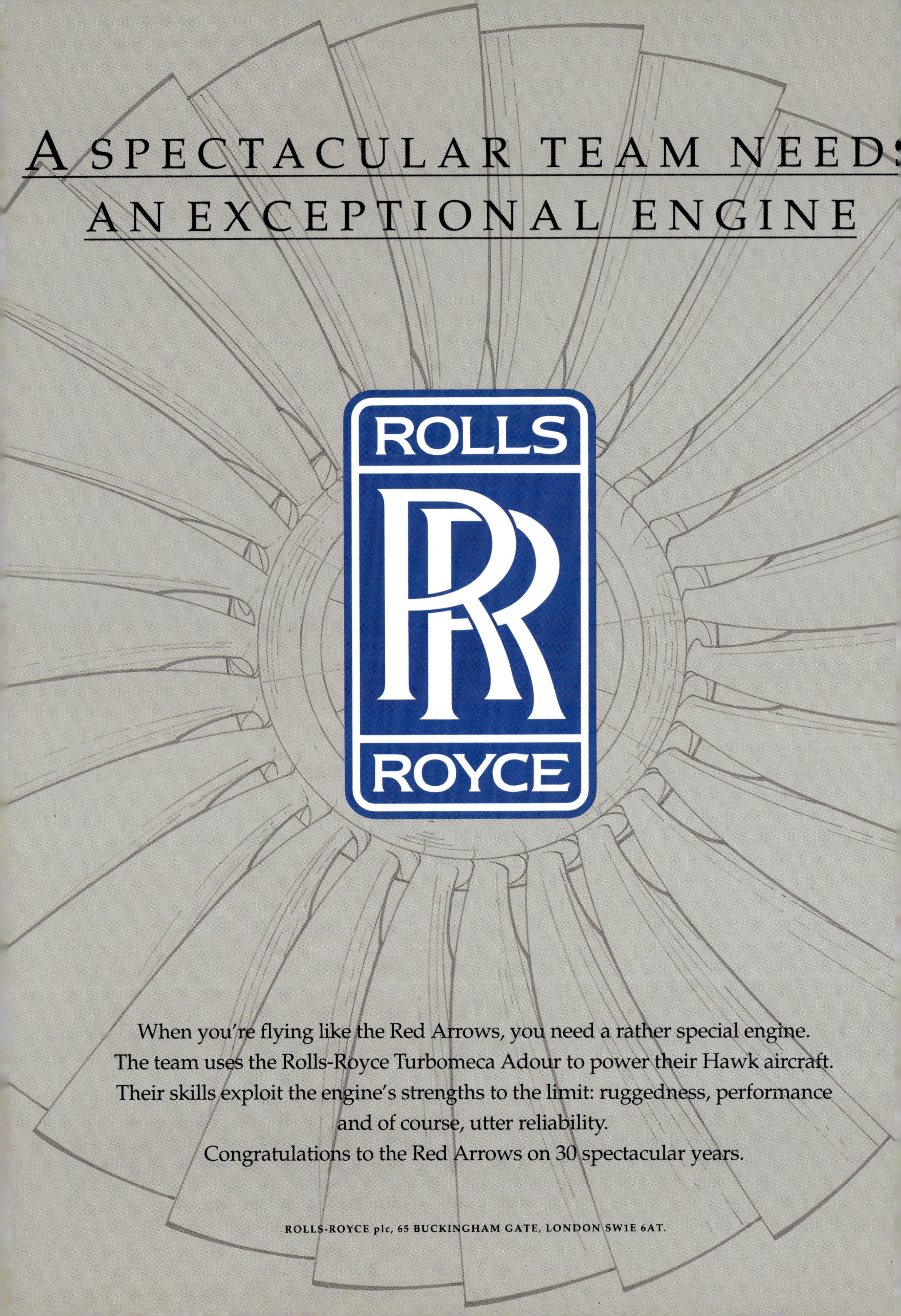
A SPECTACULAR TEAM NEEDS
AN EXCEPTIONAL ENGINE
ROLLS
RR
ROYCE
When you're flying like the Red Arrows, you need a rather special engine. The team uses the Rolls-Royce Turbomeca Adour to power their Hawk aircraft. Their skills exploit the engine's strengths to the limit: ruggedness, performance and of course, utter reliability.
Congratulations to the Red Arrows on 30 spectacular years.
ROLLS-ROYCE plc, 65 BUCKINGHAM GATE, LONDON SW1E 6AT.

PETER MOBBS

Chapter Four: HAWK — A SUCCESS STORY

JOHN OATEN

Brought to international fame by the Red Arrows, the Hawk owes its birth to another famous aircraft, the Jaguar. It was the latter aircraft that had been projected with the specific tasks of replacing the Gnat (and eventually the Jet Provost) in advanced flying training, and the Hunter then being used for weapons training. The Jaguar proved to be a success in its main role — that of ground attack — but turned out to be rather expensive as a pure trainer. So a new design had to be sought as quickly as possible since the Hunter, and particularly the Gnat, were quickly coming closer to the end of their service career.

The Ministry of Defence (MoD) issued Air Staff Target 397 in January 1970, calling for a basic/advanced trainer to replace the types already mentioned, then the main training types in service with the Royal Air Force (RAF). Hawker Siddeley (HSA) presented its HS. 1182 while British Aircraft Corporation offered the P. 69. By October 1971 the choice had been made in favour of the HS. 1182, later to be named "Hawk", without as much as requesting a prototype. The aircraft to be used for initial flight trials had to be an aircraft rolled out of the production line.

In March 1972 HSA was rewarded a contract "off the drawing board" for 175 examples (XX156–205, XX217–266, XX278-327, XX329–353) plus an initial pre-production machine, XX154. Five further production aircraft (from within the total order) were to be kept back and used for the flight development programme, on completion of which they had to be brought up to full production standard and delivered to the RAF.

Service requirements stressed ease of maintenance and reliability of airframe, engine and all supporting equipment. In fact it was required that mean time to rectify failures had to be one hour, and 90% of any such failures had to be capable of rectification within 3 hours. Further aims of scheduled servicing included:

Before Flight: simple checks to be completed by one man in not more than 20 minutes.

Turn-round: in the flying training role, to be completed by one man in not more than 20 minutes.

After Flight: servicing, including servicing actions, to be completed in a maximum of 0.75 man-hours.

Second Line: the aircraft had to be designed for a maximum of 1.5 direct servicing man-hours per flying hour. Scheduled bay servicing of components was not to exceed 2 man-hours per flying hour.

Component Lives: system components had to be designed for a life of 6,000 hours without intermediate overhaul.

Engine Blade Inspection: easy access had to be provided to permit visual examination of engine blades.

Engine Change Time: time for preparation of the aircraft, engine change, adjustments and engine run were required to be within three hours.

Fault Diagnosis & Component Change Time: where practicable, all systems had to utilise the concept of fault location down to easily replaceable Line Replaceable Units (LRU). Where the predicted defect rate of components was 0.1 per 1,000 hours or greater, special consideration had to be given to the ease of maintenance, repair or replacement of such components.

Inspection: primary and secondary structure and components had to be made readily accessible for visual inspection.

The first Hawk (XX154) was built on production jigs — probably making the type the first British military aircraft to enter production without prior construction of a prototype. The new trainer rolled out at Dunsfold on August 12, 1974, finished in standard Training Command white-grey-red colours.

MAIDEN FLIGHT

The last few weeks of preparation before the first flight were characterised by intense activity for the Hawk team at Kingston and Dunsfold aerodrome. On August 21, Hawker Siddeley chief test pilot Duncan Simpson started a series of high speed runs to satisfy himself with the behaviour of the aircraft on the run-

ARTHUR GIBSON

way up to nosewheel lift-off speed. In between each run the brakes were examined and the temperatures recorded; the anti-spin chute was tested and on the final run, the tailplane power was assessed at just below lift-off speed.

Early that same evening Simpson was satisfied and pronounced himself ready to go on the maiden flight. The forecast weather for the following day was not encouraging. The chase aircraft for this flight included a Royal Aircraft Establishment (RAE) Bedford two-seat Hunter flown by another Hawk Project Test Pilot, Andy Jones with Rob Addie from Armament and Aircraft Experimental Establishment (A&AEE) Boscombe Down as photographer. The second machine was the company's own Harrier demonstrator G-VTOL flown by Deputy Chief Test Pilot, John Farley accompanied by HSA's Chief Photographer, John Tweddell.

The Hunter took off first into a covered sky with cloud base at about 5000ft; however, the general flying conditions were excellent and at least an hour was available before light conditions could become a potential problem. At 1818hrs Duncan Simpson lifted the Hawk into the air for the first time and proceeded to complete a flawless 52 minutes sortie during which undercarriage, flap and airbrake operations were carried out and the aircraft's behaviour assessed up to 300kts and 25,000ft. Stall approaches were also carried out and the final landing presented no difficulties.

Testing Time

The next day began with a flight by Simpson, followed by another flown by Andy Jones. The aircraft remained fully serviceable and the flight envelope was rapidly expanded to 400kts and Mach 0.8 to 35,000ft and over 5 g. Three flights in 24 hours for a new aircraft must have constituted a new record. Six more flights were flown over the following three days accumulating 11 hours flying time. During one of these flights Jones was accompanied by second Project Pilot, Jim Hawkins who made his first "in-flight" assessment of the rear cockpit. Andy and Jim were ex-RAF test pilots, qualified weapons and flying instructors who were both to play a major part in the development and clearance of the Hawk for service in the RAF and the Red Arrows.

Duncan Simpson flew XX154 to Farnborough on its ninth flight, and took part in the flying display on all eight days of the show. The weather was appalling for most of the week but the Hawk remained fully serviceable throughout. He recalls that on arrival at Farnborough two Red Arrow pilots were first to greet him and were soon crawling all over XX154. "When can we get our hands on it?" In fact, it was six years later, in 1980 – almost to the day – that the Arrows gave their first performance in the new Hawks at Farnborough International.

On September 10, Hawk XX154 made its last flight of the initial series and was then laid up for three

TESTING THE HAWK

In the late 1960s, with the Gnat reaching the end of its life as an advanced trainer, the RAF realised the urgent need for a new aircraft to take over the flying and operational training role.

At Kingston, Hawker Siddeley had the strongest team to design, develop, build and produce just such an aircraft. Many of that team were 'Hawker' people who had been through the Hunter and Harrier – some even the Hurricane – and they had inherited many of the key members of the Folland organisation who had created the Gnat.

The collaboration between Kingston and the RAF 'trainers' was excellent and from 1970 the design of the P1182 proceeded through its various stages; this story is well documented in other places.

Some held the view that the new trainer would be 'easier' than the Harrier, which was not only a new aircraft, but a revolutionary new concept in the military field – maybe so, but the Hawk – if it were to succeed at home and overseas – had to be highly competitive in every flying training, with defence and attack capability in its own right.

The foremost task was to win the T Mk.1 contract for the RAF. Dedicated effort and enthusiasm were required from both Hawker Siddeley and the MoD. Costs were examined and re-examined.

It was an exciting time for all of us at Kingston and Dunsfold. It had been said that we would never again create a new British military aircraft on our own; we had to prove this wrong, and we had some very clever and experienced people to do it. The enthusiasm for the project began to grow in the RAF, the prospect of a new British trainer after so many years. Occasional calls from my friends in the Red Arrows, some of whom considered that the Hawk was being specially built for them!

I visited Kingston regularly with Andy Jones and Jim Hawkins for design meetings, cockpit layout discussions – often with RAF trainers – and to inspect XX154 in its various stages of construction. Tremendous efforts were being made to ensure a first flight on time, with an eye firmly on the Farnborough Show. Final assembly at Dunsfold went well and on August 21, 1974, I was privileged to fly the aircraft on its first flight after all the preliminaries had been completed.

First impressions? Smooth, comfortable – everything worked as planned – felt good. I was impressed by the excellent vision from the spacious cockpit as I took the occasional glance at the reassuring sight of Andy Jones in the Hunter and John Farley in the Harrier; both in turn keeping a very close watch on the Hawk.

Back to Dunsfold, evening drawing in. A gentle flypast for the few designers and builders who were there to watch, a circuit into the first landing and the now familiar final approach and touchdown characteristics being experienced for the first time. Two good flights the following day. Both Andy and Jim flew the Hawk during the following week and on August 29, I took it over to Farnborough on its ninth flight. It remained serviceable and flew on each of the eight show days; the weather was appalling and I must confess I experienced a few 'corner points' in the flight envelope rather sooner than I would have wished!

I reported to the Hawker Siddeley main Board of Directors some four weeks after the initial flying – I sounded

XX156, second production Hawk, during hot weather trials at Malta in June and July, 1975

a note of optimism but caution. The basic aeroplane and engine were right for the RAF and we were to build 175 T Mk.1 Hawks. But this was only the beginning. Intense company effort, expertise and funding were going to be required if we were to beat the opposition, notably the AlphaJet. Over the next two years that effort was forthcoming, and success was beginning to show. G-HAWK was built with Industry funds and served for development and sales demonstrations at home and abroad. Andy and Jim flew an intensive development programme; changes were made literally overnight, if necessary. The basic handling was improved with particular reference to weapon carriage and aiming, and one of the most searching stalling and spinning programmes was made – calling on all the lessons learned from the Hunter, Harrier and Gnat.

The overall performance was so much better than specified or predicted. I remember the speed envelope being expanded rapidly, and announcing to Kingston that we would be transonic shortly.

"Oh, but we have no clearance, it is not required."

"Well, get it, and quickly, because we are going there!"

In fact, the Hawk was flown and cleared to a no-limit Mach Number of about 1.1 (True) by diving it vertically from 48,000 ft. It was also self limiting to about 570 kts at low speed. With an 8g clearance and a full mishandling and spinning clearance, perhaps the designers' dream had come true!

During this time first priority was to obtain the service release and to deliver the first aircraft to RAF Valley. When I delivered XX163 on November 4, 1976, with my old friend Sir Alex Roe – the Commander-in-Chief – in the rear seat, I felt we had achieved our first significant goal. We were welcomed at a very dark and wet Valley by Group Captain David Thorton and his team of instructors. The rest of the story is well known!

Plans for the Red Arrow Hawks were well on the way when I retired from flying in 1978, and the task of preparing their aircraft went to Albert Whitehouse and his splendid team at Bitteswell.

I was then posted to the SBCA where one of my first responsibilities was the Farnborough Show in 1980.

Imagine my feelings when I saw the Red Arrows in their new Hawks performing at Farnborough for the first time. It was a marvellous moment – and almost exactly six years to the day since the aircraft flew in the 1974 Show. It brought back memories, some of which I have recorded here, of the creation of one of the most successful British military aircraft.

The Red Arrows have made a significant contribution to this success – all over the world – and long may they continue to do so.

Duncan Simpson
Test Pilot, Dunsfold
1954-78
Chief Test Pilot,
1970-78

BRITISH AEROSPACE

BRITISH AEROSPACE

months for a major expansion of the test instrumentation fit. It was back in the air in December with the aim of extending the usable flight envelope: developing low speed handling characteristics, investigating handling at intermediate speeds and checking the various systems. A number of interesting points emerged during this initial period of flying. The serviceability of the aircraft proved remarkable — 25 flights were made with only two very minor faults, neither of which caused any delay. A secondary flight instrument had to be changed and there was a snag with one of the aircraft batteries.

An important step was made in the test flight programme on February 26, 1975 when Hawk XX154 achieved supersonic flight four times during two flights — both on the same afternoon — lasting 93 minutes and 90 minutes flown by Duncan Simpson and Andy Jones respectively, at Dunsfold. On the following day the aircraft accomplished another supersonic run at the end of a day's tests which had included a flight of two hours duration on internal fuel alone. Moreover, the aircraft's serviceability record remained outstanding; in the space of those 24 hours XX154 had flown for 5.5 hours during which it went supersonic five times. Aims of the flights during this period included high Mach number investigation, stalling and high g turns. The aircraft achieved an indicated speed of Mach 1.04 at altitude and 550kts at low level while at the other end of the spectrum it was flown down to an 84kts stalling speed.

Designed for a safe life of 6,000 hours, it was essential to test the primary structure for no less than 30,000 hours to a fatigue spectrum more severe than that applied to any British fighter aircraft produced up to that time. By March this part of the Hawk programme was advancing on schedule in the structural test frame at Kingston-upon-Thames. Other aspects of the ground test programme included bird strike tests, one of which involved a 2lb bird hitting at 450kts, cabin pressure testing and resonance testing.

The second aircraft (XX156) flew on May 19, 1975 and was distinguished by its standard RAF tactical camouflage finish later to be applied to Hawks delivered to Tactical Weapons Units (TWU). This aircraft was chosen to undertake preliminary hot weather trials and on June 26, XX156 arrived at Luqa, Malta (via Nice), for three weeks of these tests. With temperatures showing 33° Celsius, HSA test pilot Jim Hawkins flew the Hawk through a carefully planned programme to examine the aircraft's performance and air conditioning in high Mediterranean ambient temperatures. Prior to flying, the programme called for engine ground runs in the highest temperatures experienced up to that time by the Hawk followed by flights shared between an HSA pilot and another from Boscombe Down. Performance of vital components in dramatically different environmental conditions was also monitored, while the aircraft operated with a 20 minute turn around between sorties.

This was followed by four days of familiarisation flying with the Egyptian Air Force at a base near Cairo where it was also flown by MiG pilots and two members of the Air Academy. Temperatures here soared to 40° Celsius while the Hawk performed unhindered nine sorties of 50 minutes each plus two demonstrations shared between HSA pilots Hawkins and Don Riches.

XX157, the third production machine, was the second to fly on April 22, 1975 following completion of resonance testing of the second Hawk. It was also the first to go overseas having been displayed at the Paris Air Show soon after. This machine cleared the way for the further expansion of the flight test envelope. A fourth Hawk (XX158) joined the flight test programme, mainly aimed at performance and spinning trials. Two more Hawks followed; these were delivered to the Aircraft and Armament Experimental Establishment (A&AEE) at Boscombe Down to be flown by RAF pilots.

Throughout the Hawk's test period it became obvious that the new design was destined for success. The near snag-free experimental period clearly indicated that MoD standards were exceeded, some by a substantial margin. This was also reflected in the manufacture of the first 60 examples for the RAF which proceeded ahead of contract time-scale.

Production was shared between the Hawker Siddeley factories at Kingston (main design and production centre), Brough (wing, tailplane and fin) and Hamble (rear and rear-centre fuselage units, nose cone, canopy and windscreen) and built up to a rate of four aircraft per month for the RAF by the end of 1977. Hawk XX158 was in fact the subject of the final delivery, made on March 17, 1982 more than a month after the last production aircraft (XX353) had been handed over on February 9.

To fulfil the delicate transition period of trainer pilots onto the Hawk, the MoD awarded Redifon Flight Simulation Limited an order for five Hawk simulators at a cost of £2.5 million in 1975. These simulators are containerised for complete mobility and began to train future Hawk pilots in mid-1976, a few months before the first aircraft went into service.

Three Hawks, three schemes: the Hawk in the foreground wears the original trainer scheme, which has now been modified to carry dark blue on the top of the fuselage decking, fin and rudder. Also defunct is the defence scheme of Dark Sea Grey and Dark Green (central aircraft) which has been replaced by the overall Light Grey (extreme left) now in general use for the TWU squadrons

A Sharper Bite

In 1979 the MoD announced its intention to modify a substantial number of Hawks T Mk 1 to allow them to carry two AIM-9G or AIM-9L Sidewinder air-to-air missiles, together with BL755 cluster bombs. Flight clearance for the installation had already been obtained by British Aerospace. The object of the Sidewinder installation was to give the TWU Hawks a secondary

Following the modification of all existing Hawks to take the AIM-9 Sidewinder air-to-air missiles, the Red Arrows Hawks were also modified. Since the ventral tank, which contains fuel for smoke generating during displays, can also be changed to a fully operational cannon, as on the standard T.Mk.1A, the Red Arrows Hawks can fully perform defence interceptor duties should the need arise

BRITISH AEROSPACE

BRITISH AEROSPACE

Above:A grey-camouflaged Hawk armed with the belly gun pack and two practice missiles under the wing pylons

air defence role, so that in an emergency these aircraft could be dispersed to operational bases and flown by the weapons instructors.

On January 31, 1983 the MoD contracted BAe to convert 88 Hawks T Mk 1 to T Mk 1A standard by modifying the wings to accept an AIM-9 on each inboard pylon (Mods 680 and 717). This also required the fitting of a Missile Control Panel in the cockpit (MCP). While this modification was being made, the opportunity was taken to extend the wiring to the outer wing positions, as the RAF had originally elected to buy the aircraft with only the inboard pylons operative. The three-year programme was completed on May 30, 1986 with the re-delivery of the last aircraft (XX256) to be modified. The aircraft flown by the Red Arrows were also converted.

The Hawk In Detail

Certainly no beauty contest contender, the Hawk may not have the Hunter's sleek fuselage or the Gnat's grace, but it must be remembered that it was designed and built as the advance flying and operational trainer for the RAF and forces overseas. Pilots trained on the Hawk must be capable of progressing directly to their squadron aircraft and it therefore had to have a relatively large cockpit to give the right 'feel' and environment. It was inevitable that there would be a requirement for additional equipment, particularly with the navigation and weapons fit. However, it does have a special place in the hearts of all those who fly and maintain it for they know that it has consistently won selection for overseas Air Forces – and the US Navy – against the fiercest competition. In many cases the Red Arrows contributed to this success.

The Hawk fuselage is an excellent example of ergometric design, starting from the tandem seat configuration with the raised rear seat providing an exceptional field of vision, and proceeding through the layout of equipment which is easily accessible from the ground. Its one-piece, all moving tailplane is drooped unaesthetically (10° anhedral) to combine the required mean height above the wing plane with straightforward mounting and actuation. The fin and rudder are positioned well forward in relation to the tailplane and provide excellent spin recovery characteristics by ensuring that the rudder is never completely blanked.

The moderately swept wing mounted low on the fuselage is constructed as one complete unit attached by only six bolts, making wing removal a speedy and straightforward operation. The wing has 2° dihedral and trailing edge double slotted flaps. This truly remarkable lifting surface has given the Hawk the edge over its main rival, the AlphaJet, in terms of Mach numbers and operational ceiling and is the result of experience accumulated by HSA on advanced sections for swept wings, beginning with Harrier and Trident work in the early 'sixties.

Built following the conventional frames and stringers method, the aircraft has a sufficiently generous fuel tankage to permit two training sorties without refuelling, and still retain a reserve for an emergency diversion. From front to rear, the fuselage is made up as follows: the front section which accommodates two equipment bays and a pressurised cabin containing two cockpits; a centre section containing the engine (Adour Mk 151 turbofan), a fuselage fuel tank, a gas turbine starting (GTS) system and a ram air turbine (RAT); the rear fuselage houses a jet pipe bay and has an airbrake hinged to its undersurface.

Cockpit: A retractable step, a tone-in step and an extending step on the port fuselage side gives access to the cockpits. Each cockpit is equipped with a fully automatic Martin-Baker Type 10B rocket assisted ejection seat with zero speed/zero height capability. These seats can be fired individually from each cockpit or in sequence by a command ejection system initiated from the rear cockpit. This command system is preset on or off as required.

A single, sideways-hinged (to starboard), manually operated cockpit canopy is fitted. It can be jettisoned, but embodies a miniature detonating cord (MDC) to shatter the canopy transparency. On ejection, an interconnection between each ejection seat and the MDC fires the detonation cord to ensure that the transparency is shattered early in the ejection sequence. The MDC can also be operated manually from inside or outside the cockpit to facilitate escape on the ground. A dividing internal windscreen, integral with the canopy, protects the occupant of the rear seat if the front half of the transparency is shattered (especially in case of a bird strike).

Cabin pressurisation and air conditioning systems use air supplied from the engine HP compressor via heat exchangers and a cold air unit. Engine compressor air is also used to inflate the cockpit canopy seal and for inflation of anti-g suits. Ram air can be introduced to ventilate the cabin if malfunction of the system occurs. The pressurisation and air conditioning system is controlled from the front cockpit.

Cockpit Controls and Equipment: The layout of each cockpit is similar. Full control of all systems is from the front cockpit with override facilities provided in the rear cockpit for the appropriate systems. When flown solo, the front cockpit is used, special preparation of the rear cockpit, in such cases, being unnecessary apart from usual cockpit safety checks.

Controls and equipment in each cockpit are grouped on consoles and panels as follows:

a Left console — throttle, engine starting, electrical and flying control systems

b Main panels
 Left: weapon selection and UHF
 Centre: flight instruments and weapon sighting
 Right: engine instruments

c Right console — avionic equipment control units.

Oxygen System: A gaseous main oxygen supply is provided, via a personal equipment connector (PEC) and a seat-mounted demand-type regulator, for each occupant. Each cockpit has a supply gauge and a flow indicator. Warning of low pressure in the oxygen supply is given on the central warning panel (CWP).

Electrical Systems: An engine-driven 9 kW DC generator supplies an Essential Services busbar via a Generator busbar. Two batteries provide power for engine starting and, following generator failure, for those services essential for the normal operation of the aircraft, the batteries are individually switched to the Essential Services busbar.

Two static inverters, supplied from the Generator busbar, provide the main AC power requirements; in addition, some sections of the equipment are supplied from individual static inverters. An additional static inverter is installed in the T Mk 1A to provide power for the armament installation. An external DC power supply can be connected for aircraft servicing purposes and to supply power for operational readiness state.

Central Warning System: A central warning system (CWS) indicates system failures and events which require prompt action. The failures or events are classified and appear as red or amber captions on a central warning panel (CWP) in each cockpit. A light in the head of an engine fire extinguisher button, on the CWP, illuminates to give additional warning should a fire develop in the engine bay. Attention lights, either side of the CWP flash in association with the illumination of any caption; the lights in both cockpits are cancelled when any one attention light is pressed. All red warnings are accompanied by an audio tone in the headphones.

Fuel System: All fuel is carried internally, in a flexible fuselage tank (180 Imp.gal) and an integral wing tank (175 Imp.gal). Total fuel contents are indicated on a single gauge in each cockpit. Fuel transfers automatically from the fuselage to the wing tank and thence to a collector section of the wing tank; a negative g compartment, at the forward part of the collector tank, houses a booster pump. The aircraft fuel system is pressurised from an engine air bleed.

The booster pump, which has its own electrical inverter, supplies fuel to the engine fuel system and to the fuel system of the gas turbine starter (GTS). A single pressure refuelling/defuelling point is positioned near the front of the port air intake trunk.

Engine: The Anglo-French Rolls-Royce/Turbomeca Adour 151-01 non-afterburning turbofan engine, rated at 5,200lb st (231kN at International Standard Atmosphere – ISA – sea-level conditions) has been chosen for its excellent fuel efficiency and a proven track record with the RAF in the Jaguar. The Red Arrows Hawks have the modified Adour 151-02 with faster throttle response, but power output remains unchanged.

The Adour has a two-stage low pressure (LP) compressor driven by a single LP turbine, and a five-stage high pressure (HP) compressor driven by a single-stage HP turbine. Installed in the aft end of the centre fuselage, it has an air intake on each side of the fuselage, providing excellent ground clearance ensuring that foreign object damage (FOD) is reduced to a minimum. It is started by the GTS system which is operated from the aircraft batteries, thus not depending on any external devices.

Fire detection and warning systems are embodied for the engine bay and the air producer bay and there is an overheat detection system for the jet pipe bay. A fire extinguisher facility is provided for the engine bay only.

Hydraulic Systems: Two independent hydraulic systems, N° 1 and N° 2, supply hydraulic power to tandem actuators in Powered Flying Control Units (PFCU) and for general services. A ram air turbine (RAT) extends

into the airstream automatically and maintains pressure in the N° 2 system if the main system pump fails.

The N° 1 system also supplies power for the normal operation of the landing gear, wheelbrakes, flaps and airbrake. N° 2 system pump is automatically offloaded to allow an adequate engine windmilling speed to be attained when an airborne engine relight is attempted.

Landing Gear: This consists of two mainwheel units and a nosewheel unit; the mainwheel units retract inward into wheelbays in the wing; the nosewheel unit retracts forward into a wheelbay in the front fuselage. Landing gear selectors and position indicators are positioned in both cockpits, but the controlling selector depends upon the setting of a control transfer button in the rear cockpit.

In case of failure of the normal system, the landing gear can be lowered by a nitrogen operated standby system. Mainwheels have hydraulic brakes, operated by toe pads on the rudder pedals, with differential braking action. An anti-skid facility is incorporated.

Flying Controls: Ailerons and tailplane are fully operated by the two hydraulic systems and artificial feel is incorporated in the control circuits; there is no manual reversion facility. The rudder is manually operated and, thus, needs no artificial feel; a rudder lock is in the front cockpit. Trim is provided for all controls but out-of-trim forces are easily held if a trimming system fails.

From the front cockpit, flaps can be set to up, mid or fully down; from the rear, they can only be selected to up or fully down. A nitrogen-operated back-up system is available should the normal system fail.

The airbrake, situated under the rear fuselage, can be controlled from either cockpit. An interlock in the landing gear system prevents extension of the airbrake when the landing gear is selected down, thus avoiding any ground damage.

XX172/172 in company with sister ship XX238/238 from the RAF Central Flying School painted in this striking variation to their standard colour scheme for the 1986 display season

Flight Instrument System: The Hawk has an Attitude and Heading Reference System (AHRS). Attitude information in pitch and roll is presented on a main attitude indicator in each cockpit. Gyromagnetic compass, Cossor CNS 632 Instrument Landing System (ILS) and Cossor CAT 7000 Tacan range and bearing information can be displayed on a Horizontal Situation Indicator (HSI) in each cockpit.

Each cockpit is equipped with a standby compass, a turn and slip indicator, a Directional Gyro Indicator (DGI) and a standby attitude indicator.

Communications: Multi-channel voice communication equipment using UHF and VHF are installed. Transmit and receive facilities are available in both cockpits but frequency selection can only be made from the front cockpit. UHF (AN/ARC 164) and VHF (AN/ARC 115) communications, intercom and the audio inputs from Tacan and ILS equipment are integrated and controlled by a Communications Control System (CCS) which has a station box in each cockpit though control for both is situated in the front position.

A two-channel standby UHF (D403M) transceiver is provided, with channel selection, transmit and receive facilities in each cockpit. A Sonar Locator Beacon (SLB) Type 17638 is in the ram air turbine bay (post-Mod 1029). The T Mk 1A has a telebriefing facility for use during operational readiness periods. Post-Mod 1015, an anti-jam (A/J) facility is available as an aid to electronic counter-counter measures.

An IFF/SSR installation (Plessey PTR 446), controlled from the front cockpit, provides identification and coded flight level information to interrogating stations.

Lighting: The Hawk has normal and emergency cockpit lighting. External lighting includes a landing/taxiing lamp in the transparent nosecone; an indicator light, on the nosewheel leg, comes on to confirm to a ground observer that the landing gear is down and locked.

Ice and Rain Protection: Engine bleed air is used to de-ice the engine LP compressor nose fairing. The nose

BRITISH AEROSPACE

TIM LAMING

XX295/295 photographed during a typical training sortie out of RAF Valley, early in 1990

probe is electrically heated to prevent ice formation in the pitot-static tube. Curvature of the windscreen provides a measure of rain clearance for frontal vision.

Armament Installation: As a weapon trainer, especially with the RAF's Tactical Weapons Units (TWU), the aircraft armament installation provides for the carriage and release of rockets and practice bombs on two wing pylons, and for the firing of a 30mm Aden Mk 4 cannon with 120 rounds, carried in an under-wing pod mounted on the fuselage centreline. The T Mk 1A is additionally equipped for the carriage and release of AIM-9 (G or L) Sidewinder air-to-air missiles and cluster bombs (BL-755) on the wing pylons.

A Weapon Control Panel (WCP) is in the front cockpit and a Weapon Monitor Panel (WMP) is installed in the rear. A Sidewinder Missile Control Panel (MCP) and a bomb spacing intervalometer are situated in the front cockpit of the T Mk 1A. Weapon aiming is by means of an ISIS D-195R optical sighting system in each cockpit; ranging information is not provided. A recorder camera (Telford 1007/10) can be fitted to the sight head in the front cockpit. A gun firing trigger and a bomb/RP release/missile launch button are on the handgrip of each control column. A master armament safety switch (MASS) is in the front cockpit.

Ammunition used by the TWUs is practice round (ball) and high explosive. Normally carried on the Hawk's port wing inner pylon is a CBLS 100 Mk 1 (Carrier, Bomb, Light Stores) launcher for practice bombs. This is usually equipped with up to four 3 kg bombs which match the ballistic characteristics of retarded 1,000 lb bombs, despite their small size. Each of the four underwing pylons and a pylon in place of the ventral gun pack is capable of carrying a 1,000 lb load. Total external stores load is 5,660 lb. The Matra 155 rocket launchers each with 18x2.75in ground attack rockets, were used by Hawks but this weapon has now been withdrawn from RAF combat use.

Accident Data Recorder: An Accident Data Recorder (ADR) provides a continuous tape loop in a crash-protected case, which records information from a data acquisition unit (DAU). The tape has a recording duration of three hours and thirty-five minutes.

Into The Training Role

XX161 was the first Hawk to join, albeit unofficially, the RAF when it was flown on April 1, 1976 to Valley, on the island of Anglesey (Wales), for a period of familiarisation. It was on November 4 of the same year when XX161 and XX163 were officially taken on charge at N° 4 Fighter Training School (FTS) at RAF Valley (a detachment from the CFS, Scampton), starting the process of replacing the Gnats. Other Fighter Training Schools are N° 6 FTS based at Finningley, South Yorkshire, and N° 7 FTS at Chivenor, Devon.

After they complete their basic stage on the turbine-engined Shorts Tucano student pilots are streamed into one of three groups. Those who make it to Group One continue on a course for "fast-jet" flying — Tornado, Harrier, Jaguar. Advanced Flying Training (AFT) with N° 4 FTS occupies 17-18 weeks, during which the student pilot flies about 75 hours on the Hawk, plus twenty-one more in a simulator to complete the course on the T.Mk 1.

The Hawk's attributes are highly appreciated by FTS Instructors. The aircraft is easy to fly, especially for those with a natural aptitude towards fast-jet flying; some students, of course, do not cope and have to change over to a different Group. Each course starts with five weeks of Ground School, with some 160 hours intensive preparatory study for the equally intense flying period. Half-way through the Ground School the student is ready to take to the air. The first flight is just a joy-ride, with the flying course proper starting with Exercise Two. Initial training trips deal with the effects of controls, leading to stalling, and basic aerobatics.

By Exercise Four the student is performing the start, take-off and climb and flying to a diversion airfield. The Hawk's 'long-legs' are put to good use; airfields as far away as St Mawgan in Cornwall or Lossiemouth in Scotland are often used as diversion airfields. After a long Military Training Area sortie (MTA), a last minute diversion due to weather or a blocked runway, allows the Hawk to reach safely such distant diversions, with something like a 200kg fuel remaining in the tanks after landing at Lossie!

A Progress Check is scheduled for Exercise 28 while the Instrument Rating Test normally occurs at Exercise 30, concluding the basic Convex (CONVersionEXercise) Phase of the syllabus, with 20:40 hours flown with an instructor and a further 8:40 hours solo. A birdstrike exercise is prepared for Exercise 38 and Exercise 51 involves a Final Navigation Test. Five or six more flights are planned to give the student that finishing touch leading to the Final Handling Test. This final test simulates a front-line sortie; take-off as a two-ship formation, do a tactical formation, break away and go solo, do some low-level navigation, then up to medium level, aerobatics and some circuits

Following graduation pilots went to one of the two Tactical Flying Units, N° 1 at Brawdy and N° 2 at Chivenor to do their weapons training before joining an Operational Conversion Unit (OCU). One or two per course were usually 'creamed-off' and selected to go to the Central Flying School (CFS) as a first-tour Qualified Flying Instructor (QFI). Training of QFIs for the Hawk is the task of the CFS with its headquarters at RAF Scampton, Lincolnshire.

Weapons Trainer

From January 12, 1978 onwards, TWUs received their first Hawks in replacement of the Hawker Hunters in the weapons training role. After emerging qualified from the N° 4 FTS airmanship course, trainee combat pilots proceeded to a TWU where they learned to fight as well as fly.

Initially the RAF had only one TWU, located at Brawdy on the south-western coast of Wales. On July 30, 1978 this was renamed N° 1 TWU. An offshoot, N° 2 TWU, was established in Scotland and flew Hunters

RAF VALLEY

Two schemes from the same unit, that of N° 74 Sqn from RAF Valley. XX319/TF (above) is seen in the grey scheme while XX171/TK (below) carries the Red, White, Blue and Grey scheme. The latter was photographed at RAF Scampton in December, 1993 when it temporarily replaced one of the Red Arrows aircraft which was undergoing extensive winter maintenance

R.J. CARUANA

RAF VALLEY

All-black XX226 displaying two different styles of markings, the first (above) belonging to N° 74 Sqn, as the tiger on the tail clearly indicates, while the second (left) shows it as the RAF Valley Solo Hawk Display aircraft for 1993

until April 1, 1981 when it moved to Chivenor, Devon, where a detachment of N° 1 TWU had already been stationed since August 1, 1980. From April 1981 the enlarged organisation, entirely Hawk-equipped, became known as N° 2 TWU. Each TWU comprised two 'shadow' squadrons, and their aircraft carried the colourful fuselage markings of four distinguished RAF fighter squadrons. N° 1 TWU comprised N° 79 and 234 Squadrons while N° 63 and 151 were within N° 2 TWU.

Both N° 2 TWU squadrons and N° 234 of N° 1 TWU provided students with a 54-hour introduction course to air combat before passing to an OCU to convert onto the combat type they would fly in front-line service (N° 226 Jaguar, N° 229 Tornado F3, N° 233 Harrier or TTTE/TWCU Tornado GR1). A creditable 90 per cent of pilots passed the TWU course, many going straight to front-line Tornado squadrons.

N° 79 Squadron of N° 1 TWU was more specialised and dealt with more experienced personnel. Its 'A' Flight provided a 40-sortie refresher course for officers returning to Hawk flying, this totalling between 33 and 53 hours, according to past experience. The squadron's Weapons Instruction Flight ('B' Flight) produced Qualified Weapons Instructors (QWI) for the Hawk in a 65-sortie/56-hour term. Additional tasks included target-towing and dissimilar air combat-training (DACT) for a variety of aircraft.

Early in 1992 it was announced that the AFT and TWU training courses were to be amalgamated into one 100-hour 'Mirror Image Programme' (MIP) to be run concurrently at Valley and Chivenor, Devon. This, in fact, meant that N° 4 FTS would add to its syllabus a TWU course following its usual AFT, and the TWU at Chivenor would begin its course with an AFT! With this modification in training courses, the units within these schools were also modified. At the time of change-over N° 4 FTS incorporated N° 74 (Reserve) Squadron — using the style N° 74 (Tiger) Squadron; originally it had been planned to name the second unit N° 208 (R) Squadron. Since this change could not be effected until mid-1994, it was decided to use the designation of N° 234 (Reserve) Squadron. At Chivenor the units within N° 7 FTS became known as N° 19 (Reserve) Squadron and N° 92 (Reserve) Squadron.

Both flying training schools fell within Support Command as from April 1, 1992. Meanwhile, N° 1 TWU at Brawdy had closed down by the end of August, with its Hawks T Mk 1A being taken on by 4 FTS at Valley to add 'teeth' to its new combat secondary role. This brought great changes to Valley, where the new 'armed' Hawks began arriving in May. MIPs kicked off for the first time at Chivenor and Valley on 31 September of the same year. The transition was not as smooth as one would have expected it to be.

While Valley has a good diversion airfield nearby (RAF Mona), it proved rather far away from the weapons ranges at Pembrey in South Wales; Chivenor, while within easy reach of Pembrey, lacked a suitable relief airfield, so important in the initial part of the AFT course. So it was decided to detach 4 FTS students, instructors and aircraft to Chivenor for the weapons phase, straining somewhat N° 7 FTS resources until these were expanded towards the end of 1992. To relieve congestion, 7 FTS began detaching students at the early part of their AFT course to RAF St Mawgan on a daily basis.

Excepting for the amalgamation of AFT and TW courses, the training methods have remained very similar in the case of the former, while the weapons phase now usually consists of 20 flying hours dual and 15 flying hours solo together with 8 hours of simulator training. Changes had also to be applied to the QFI courses which have been reduced from 60 to 45 hours with CFS, a similar time on a Mirror Image Pre-employment Tactics Training course and finally 15 hours allocated to tactical instruction. Three more months training at the Chivenor Weapons Instructor Flight are needed to reach Hawk QWI standard.

New Role

Latest role assigned to the Hawk in RAF service is that of dedicated target tug. Wyton-based N° 100 Squadron (18 Group, Strike Command) finally began phasing out its venerable Canberras on September 6, 1991 when the first of 12 Hawks arrived at the base in full squadron markings. The squadron, which provides aerial targets, had flown several versions of the Canberra since 1972. The first Hawk delivered, XX195/CA, is one of six T 1A aircraft donated by the two TWUs, the others being T 1s from Support Command. No special trials had been necessary as the Hawk towed banner targets regularly at Chivenor and Brawdy.

The Hawks tow banners for fighter gunnery, but cannot operate with the podded Rushton winch which allowed Canberras TT.18 to tow sleeves or the infra-red emitting missile-shaped target used to train Rapier SAM crews. Other roles remain the same, including acting as enemy aircraft for the benefit of Tornado navigators. Regular detachments are maintained in Akrotiri, Cyprus, for Armament Practice Camp support, as during the Canberra days.

Miscellaneous Units

Several Hawks were, or are still, operated by various trials establishments. Three late-production T 1s (XX341, XX342, XX343) were delivered to the Empire Test Pilots School (ETPS) at Boscombe Down in 1981 finished in the famous Raspberry Ripple scheme of red, white and blue used on all aircraft owned by the MoD PE (Procurement Executive). The ETPS aircraft had a number of special items of equipment, including extra instrumentation and displays in both cockpits, a digital data recording system and a voice warning system for use during spinning exercises.

Early in 1984, the College of Aeronautics, Cranfield Institute of Technology, was awarded a contract by the MoD PE for design, manufacture and installation of a Variable Stability Flying Control System in one of the Hawks of the ETPS. The Hawk in question, XX341, was used as a back-up for the other two in daily use. The installation enables student pilots to experience inflight simulation of variable aircraft handling qualities, and flight control and display system dynamics over a wide range of flight conditions. BAe's EAP (Experimental Aircraft Programme) prototype and the forthcoming European Fighter Aircraft (EFA) are variable stability aircraft and their handling qualities can be simulated on the specially modified Hawk. The project, known as ASTrA (Advanced System Training Aircraft) incorporates the latest in microprocessor display and control system technology. The ETPS is thereby able to train for the future on a comparatively cheap aircraft, and at the same time have a safety pilot in the Hawk's rear seat equipped with the traditional type of control linkages. An A&AEE Hawk T.1, XX156, has also been converted into a Variable Stability aircraft in common with XX341 for use by the ETPS.

The Hawk is also operated by N° 6 FTS (Support Command), a navigator training unit at Finningley, South Yorkshire. Of course, the most famous of all Hawks are those used by the Central Flying School at RAF Scampton, Lincolnshire, by the Red Arrows aerobatic team.

XX312/CF, one of N° 100 Sqn's Hawk target tugs carrying the unit's 'skull and crossbones' motif on a highly decorative yellow and black fuselage top decking

100 SQUADRON, RAF

BRITISH AEROSPACE

HW-338

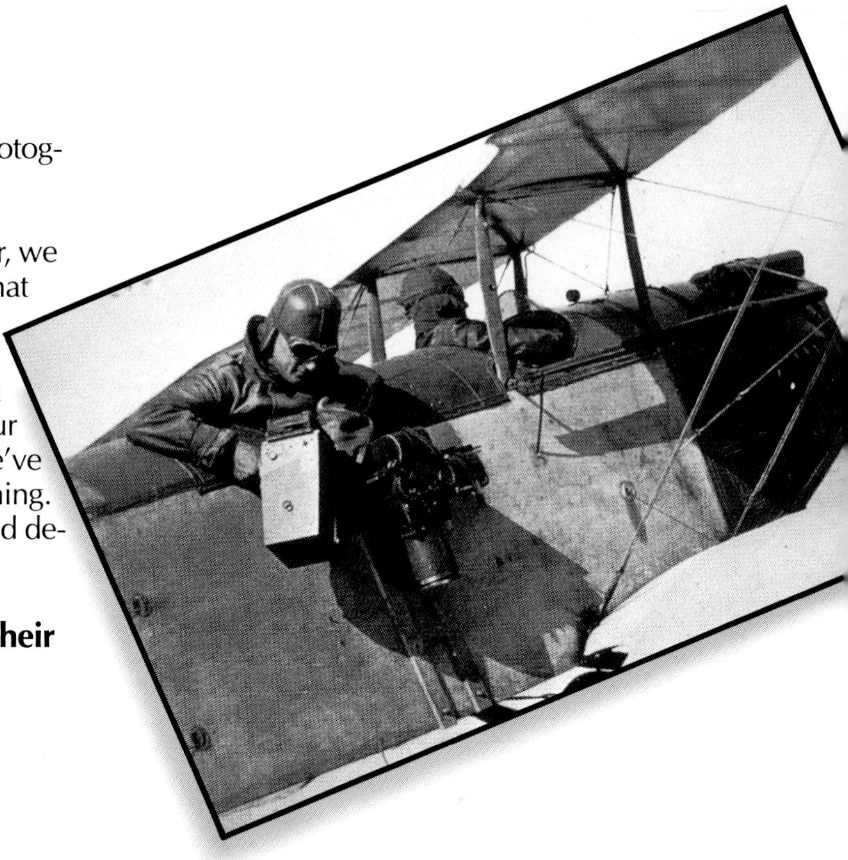

BRITISH AEROSPACE

Export Hawks

Fulfilment of the 175-aircraft order for the RAF was not the end of the Hawk's history. In recent years we have seen this aircraft retain its lead over all competition even on the export front. The two-seat Hawk Series 50 and 60 have achieved excellent sales to countries which include Finland, Kenya, Indonesia, Zimbabwe, Dubai, Abu Dhabi, Kuwait, Saudi Arabia, Switzerland and South Korea. In its T-45A Goshawk version, the aircraft has been selected (out of six contenders) by the US Navy to fill a jet trainer requirement of just over 300 aircraft. This extraordinary achievement by a British design was the result of successful teamwork by British Aerospace, Rolls-Royce and McDonnell Douglas. The latest developments are the two-seat Hawk series 100 enhanced ground attack version and the single-seat Hawk Series 200 dedicated combat derivative.

The Hawk 100 retains the well proven trainer reputation, but now has air-to-air and full air-to-ground capabilities (with a seven-station wing), allowing pilots to be introduced to a modern combat avionic system, with electronic multi-function displays linked to an avionic/weapons systems digital databus. A high performance inertial navigation system and head-up display/weapon aiming-computer are combined with Forward Looking Infra-Red (FLIR) sensor and laser range finder, to give a highly accurate, poor

Two countries which have taken the Hawk into their Air Forces are Indonesia (above) with the Hawk 50 and Dubai (below) with the Hawk 60. The latter shows its long legs thanks to the underwing long-range fuel tanks

BRITISH AEROSPACE

BRITISH AEROSPACE

The Hawk 100 left the British Aerospace aerodrome at Warton in Lancashire on October 30 for a tour which lasted 52 days and touched 15 countries. The aircraft flew 92 times, of which 42 were VIP demonstrations, 22 airshows and 28 ferry flights – a total in excess of 40,000 miles. Apart from essential routine checks before and after each flight, the aircraft used one set of main wheel brake pads, two sets of tyres and the engine used four litres of oil

JOHN VISANICH

weather/night operational capability. The aircraft is in service with the Air Forces of Abu Dhabi, Oman, Malaysia and Indonesia.

A single-seat, radar equipped, lightweight multi-role combat aircraft, the Hawk 200 provides comprehensive air defence and ground attack capabilities. This variant benefits from the operational experience gained with the Hawk family and, in addition, incorporates the latest cockpit displays and sensors. The Hawk 200 is fitted with the well proven Westinghouse APG-66H Pulse-Doppler multi-mode radar, which offers outstanding air defence and air-to-surface attack capability. The

Above: Hawk 100 ZA 101 seen at Malta in September 1988 during a technical stop while performing an export promotional tour. It is here seen in an experimental all-white scheme

Below: ZJ100, in tactical brown and green camouflage, flying over Qatar in the United Arab Emirates

BRITISH AEROSPACE

BRITISH AEROSPACE

Two demonstrator Hawks 200, in all green scheme (right) and in two-tone grey (below)

Hands-On-Throttle-And-Stick (HOTAS) controls and weapons control panel are identical to those fitted to the Hawk 100, thereby continuing the commonality concept. A wide field of view HUD projects navigation and weapon aiming data into the pilot's field of vision under the control of the HOTAS system. Hostile radar emissions are displayed on the HUD and Multi-Purpose Display (MPD) and flare and chaff dispensers complete the aircraft's comprehensive self-defence capability. An option already specified by some customers is the bolt-on inflight refuelling probe. An Auxiliary Power Unit (APU) gives the aircraft the possibility of operating away from its home base, making it independent of most ground equipment which are usually necessary. Hawk 200 is therefore capable of performing air defence, close air support, interdiction and maritime attack duties, together with a very useful reconnaissance role. Oman, Malaysia and Indonesia have Hawks 200 on order with future orders from Brunei and Indonesia being a very likely possibility.

R.J.C.

JOHN VISANICH

BRITISH AEROSPACE

THE HAWK COMBAT COCKPIT

The cockpit and its equipment in the Hawks flown by the Red Arrows are essentially the same as in the standard trainer version. In contrast the attack versions of the Hawk, such as the 100 and 200, have instruments and controls to match the needs of a first-line combat aircraft. These include HOTAS (Hands On Throttle and Stick) controls. Another variant of the basic aircraft is the T-45 Goshawk of the US Navy. This is used as the lead-in trainer for the carrier-borne F/A-18 Hornet.

Before describing the combat Hawk cockpit it is worthwhile considering the interface between pilot and aircraft. Fundamental to flying high performance aircraft in all degrees of visibility, from the 'near impossible' to the intense sunlight of high altitude, is the conflict between 'inside' and 'outside' information. The former is provided by instruments and displays, physical sensations experienced by the pilot and aural inputs. The 'outside' information is what the pilot sees of the real world outside the aircraft. Obviously in poor visibility the real world is neither very real or apparent. Of importance is the fact that if a pilot has to look down at an instrument panel when flying at, say 500 knots the aircraft will be moving towards features on ground at nearly one nautical mile every six seconds.

BRITISH AEROSPACE

Above: The front cockpit of the Hawk 103 with the Head-Up Display (HUD) at the top centre. Immediately below the HUD is the Multi Purpose Display (MPD)
Below: The Smiths Industries Head-Up Display for the Hawk 100/200

MICHAEL HALL

The controls and instruments in the Hawk 100 and 200 are designed to keep the pilot aware of everything that is happening both inside and outside the aircraft: in other words, to maintain situational awareness. The electronic displays need to operate over a wide range of conditions ranging from low-level in a stormy North Sea night to high altitude sunlight.

The instrument panel in the combat Hawks is dominated by the Head Up Display (HUD). Immediately below the HUD is the colour Multi-Purpose Display (MPD) and the monochrome Multi-Function Display (MFD). These three displays present over 90% of the information needed by the pilot. The position of the controls and displays are classified according to their importance. The HUD is placed in the primary position, high up directly in the forward field-of-view of the pilot. Secondary locations, outside the pilot's forward field-of-regard, contain the head-down electronic displays for navigation, engine, weapons and other systems information. Rarely used indicators and controls are given tertiary areas at the extremities of the pilot's vision and reach.

The HUD includes a collimated optical system. Early in

the history of aerial combat an alternative was found to the 'rifle' method of aiming a gun whereby the pilot's eye, a back-sight and fore-sight and the target had to be aligned. The alternative used the optical principle of collimation. In a collimated sight the aiming symbols are focused at infinity. An early example is the Aldis sight which became a familiar item of equipment mounted in front of the windscreen in the biplane fighter era. It looked like a telescope but there was no magnification. The Aldis was superseded by the optical illuminated reflector sight in the late 1930s. The collimated aiming symbols were projected onto a sloping glass screen into the pilot's forward line-of-sight. In its refined version, the gyro gunsight compensated for the relative movement of the target, thus allowing for deflection, i.e. leading the target.

The advent of the electronic computer suitable for use in aircraft in the 1950s prompted the development of the electronic head-up display. The modern digital computer in the aircraft receives data from the aircraft sensors of airspeed, altitude, heading, attitude, accelerations, velocities, navigational data, target and weapons data and many other inputs. The Smiths Industries display processor/mission computer calculates the solutions for flight, navigation and weapon aiming. The symbols and alphanumeric characters are produced by a graphics generator and displayed on the face of a high brightness CRT. The display is collimated, focused at infinity, and projected onto a sloping glass screen in front of the pilot. The pilot therefore sees the essential information overlaid onto the view ahead. Both the display of symbols and alphanumeric characters and the view ahead are kept in focus.

Immediately below the combining glass of the HUD is the data entry panel. Its keys and switches enable the pilot to select the modes of the HUD to match the operation of the aircraft and input navigational data. In addition, the brightness of the HUD symbology is set by the pilot and the level is automatically varied under the control of a light sensor.

The attack versions of the Hawk do not have an array of conventional pointer-on-dial instruments which have a single unchanging function. These instruments, which include the attitude director and horizontal situation indicators, are replaced by a Smiths Industries 5" x 5" colour CRT Multi Purpose Display. Around the periphery of this 'head-down' display are 'soft' keys which enable the pilot to select the format and type of information. As its designation 'multi purpose' implies, it can be used to display flight, navigation and systems data from the engine and fuel systems and from the radar warning receiver. In effect it is the equivalent of an office computer. This analogy is apt because a modern aircraft like the Hawk is a flying computer. The majority of its sensors and systems are generators and users of digital data.

The other electronic 'head-down' display in front of the pilot is the GEC Marconi Avionics Multi Function Display. This is a monochrome CRT unit used to display Forward Looking Infra Red, forward radar and radar warning sensor information. This CRT unit gives a high brightness, high resolution display which can be viewed by the pilot even when the cockpit is flooded with the intense sunlight of high altitudes.

A feature of the combat Hawk cockpit is the overall arrangement of the controls so that the pilot can fly the aircraft HOTAS: Hands On Throttle And Stick. This includes controlling the navigation/attack system. The throttle lever 'grip' is equipped with six different 'finger-tip' switches and controls. The control column, the 'stick' has seven 'finger-tip' controls. These enable the pilot to concentrate on 'head-up' information during critical phases of flight; such as air-to-air combat or when attacking a ground target.

Without these avionic systems the pilot's workload would be excessive.

L.F.E. Coombs

The rear cockpit of a Hawk 103 showing the repeater display of the HUD. Its associated data entry panel is on the right of the main instrument panel and below the HUD is the MPD

BRITISH AEROSPACE

HAWK T.Mk.1/1A SCALE PLANS

Drawings by Richard J. Caruana

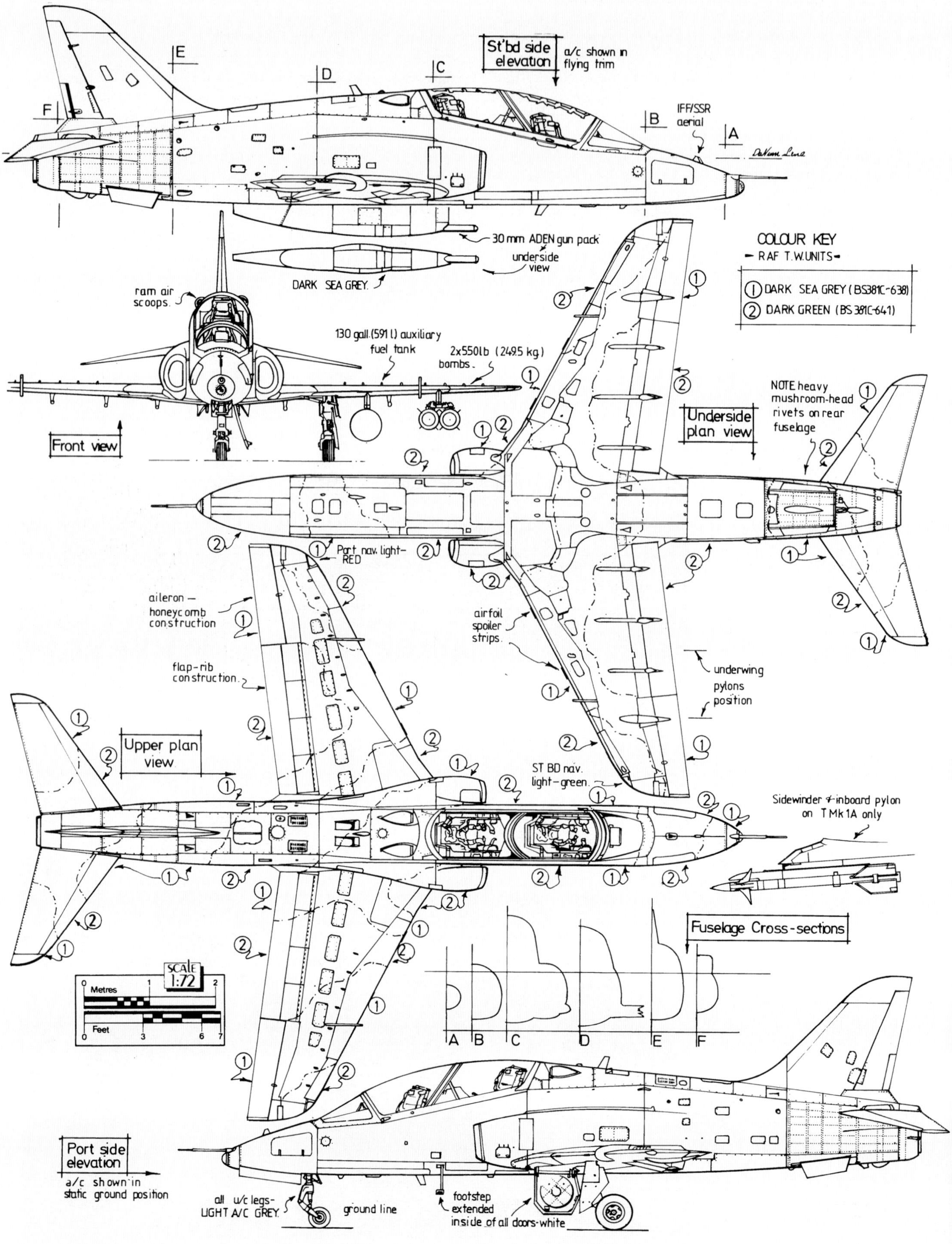

RED ARROWS HAWK T.MK.1A CLOSE-UP

Above: Front view showing the nose probe and nosetip light
Below: Cockpit area: note the pilot's and technician's names in white under the windscreen

Feature Photographs by
Richard J. Caruana

Hawk rear end with the three smoke generating pipes hanging down in the jet efflux

Rear view of the standard Aden cannon pod converted to carry the diesel and dyes which is ducted to the jet efflux to create coloured and white smoke

Nosewheel undercarriage leg and wheel

Port mainwheel undercarriage and door. Note front and back chocks

RICK BREWELL

Chapter Five: WHAT MAKES A RED ARROW

RICK BREWELL

Today's Red Arrows are the latest in a long pedigree line extending over seventy years into RAF history. Every year hundreds of thousands look up at the sky and marvel at the skill of the pilots. In the best traditions of 'showbiz', the Red Arrows combine artistry with danger yet the standard of excellence necessary to be a team member is far above the normal standards required for even the most dangerous acts.

Wing Commander David Hamilton's designation is Wing Commander Royal Air Force Aerobatic Team (RAFAT)*. He is not in command of the squadron but he supervises the team on behalf of the Commandant of the Central Flying School (CFS) and ensures that the team follow directives and standard operating procedures. With a team of high quality, highly motivated volunteers he admits that his job is hardly an onerous one. To a certain extent he is somewhat 'on the outside looking in', and therefore the ideal person to give an insight not only into the people involved but also into the squadron as a whole. The obvious leading question, therefore, was "What makes a Red Arrow?"

He explained that a Red Arrows pilot in the fullest sense must have a combination of impeccable flying skills, good mental attitude and strong character. All these three qualities have to be combined in a particular way. Flying skills on their own are certainly not enough. Many pilots possess the necessary level of skill but what is really required is the ability to apply that skill continuously throughout the season, to have the discipline to perform to that level under various conditions and to combine that skill with getting on with people within the team because they live on top of each other for so long. On the other hand it is also necessary to be able to get on with people outside the team because of the Public Relations aspect of the job. The Red Arrows pilot is constantly under the microscope. He must be able to live with that. He must also be an ambassador when meeting people from all walks of life ranging from adulating fans to senior officers of his own armed forces, foreign armed forces, politicians and other personalities. The pilot has to be able to maintain an image both in the air and on the ground – a rare combination which not everybody possesses.

The selection process starts every year with a signal being issued in mid-December asking for people to volunteer for the job of pilot with the Red Arrows.

* Subsequent to being interviewed, David Hamilton was promoted to Group Captain and posted to NATO HQ, Brussels. His successor is Wing Commander Terry Yarrow

'Volunteer' is the operative word as it is traditional that everybody who joins the team is a volunteer. To apply the pilot has to fulfil several criteria. In particular he must have a fast-jet background, he must have completed an operational tour and he must have been graded by his squadron commander as above average as an individual both in the air and on the ground.

Each year over fifty applications are received. These will be scrutinised by the Commandant of the CFS, the Wing Commander RAFAT and the Squadron Commander. After careful scrutiny the list will be trimmed back to about eight or nine based on local knowledge of the applicants as well as their service records. The team members are also asked if they have any thoughts on the individuals who have applied.

It is normally quite easy to trim the list down to eight or nine because not everybody who applies fulfils all the required criteria. The chosen few are then invited to spend a week at RAF Scampton where they are looked at by the other team members in both a social and a work sense. They are also given a flying test even if they have not flown in a Hawk before.

"I was a bit reticent about this when I first heard of it but I found out that you can tell if the chap has that little bit extra to get in there and hang on in the formation," explained Wg Cdr Hamilton. "The chosen few do a sortie in the back seat on the wing of the leader flying as a pair and he loops and rolls them. He does the sequence twice. What the leader is really looking for is the learning curve – to see what the pilot has learnt from the first loop and roll, not making the same mistake. I was quite impressed and soon found out that you really can tell a great deal from that first quick look at somebody".

The applicants are then given an interview where they sit in front of the same three people who scrutinised their applications. Here they are asked all sorts of questions in order to find out a little more about their character. The questions range from:

"Why do you want to be a Red Arrow?"

"What would your answer be if someone accused you of being a posing Red Arrow?"

"Which of the other eight applicants would you select to join the team and why?"

At the end of the interviews the list is whittled down to two or three, depending on how many pilots are needed.

Every year two or three pilots are changed having finished their three-year tour, ensuring that there is a continuous topping up of fresh people. If one talks to team members they will agree that three years is long enough! It may be exciting, challenging and good fun and they certainly see a lot of places but by the time the third season arrives it begins to drag somewhat. Halfway through the third season the pilots are really having to work hard to maintain the required standard of excellence.

A display itself only lasts for about 21 minutes and the whole sortie about 25 minutes. Yet during that time it is incredibly intense flying, to a degree that no other pilot in the Air Force ever encounters. On a combat mission the pilot may fly that accurately for probably only one or two minutes during the weapon delivery phase. If the combat pilot is doing instrument flying he does have to fly accurately but he is not in such a dynamic situation. This makes the whole scenario strange for the display pilot, particularly during the first year.

"The chosen few do a sortie in the back seat on the wing of the leader flying as a pair and he loops and rolls them"

KEVIN JONES

"You won't find one Red Arrow pilot who doesn't admit to having to work hard during the first year. Even the guys who are weapons instructors in the Harrier and who are used to teaching precision weaponry will then come here and find it hard to just fly an aeroplane, because that's all they're doing, only flying aeroplanes. Most fighter pilots today are just operating a weapons system but to concentrate on that degree of flying required of a Red Arrow is very hard work physically – initially because you're under g a lot, which you are not during combat flying. The mental strain is so tremendous that you will find that at the end of a week the new guys are absolutely exhausted," explained the Wing Commander.

The pilots work hard in short periods. During the display season they are always on their guard and there is no way in which they can 'let their hair down' in public as someone will always spot a Red Arrow. "When you see the chaps go to the crowd after the display, some people misinterpret it and think that they are showing off. They certainly are not – the crowd loves it. You can see the crowd go towards them as though they were superstars but the guys have to keep their feet on the ground because of that. What you wouldn't want to happen is for somebody to get carried away by being a Red Arrow. This is something we have to look for in their temperament. No one should ever think that he is a little bit more important than he really is because he is team member. When he is flying with the team, and because of the way they fly, each member of that formation trusts the other implicitly to be in his right part of the sky. Most of the time they are not looking at the guy closest to them and that is a very important aspect. Being on the evaluation board is not an easy thing because apart from ensuring that the applicant fulfils the necessary criteria you just have to have a feeling that the particular person will fit in," says Hamilton.

When the pilots finish their tour, most are happy to get back to the real world of the RAF. The majority go back to normal units and as the people who are selected for the team are usually sharper, they are most likely to get promoted to squadron leader. The members who left the team at the end of the 1993 season have all gone back to be flight commanders; one went to Tornados F.3, one to Jaguars and one to Harriers. Undoubtedly one will find that those three have enjoyed their years of glory and of showbiz but they are happy to get back to being normal operators. They certainly will not find life as hard as it was during their three-year tour. Strange as it may seem, being a Red Arrow does not count a great deal career-wise. It is not looked upon as a career posting; although it does not inhibit a pilot's career, it does not advance it either. It is, in fact, looked upon as a neutral career move because it takes the officer away from the mainstream Air Force for three years.

Every three years a new team leader has to be selected and unlike the recruitment of normal team pilots, no applications are invited – the team leader is simply picked. Past members of the team are looked at and an unofficial shortlist is circulated. The names on this list will be there as a result of former team members having expressed a desire to lead the team at a future date. This is tantamount to volunteering in the best tradition of the Red Arrows; it is also required that a team leader has to be Squadron Leader in rank and ideally must have done a tour in this rank thus acquiring the necessary experience of dealing with people.

It is a prerequisite for a Team Leader to have served a full tour as a Red Arrow. Nowadays it is also somewhat of a necessity that the chosen candidate had during his tour led the Synchro Pair as well. This means that the new leader will have spent one year as an ordinary team member, one year as Synchro Two and one year as Synchro Leader. Of course, not every previous Synchro leader goes back to lead the team but the ones that do have all the necessary experience.

Wing Commander Hamilton says that "the important thing about having been Synchro Leaders is that they have led the back end of the formation. The Synchro Leader will have led the back four so he's had a bit of leading and he's also led the synchro pair which is the most dynamic part of the Red Arrows display. I think that to come straight in as a Red Arrow leader never having done synchro is possible if the chap is good enough. To come in and be an aerobatic team leader without ever having been a team member would not be impossible but it would be very difficult, particularly in getting the trust of the rest of the team".

As a team the Red Arrows are in a continuous state of evolution. The members move within the team every year. In days gone by, pilots used to start at the back of the formation and work forwards; today they start at the front and work back. Modern thought is that you put the two new pilots next to the leader in Number Two and Number Three slots. Having been given their slot, the pilots normally stay on the same side even though they move backwards each year. If there happens to be a third new pilot, as there is for the 1994 season, he is normally placed in the Number Four slot placing him two out from the leader and therefore making life very hard for him. Unlike the others he may stay there for two years and if he does not get picked for Synchro Pair his next move will probably be to the outside of Number Four. His next year would probably take him to Number Eight. The best pilot of the intake is usually chosen to join the Synchro Pair and he will go from whatever position he is into Number Seven, the following year he will move forward to take the position of Number Six, Synchro Leader.

At the Red Arrows Squadron there is never a dull moment. The season lasts from April to late September. Normally the team will then have three weeks block leave except for the new pilots who will have taken their leave before joining the Arrows. They will also have spent the last two weeks of the previous season sitting in the back seat during displays in the slot that they have been allotted for the next season.

RICK BREWELL

Here they will pick up all the hot tips from the experienced pilots. Red Arrows flying is very personal and although some things are laid down there are many personal hints that will be invaluable to the new flyer. The team leader will only take two weeks leave. He then comes back and starts with the new pilots. He will take them up and gently start them off at 3000ft looping and rolling, gradually bringing them down to 1000ft, then down to 500ft and then down to display height of 300ft.

Whilst he is doing that the other team members come back, he adds them on and they gradually work the sequence. Whilst that is going on, Number Two of the previous Synchro Pair (who has become Synchro Leader) picks up his new synchro pilot and works him into solo aerobatics, eventually down to 100ft. Once he is down to that level he will start timing runs with his leader and then they both go off together and practise their part of the display.

The situation now is that the main formation is building itself up into a seven-ship formation and the Synchro Pair is getting its act together. Then the next step is for them to come into the main formation. This happens after about two and a half months and around mid-January the team will fly in a full nine-ship formation for the first time. This first flight is a very major step forward for them all. From now on training will take the form of display practice and all nine will be concentrating on honing down the sequence.

To make life even more complicated the Red Arrows have three different displays which they give, depending on weather conditions – the full show, the flat show and the rolling show. During this stage of training the leader will continually intersperse portions from each show because the Red Arrows are the only aerobatic team that can get airborne and change from a flat to a rolling, to a full depending on the weather. Typical British weather could, and often does, change after the team is airborne. Because of this the leader can adapt the show according to what the weather is doing in real time. This causes a big strain on the leader and it also necessitates particular rigid training schedules because the team must be able to switch from one type of show to another immediately. During training he will do that on purpose even though the weather may be good, as the team members must always be prepared for the unexpected. The leader really has to get a hold of his pilots' minds because they are anticipating all the time; they must know where they are in a sequence, they do not just blindly

RICK BREWELL

follow the leader because the movement is so quick when the leader calls, that they must know what they are going to have to do before he calls it. All this is a very important part of the work-up phase as on the day they could be switching from one display to the other quite often.

The next step in the training phase is a visit to Cyprus in March. This is the ideal venue for several reasons. Apart from the advantage of getting the whole Squadron away, it gives the ground engineers practice in packing and loading, something that they will be doing regularly during the display season. A major advantage is that good weather being guaranteed, the leader can at last get in the full practices that might have been difficult due to the weather in the United Kingdom. With good weather it is he who dictates what to do whereas at home it is often the weather which has the final say.

The large Sovereign Base Area in Cyprus also offers an added advantage in that being as large as it is, the leader can move the datum point around. This enables the team to practice its shows according to the terrain; it may be a cliffside show, an airfield show or, by going off a little bit to the left, a combination of both a land show and a sea show. The leader can vary the show without having to pack up and move to another site. A particularly important advantage is that for the first time the pilots now get to learn how to live together because that is how it will be during the season.

The innocent bystander will realise that there is always an element of danger in formation flying, but how dangerous is it really? David Hamilton explained that: "the manouevres themselves aren't dangerous but flying close to the ground is, for the mere fact that if you make a mistake you have little time to rectify it before you hit the ground.

Actual display flying is not dangerous. However, even one man flying alone gets more dangerous the closer he gets to the ground; when you have a number of planes flying together then the degree of danger increases, but formation flying is not dangerous so long as it's done to the level of expertise to which the Red Arrows are trained. They all have escape manoeuvres and even though it might not seem so they have enough space between to eject in case of an emergency. Most accidents happen close to the ground because at 1000ft you've got time to recover. Compared to a front line squadron which does low level flying, the accident rate of the Red Arrows is infinitesimal".

All photographs on these two pages are by Sgt Rick Brewell, ABIPP, RAF Public Relations, Ministry of Defence

Above: Instruction in the use of the oxygen mask

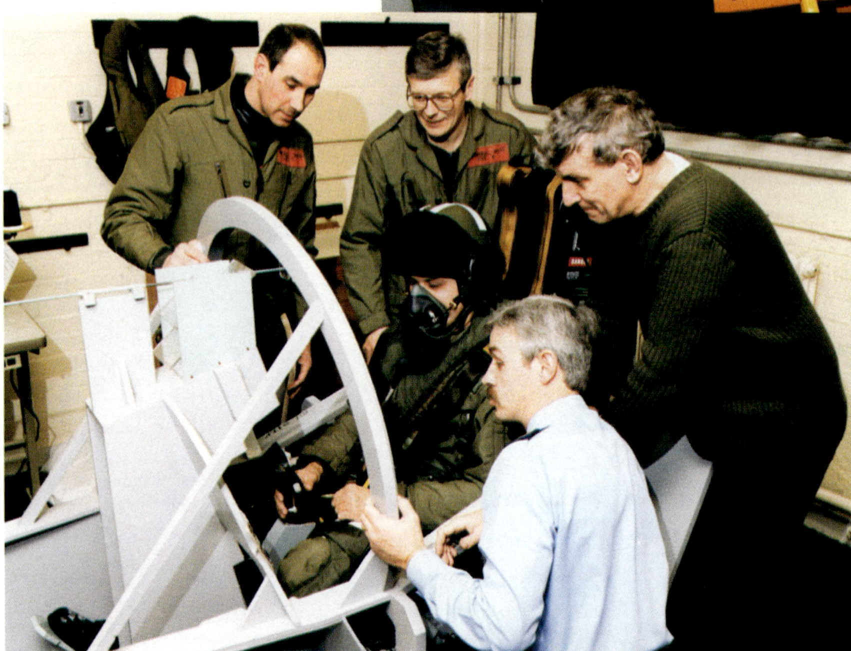

Left: Cockpit familiarisation

Below: Decompression chamber – to experience Hypoxia and rapid decompression

Right: Parachute drill

Below: Ejection seat drill (part charge used only)

Right: Dinghy drill

From the 1994 season, Squadron Leader John Rands is the officer commanding RAFAT (Red One). As a squadron commander he is totally in charge of all the troops from pilots to engineers. He left Scampton in 1989 after having led the Synchro Pair and then spent four years flying Harriers. This was followed by an executive tour as a flight commander on a squadron. "I personally would not have liked to come to this job without that training. There is so much to learn other than flying at the executive level. The difference here is that to a point I am my own boss but the Red Arrows are very much a political thing in many respects. There is a lot of interest from the upper echelons and we have a lot of visits from senior officers".

R.J. CARUANA

Sqn Ldr John Rands (left) with members of his team walking back to their briefing room after an afternoon training sortie at RAF Scampton in December, 1993. These sorties are often curtailed by bad weather unlike the training period at Cyprus where weather conditions are excellent

Understandably the difference between being a team member and team leader is quite marked. John approached his new command with a certain amount of trepidation. "What was foremost in my mind was that although I had been here before and done a fairly reasonable job, would I now be able to fly the aeroplane as well as I did then? Another strange thing is having people flying on your wing so it takes a bit of time just to settle in and have the confidence to do things in the aeroplane. Also, as the new guys are finding out now, it's very much a new game for me being at the front. I've therefore got to be completely receptive to everything the boys say because little snippets like how I'm flying the aeroplane and how things can be made better are my most important guide. It's difficult for me to try and imagine what it looks like from inside their cockpit unless they tell me".

The responsibilities of a Squadron Commander are very wide-ranging and John Rands intends to keep 'on top of everything'. "I've never been a very great fan of paperwork so I'm trying to get myself computer-literate. I've got a very good support cell here who look after me very well but if people write to me then I try to reply straight away or make sure that the boys reply. I have people on my staff who are very competent but I still like to make sure that everybody is doing the right thing so that if somebody came to look at us very closely we'd be whiter than white!

"It's important for a commander to know everything about everybody. The whole gamut of responsibility is much, much larger than the standard responsibilities of a commanding officer but one must bear in mind that the flying job takes up most of my day. I like to give myself fifteen minutes before my brief. I like to sit down and think very carefully about what I'm going to do and I also run through the brief itself because I believe that the brief should be slick and there should be no need for questions to be asked".

Admittedly, flying as leader is not an easy job but it would be even harder if it were not for the help given to the new leader by the experienced members of the team. The system of continuity that has evolved within the squadron is another major factor that eases the burden somewhat. Yet, "although I've done three years with the Red Arrows before, I obviously forget certain things. There has been a break and even though the Standing Operating Procedures are written down there is a lot of detail that isn't written which still gets taught. I was taught all that in the past but I've flown a number of different aeroplanes in the interim period and there is nobody to teach me apart from experienced guys, so I'm very willing to take advice. It all boils down to common sense and if it wasn't for their advice, life would be very difficult ".

As a new leader John Rands naturally has plans for the 1994 display season. He intends to have a relatively short, tight first half where the team stays together as nine aircraft. The team then splits, with the Synchro Pair and the seven-ship formation sharing the stage. "I am going to look at new shapes although there are not that many things you can do with nine aircraft. All we can do is some classic shapes and do them well and tight and make them look very comfortable. I like to use the vertical so we will be doing a lot of loops, a lot of rolls and a lot of wing overs to try and bring everything very close to the spectators.

"During the second half we always have to do new things but the important aspect is that they have to be guaranteeable. At Scampton we know the runway, we know the area and its easy features but we do over a hundred shows a year at some quite exotic sites and

RICK BREWELL

the show may not translate particularly well. So we have to stick to an old Air Force axiom: KISS (Keep It Simple, Stupid). When people are working very hard and the weather is not on your side, and when it's the end of a long three or four days away, you can understand that the show has to be relatively simple, not incredibly difficult. This is not a show that is allowed to succeed only some of the time, it has to work every time, look slick and be safe".

The Red Arrows are one of the only existing aerobatic teams that give more than one show a day. This is obvious during Battle of Britain week when they travel the whole length and breadth of the country. It is interesting therefore to find out how this affects the pilots and how much it taxes their nervous and physical ability. John Rands explained that the team can do more than one display a day without involving any extra stress. "The difference is the way the RAF goes about its business. Most pilots have come off aeroplanes where to fly three or four times a day is not unusual. Air Force personnel are probably the most flexible people I've ever met. Of course we discuss the schedule and the attitude is that if it can be done we'll do it. The beauty of it is that you've got a lot of young guys with good brains and as a supervisor you've just got to keep them in check slightly because they're running very fast. Experience tells you what works and what doesn't.

"Generally I will try and limit it to two transits and two shows though the quality does not change if we do several flights. The guys enjoy it; I myself prefer to stay busy. I have a great deal of respect for the other European aerobatic teams like the French and the Italians but we work to a different system. When I was on my previous tour with the Arrows, on one occasion we met other teams in Belgium and I think they had arrived two days previously, had a day off and practised the day before. We flew in the morning of the show having been somewhere else, we displayed, we landed, nightstopped there and then we came back home to do another show. The others had another day off, transited to Luxembourg, had another day off and then practised again. In the meanwhile, we had done a number of other shows in the UK, flew in that morning, went straight into the display, nightstopped and the next day we were on our way. I prefer our way of doing things. It keeps you fresh, keeps you busy and it doesn't tax you too much. At the end of a long season the guys may get a bit tired but they're fit and used to it. I personally believe that if you give a person just a certain amount of work he'll do it and then sit back and relax. We never get to fever pitch or breaking point but

PETER MOBBS

There's hard work to be done, both in the air and on the ground. For the pilots there is plenty of planning before each sortie while the boys on the ground have an untarnished reputation to uphold

there are days when we come in early in the morning and go home late at night".

As team leader one of John Rands' major considerations is to be very much aware of modern trends. Ten or fifteen years ago people would look at the Red Arrows and appreciate that there was actually a person flying the aeroplane and doing marvellous things with it. Today people are used to seeing things that are fantastic; they watch films like 'Jurassic Park', they are continuously bombarded with electronic wizardry, they even fly their own fighter plane in arcade games. Images and skills that once were purely imagination are now real so that when they see nine aeroplanes flying in formation they might think nothing of it. Because of all this it is essential that the aerobatic display is reduced to such a fine art that spectators are made to realise that, after all, it is a question of human endeavour, skill, eye and coordination and that it takes a great deal of courage on the part of the pilots.

John admits that "the stress of flying, the constant need to achieve nothing but excellence and the regular exposure to the public can have a psychological effect on the pilots. But they have to keep their feet firmly on the ground. I don't have any problems as my pilots are here because they are stable extroverts. When we interview the guy for the job we have his service record which shows us how he has built up his maturity over the years. However, it is important for people to realise that these are very normal guys – cut them and they'll bleed. And they're no different from anybody else, they're just very fortunate that they are doing a job they enjoy".

Wherever the Red Arrows go, people want to know them, want to shake their hand, want their autograph. At the end of a long day when all the lads want to do is put their feet up, watch the video and get the debrief over and done with, they still have to maintain their image, they have to keep smiling. The crowd expects it of them. After all, they are the famous Red Arrows.

M.B.

RICK BREWELL

TRAINING ON THE HAWK

TIM LAMING

Tail-chasing the Hawk in a wide loop. Anyone for 6-g?

RAF Valley, on the southern coast of Anglesey, is the home of N° 4 FTS, one of two Royal Air Force Flying Training Schools where 'wannabe' bomber pilots learn to use the British Aerospace Hawk as an advanced trainer aircraft and as a tactical fighter and attack aircraft. Until recently, the RAF trained its fast jet pilots in a two-stage process, completing advanced flying instruction at Valley, before progressing to Brawdy or Chivenor for tactical weapons training. These courses have now been combined, and both Valley and Chivenor operate identical courses, teaching Tucano pilots to become very competent fighter-bomber Hawk pilots. A Royal Air Force instructor explains:-

"We have now started the new combined syllabus, and although there have been some changes to the course, the students are effectively doing the same training that they would have done under a separate FTS and TWU arrangement. There is a clear-cut division between the flying training and tactical training elements of the 4FTS course, but the distinction is rapidly disappearing. However, it is naturally important to keep the students on a learning curve, and the advanced flying skills will obviously have to be learned before we introduce the tactical training, so what we have essentially done, is to join the two courses together, rather than mixing them.

"There are still some general handling sorties within the tactical phase of the course anyway, so the new system is mixed, but only in as much as the whole course is done in just the one squadron on one airfield, and the training is much more of a continual learning curve. The student comes here without having flown the Hawk, and he leaves having dropped bombs and having flown air combat. The flying hours are somewhat reduced when compared to the old arrangement, but we haven't removed anything of any significance from the course. Because the students aren't changing stations after the advanced flying phase, we don't need to fly any familiarisation sorties after changing base, so we've saved on duplication. Some sorties have been lost though, but maybe only one or two less within the actual training elements, so nothing significant in that sense.

"We're anticipating a drop in the number of students passing through here, but so far we haven't seen any real reduction. We aren't working any less than we ever have done before, but we are talking about smaller courses in the future, reflecting the reduced commitments of the front-line squadrons.

"The students all fly the same course, and there is no distinction between the potential fighter pilot or bomber pilots. We don't divide them into the two categories like we did a few years ago, and they all do the same combined course. At the end, we will decide where to post them. There is an advantage in this system, in that aircraft like the Tornado GR1 and Harrier do sometimes fly combat, and we can give the student an overall impression of everyone's role, and that will be of benefit to the student when they fly an operational type. When the student leaves Valley or Chivenor, it's fair to say that he will have learned more than just the basics. He will have learned how to lead an advanced air defence sortie, using a ground intercept controller, using Sidewinders and so on, and he'll have led a simulated attack profile, with a bounce aircraft trying to put him off track. That's a fairly demanding sortie, so the student is pretty capable by the time he completes the course. Moving to the Operational Conversion Unit is perhaps something of a quantum leap however, in terms of the aircraft that he'll be flying. It's often said that the Tornado is just a big Hawk, but believe me, it is a big Hawk, in the same way that you could say that a bus is just a big van. The operating constraints are different. You'll fly in bigger formations, maybe six-ships or eight-ships, and you'll fly further, maybe refuelling from a tanker, so the sorties will become more complicated".

TIM LAMING

Above: A 4FTS student prepares a descriptive slide, prior to presenting a pre-flight briefing

Certainly, the 'Top Gun' movie image of the modern military 'fast-jet' pilot is quickly shattered at Valley, where there is no time for anything other than plain hard work. The N° 4 Flying Training School syllabus is tough, and not every student will survive the course. Those who are successful will be posted to an Operational Conversion Unit (OCU) where they will continue their training on the aircraft type which they will fly when they are finally posted to an operational squadron. However, there's no doubt that by the time each student leaves Valley (or Chivenor) they are already very capable. Towards the end of the course, the student will lead an SAP sortie, a Simulated Attack Profile which is a particularly arduous mission designed to resemble closely a 'real' operational attack sortie.

The ultimate aim of a sortie flown by a strike/attack squadron, is to deliver weapons accurately onto a designated target. The request for an attack sortie usually comes in the form of an Air Task Message (ATM) and this, together with a target photograph (if available), the Intelligence Officer's briefing, the Ground Liaison Officer's briefing and the meteorological forecast, provides all the information necessary for planning the attack.

The Air Task Message will include, amongst other things, the details of the task, the time over target (TOT), the position of friendly forces, the number and type of aircraft to be used, and the weapons load to be carried. The Intelligence briefing will include details of the positions of any SAM (Surface to Air Missile) and AAA (Anti Aircraft Artillery) areas, the details of enemy fighter defences and CAP (Combat Air Patrol) positions, target information from previous attacks or reconnaissance sorties, enemy radar coverage, and escape/evasion and SAR (Search And Rescue) cover.

For a Close Air Support mission, a briefing will normally be given by an Army GLO (Ground Liaison Officer). He will provide details of radio frequencies, control agencies and callsigns, the position and description of Contact Points (CP's) and Initial Points (IP's), the position of friendly and enemy forces, the type of target marking (if any), and the position of entry and exit 'gates' in the area. Finally, the meteorological briefing will cover the weather conditions at base and at the diversion airfield/s, route weather, winds, and contrail heights if any high level flying is to be conducted.

Below: Two BAe Hawks T.Mk1 from N° 4 FTS pictured during a sortie from home base, at RAF Valley, in September, 1990

TIM LAMING

TIM LAMING

Because of the large amount of planning involved in an attack sortie, the leader of the mission (in the case of an SAP, this will be a student) must work back from the time over target (TOT) and decide how long can be spent on planning and briefing. He must study the target maps and photographs, formulate an attack plan, and decide on tactical procedures. He may then allocate some tasks to other members of the squadron, such as domestic information, the met. forecast, route planning and map preparation, fuel calculations, copying the attack plan and target maps, and weapons briefing. It is important to arrange the planning sequence correctly, otherwise the time taken to plan the sortie can become unnecessarily protracted.

For a typical SAP mission, an instructor will provide the student with a target, from a range of around sixty potential sites situated around the UK (mostly in the West). The instructor will provide all the relevant details which would be included in a 'real' ATM, and the student is then expected to assemble an SAP plan based on the information. He will firstly plan the intelligence and meteorological briefings, and he will then draw-up suitable maps, a low-level en-route chart (1:500,000 scale) and an IP-to-target chart (1:50,000 scale), with details of the route and all relevant intelligence included as necessary. Naturally, the route taken will depend upon the attack plan, and there are many considerations to bear in mind when preparing the SAP plan. Firstly, the available weapons must be considered, as each weapon type will require a different delivery technique. The target defences will vary in quality and quantity, and the chosen route must be designed to keep the attacking aircraft 'masked' from the target for as long as possible, but still with sufficient time for the pilot/s to visually acquire and line-up on it.

The number of aircraft is another consideration, as the student must take into account the size of his formation. It would naturally be impossible to route through narrow valleys with a four-ship SAP formation. Other considerations include the terrain surrounding the target, and the possibilities for re-attacking (if any). The best aiming point on the target/s must be chosen, so as to obtain the best effects with the available weapons. Likewise, even the sun's position can be important, in providing good illumination of the target, and obscuring the enemy's view of the attackers. Wind effect on weapons aiming and smoke travel is also important.

The IP (Initial Point) is a vital stage in the attack mission, from which the final target run is commenced. The IP by definition must be an easily-visible and unique ground feature which must be visible from a reasonable distance. Additionally, it should be between five and ten nautical miles from the target. It must be undefended, and should also provide a suitable map changeover point, thirty seconds before the IP, to give an accurate track check. The student will plan to overfly the IP on the target heading, as turns onto the IP are normally avoided (the aim is to be on track and on time at the IP).

Most SAP routes are planned 'Lo-Lo-Lo' (ie- low level throughout), and the student should take this into account when examining the target's range from base, the enemy defence positions, terrain, weather, combat fuel allowance and recovery fuel. The route should avoid built-up areas and defended areas (avoidance areas such as farms, hospitals, etc., are often classed as enemy SAM sites or similar, for the purposes of an SAP exercise). Terrain is used to hide the SAP formation as much as possible, within the constraints of the 250 feet minimum height restriction which is imposed for peacetime training. Terrain features are also used for navigation, and the most obvious features are chosen, in order to make the visual navigation as easy as possible.

Most importantly, the student is advised to plan for the unexpected. For example, a delayed take-off, bad weather en-route to, or at the target area, excessive fuel consumption, loss of contact with the other aircraft in cloud, or aircraft unserviceability. The SAP will include a 'bounce' aircraft, in the form of an additional Hawk flown by an instructor. He will assume the role of an enemy aggressor, aiming to throw the student off course and generally distract him from his planned route. Navigational errors are also possible, indeed the instructors emphasise that if the student is flying on track at all times, his lookout for enemy fighters obviously isn't good enough.

The planning stage is vitally important, as the mission will succeed or fail depending upon the quality of the pre-flight planning and briefing. The following is an extract from an SAP briefing:- "We will go as a pair, pushing out to battle formation for transit, then we'll close-up for our descent into Shawbury, and that will be a full radar-to-visual approach to overshoot and depart at low level. If I see any opportunities to cut corners, we'll take them, otherwise we'll fly down Shawbury's centreline... Flight level one-seven-zero to Shawbury, and we expect to be on runway two-three there.

"Formation is battle, and flying wing as required... For recovery we will split for individual visual recoveries back here... Birdstrike, we'll go as a pair, and I prefer to be pushed, so I'd be up front there... Low level, we're heading one-two-zero, climbing through the airways, into Shawbury for a fast speed radar-to-visual. A three hundred knot transit, and as soon as we're Victor Mike with the ground we'll overshoot and depart on one-six-zero until we're clear of LFA nine, descending to low level. What have we got by way of visuals? Well, we have an enormous two-thirty-nine double mast here just by the railway line, and this tip of land with a two-ten mast on, and then sliding down the ridge we have a pair of six-hundred-and-seventy foot masts. We don't want to hit them, and we want to be about a mile to the right of them. Then we're starting to pick up the woods, and we're time hacking on the lake in the woods just on the edge of LFA nine. Down past Bridgnorth and we obviously can't stray left, and keep an eye open for any civvies bumbling into Halfpenny Green, and we're looking to pick up the dam and the woods which feed into the bigger woods to turn onto the IP.

"We'll come off the target on one-six-six, down to the woods and low ground, around Bromyard, to pick up the distinctive ridge and the Wellington sheds complex, to turn onto our IP. Off target, we miss Ross-on-Wye and pick up the motorway, turning to come across the top of Abergavenny, fifteen-ninety-five spot height is a good lead there, and if we need to go south of Abergavenny, watch those red spots to avoid. Turning up the valley towards Brecon, we turn short of Brecon, into fighting wing if necessary, but maintaining battle if we can, as it's an air threat throughout, so I want you looking at my six-o'clock all the time. Round we go, and we've got Sennybridge mast, Llandidrod Wells, and we're starting to think about pulling up to save some gas, and then it's three-four-zero from Newtown, back to Valley.

"So, the first target is on two-one-five, at thirty-six seconds from the IP. There's a reservoir to lead us in,

TIM LAMING

RAF VALLEY

Two Hawks T.Mk1A of N° 4FTS fly over their home base at RAF Valley. N° 74 and 234 (R) Squadrons presently form the TWUs at this base

the woods abeam, looking ahead in the two-o'clock position for the next set of woods. Down past Highley, and my IP is Maxfields Coppice, and you'll be making a four-g turn through ninety degrees to get yourself behind me. Now, looking ahead I have the wood to the left, and the town on the right side, but I want to be looking for the valley line which will hopefully be quite distinctive. Then I'm looking for the wiggle in the river and then the railway line, leading us to the bridge and the complex at the target. If you look where the railway line is, I think I should be able to see where the railway crosses the river. So we're looking for the big bridge beyond the house, for our target".

The briefing continues, covering further target details, and a complete description of the second target which is included in the SAP mission. After almost an hour, the briefing will be complete, and the aircrew are ready to walk to their aircraft, after collecting their flying gear, and 'signing for the aircraft'. Out on the flightline, the conditions aren't always as glamorous as one might expect. This isn't a movie, and it's no time to make a Tom Cruise-style walk down the flightline. The weather is terrible, with driving rain and fierce winds, and the only sensible thing to do is to get inside the aircraft as quickly as possible. However, the external walk-round checks have to be completed first, while the ground crew are busy shovelling-away the pool of water which has rapidly collected inside the Hawk's open canopy. With the checks complete, the crew can climb into the rain-soaked cockpits, strapping-in before the canopies are quickly closed. After wiping rain water from the instrument faces, the start-up sequence gets underway, and in just a few minutes the Hawk's Rolls Royce/Turbomeca Adour Turbofan is quietly turning at idle speed.

After taxiing to the active runway, the two-ship formation ('Bobcat One' and 'Bobcat Two') roll onto the runway threshold and position line abreast, running engines up to full power. Although the Adour engines create a fairly considerable amount of noise, the conditions inside the Hawk are fairly comfortable, and all that can be heard through the 'bonedome' is a distant rumble, which is accompanied by a gentle airframe shudder. With a nod from the lead pilot (to cue the brake release for the wingman), the Hawk lurches forwards, and quickly begins to accelerate along Valley's runway, and at ninety knots, the control column is moved slightly rearwards, raising the Hawk's nose into the airstream. At 120 knots the stick is rotated further, and the Hawk is airborne, accompanied by the wingman, both aircraft bobbing and weaving quite significantly, in the turbulent conditions. At 150 feet, the landing gear is retracted, and the flaps are then raised, the pilot ensuring that the flaps are fully raised before reaching 200 knots.

After climbing through the cloud, the Hawks are positioned in battle formation, separated by approximately one mile. The high level transit enables the aircraft to reach a suitable 'entry gate' into a low level route without wasting fuel unnecessarily. With the assistance of a radar controller, Bobcat formation is guided through the clouds towards RAF Shawbury, where the formation leader descends into the low level phase of the mission after making visual contact with the ground. Back under the cloud cover the two Hawks level-off at 250 feet, driving through the heavy rain, literally banging and rocking as the aircraft hit continual pockets of turbulence. The conditions are terrible, and

BRITISH AEROSPACE

Four Hawks showing the different roles to which this type of aircraft is assigned. The top two are from TWU units, the one with a black fin belonged to N° 151 (Shadow) Squadron. "164" is another 4FTS machine indicating the training role, while the bottom aircraft is a representative of the Red Arrows team

occasional patches of thick low level cloud create further hazards, forcing the formation to make detours, adding to the student's navigational problems.

After passing to the right of Telford on a heading of 160 degrees, the formation approaches the first Initial Point, and at a speed of 420 knots, the student doesn't have much time to locate the position of the IP. With a 4g turn to starboard, the aircraft position onto a heading of 215 degrees, passing directly over the IP towards the target, and just 36 seconds later, the target bridge flashes by, partially obscured by thick trees. Fortunately the formation leader had successfully identified the target, and positioned the Hawk on a perfect simulated 1,000lb high explosive (retarded) bombing approach, and was quickly followed by Bobcat Two. Attacks such as this one, demonstrate that target acquisition is incredibly difficult, although level (ie non-dive) attacks do make sighting somewhat easier, as with a fixed approach altitude, the pilot can simply wait until the target 'fills' the appropriate amount of his bombsight.

Once clear of the target, both aircraft turn hard onto 166 degrees for a further two minutes, before turning right onto 255 degrees. Due south of Leominster, another turn is made, this time onto the next target heading of 155 degrees, passing over the IP at 420 knots, still at 250 feet. At one minute and eight seconds from the IP, the lead pilot pulls up to begin a dive attack, turning right sixty degrees at the top of the climb, before establishing on a 10-degree dive at the second target, in this case another bridge.

The weapons to be used on any attack will normally be predetermined by a higher authority, and three basic types are available. Firstly, the 1,000lb high explosive retarded bomb, which is used to best effect against bridges, dams, and hardened buildings. Secondly, the Cluster Bomb Unit (CBU) is used against armour, radar installations, aircraft on the ground and troop concentrations. Finally, the cannon, used against soft vehicles, aircraft, rail facilities and for flack suppression. Each weapon type is simulated during the student's training course, although the cannon is only used as an option for attacks on weapons ranges, where both practice bombs and live ammunition can be used. The type of weapon to be used will directly influence the attack tactics. Some weapons, such as cannon, rockets and unretarded bombs must be delivered in a dive, whereas the CBU and retarded bombs offer the choice of either a dive or level attack. The type of weapon will also determine the tip-in altitude, and its accuracy and damage pattern on the ground will affect the attack direction.

The basic aim of each aircraft is to maximise the time available for target acquisition and weapons accuracy, but at the same time to minimise exposure to enemy defences; contradictory factors requiring compromise. On the Hawk, the recommended profile is to pull up from low level to achieve the required 10 degrees dive angle and turn through 40-80 degrees (ideally 60 degrees) onto the attack heading. The SOP (Standard Operating Procedure) distances give a reasonable compromise of minimum exposure time together with acceptable tracking and acquisition time.

As with the level attack, an untrained observer will find a dive attack both confusing and disorientating, although it is naturally much easier to visually acquire the target once the aircraft is positioned on the final attack dive. Pulling up from the target, Bobcat Two streaks in behind Bobcat One, to complete the two-ship simulated attack, turning hard right onto 260 degrees. The ride is still rough, the weather still poor, but providing that the low level visibility is adequate, the SAP continues as planned, as the RAF instructors recognise that operational missions are unlikely to be afforded the luxury of clear skies, therefore it is important to train as realistically as possible.

After climbing out of the low level route, Bobcat One and Two transit back to Valley at high level, descending over Betws-y-Coed to run-in over the airfield at 2,000 feet and 350 knots for a battle break into the circuit. The break is made at 4g, the downwind speed reducing to 150 knots (the finals turn speed), and the touchdown is made at just over 110 knots. After taxiing back to the flightline, the crews gather for a debriefing, during which the instructor examines every aspect of the sortie in detail, concentrating on every aspect which the student can improve upon. The instructor for Bobcat One and Two's mission is suitably impressed; "He's a very good student, he was working really hard all around the cloudy areas, and the first target was a very difficult one. We had a little confusion at one stage, but he did very well, he's fine. I would say that the mission was better than average. It's not unusual to miss the targets sometimes, and that's okay as it's all a learning process. If the targets were easy ones and the student repeatedly missed them, we would naturally be concerned, so much would depend on why the student missed them, but by using hard target we are able to prove the navigation and acquisition techniques are working.

"Towards the end of the course, the students are learning to do everything as a pair of aircraft. They could do that SAP sortie easily on their own, but when they're a pair, and the student's co-ordinating two aircraft, it gets tricky. Sometimes things just tend to start happening too quickly, and the student has to think ahead. The fact that he has to organise two aeroplanes flying in battle formation, is like trying to handle an unstoppable train, and it takes a great deal of effort to keep everyone going in the right direction. Navigation is becoming almost second nature by now, but when he's working hard to stay in formation, everything tends to degrade, so he has to work even harder. When we talk about capacity, we mean the ability to prioritise, for example, he has to realise when he has to look at the map to avoid getting lost, or decide when he should be telling his wingman what to do, and so on. Capacity is vitally important, and if he can't cope with everything that's going on at the same time, then he's in trouble. Sometimes the student simply can't navigate

well at low level, but we can teach anyone if they have the capacity to learn. We tend to lose maybe just one or so students on each course, but by this stage we tend to have weeded-out most of the students who can't handle the job. We lost a student recently, and he was unable to think in three dimensions, just hadn't got the capacity to cope, so we dropped him, but he'll be offered a flying post on helicopters or transports, in all probability.

"Although the Air Force is contracting, we haven't been encouraged to be more selective, and we teach in the same way as we always have. Additionally, the new combined syllabus doesn't affect the students in any way. Much of the training is done within the OCU however, so there's no point covering everything in the advanced and tactical training course. For example, the Hawk's bombsight obviously isn't used on the Tornado, Jaguar or Harrier, so some of the training will naturally have to be done within the OCU's. The course here at Valley is different now, but it hasn't lost much other than maybe a couple of sorties, so as far as the students are concerned, things haven't really changed since the Tactical Weapons Units disappeared. The courses at Valley and Chivenor are identical, although Valley is eighty miles from the weapons range at Pembrey, whereas Chivenor is only sixty miles away, so we take the students to Chivenor for three weeks on detachment, for the weapons phase of the course.

"The students now fly tactical grey-camouflaged aircraft right from the beginning of their advanced training, and they will see people in their crewroom who are actually flying the tactical weapons aircraft, so they feel that little bit closer to the action. We've moved away from the red-and-white-trainer attitude, and that must give the students the right kind of impression, right from the start".

T.L.

Hawks T/Mk1A from RAF Valley carrying different weapon combinations, both for training and defensive roles. The aircraft in the foreground belongs to the now defunct N° 151 Sqn

BRITISH AEROSPACE

THE CENTRAL FLYING SCHOOL

MAIN PHOTO: TIM LAMING
CREST: R.J. CARUANA

R.J. CARUANA

Training aircraft of the past: The Avro Tutor (above) formed an essential element of the RAF's training establishment in the 'thirties. While the Tutor was a docile, ab-initio trainer, the Tomtit (left), though produced in very small numbers, provided the ideal platform for pilots graduating onto the fast biplanes and monoplanes then entering service, such as the Fury, Hart and Hurricane

The Central Flying School (CFS) first saw the light of day in May 1912, six years before the formation of the Royal Air Force (RAF). At the same time, the Military and Naval Wings of the Royal Flying Corps (RFC) were formed and the intention was to make professional war pilots out of men who had already gained a Royal Aero Club Aviator's Certificate at their own expense.

The first home of the CFS was a 2,400-acre site a couple of miles from the village of Upavon, on Salisbury Plain. This area was chosen because it was sufficiently off the beaten track, a valid reason for it not turning into an attraction for curious sightseers. Strangely enough the site was situated on top of a hill surrounded by valleys, dips and cliffs and this provoked an enthusiastic journalist into remarking that "one may confidently expect that those aviators who survive the gorges and ridges, the upward and downward currents, the arctic frigidity and Saharic parchedness of the Upavon School will develop into aviators of unsurpassed hardiness". Though somewhat facetious in tone this remark was to prove to be more than apt. From its very inception the CFS has numbered amongst its pupils and staff almost all of the accredited 'characters' of British military aviation. Their hardiness, sense of humour and the highest standards of flying training has drawn to the CFS pilots from over fifty of the world's air forces.

In 1912 the standard training aircraft of the RFC was the French designed Maurice Farman biplane. Its 50-horsepower engine was sufficient to propel its multitude of struts and wires but when a tall army officer named Major Hugh Trenchard was perched upon the petrol tank behind the pilot/instructor, even the normal top speed of 59 mph (95 km/h) was impossible to attain. Soon Trenchard was appointed Station Staff Officer which posed a somewhat original problem — although he had not yet been awarded his wings, his new post made him responsible for setting examination papers, correcting them and assessing the results. The decision of whether students passed or failed was in the hands of a man who had not taken the examination himself. This might have posed a problem for a lesser mortal but not for Trenchard. He simply set himself an exam, corrected it, passed himself and awarded himself his wings! From such an unorthodox beginning at the CFS, emerged Marshal of the Royal Air Force Lord Trenchard, first Chief of the Air Staff on the creation of the RAF in 1918.

Another candidate on N° 1 Flying Course was a reserve officer named Lt Robert Smith-Barry who was to become equally renowned as the creator of a revolutionary pattern of flying training. Smith-Barry was more interested in discovering the capabilities of aircraft as flying machines rather than their use as a form of aerial cavalry able to bring army field commanders information on what was happening on the other side of the hill. On several occasions the CFS was responsible for testing new aircraft and in 1914 a decision was taken by the War Office to establish an additional flight to be known as Experimental Flight CFS. It was staffed by one pilot Capt Soames and one scientist Lt Gordon Dobson, formerly the civilian meteorologist at Upavon. This pair had as their terms of reference the devising of methods for mounting guns in aircraft, developing visual signalling, bomb dropping apparatus and sights — the aerial cavalry was about to become lethal.

Before Christmas 1914 they were joined by Robert Bourdillon, a pre-war Oxford don who had developed an elementary bomb sight, and after further refinement at Experimental Flight the sight was used by the RFC throughout the First World War. The team soon grew with the arrival of several other university dons and the scientific assessment of aircraft performance became the responsibility of this flight. Experimental Flight subsequently became the Testing Squadron RFC and by 1917 its task had become too big to be accommodated at CFS and it was moved to Martlesham Heath, in Suffolk.

However by the outbreak of war in August 1914 the CFS had passed out 93 of the 153 men who did their basic flying training with the service in addition to its original task of improving the standard of already qualified pilots.

During a nine-month period during 1915-16, RFC pilots had to endure what became known as the "Fokker Scourge". Such was the efficiency of Anthony Fokker's aeroplane with its gun firing through the propeller arc that the RFC was almost driven from the skies over France. British fighting aircraft were poorly designed — mainly due to the fact that their originally intended purpose was purely reconnaissance. Yet although Smith-Barry agreed that better, more efficient aircraft should be designed, he also believed that the standard of pilot training should be improved. In November 1916 he wrote to his superiors suggesting that a school for flying instructors be opened to which all potential RFC instructors would be sent before being turned loose on pupils. "I am surprised to notice how little interest in flying is taken by so many young pilots who come out to France," he wrote, "it is suggested that the mental attitude towards flying of an instructor is reflected in all the pilots he turns out".

The officers in charge of the Training Division decided to let Smith-Barry put his theories into practice and he was given command of N° 1 Reserve Squadron at Gosport, Hants. He was also allowed to choose anybody he liked from amongst the best pilots in France for his staff. The first batch of pupils were not specially selected in any way. When the official inspectors travelled to N° 1 Squadron some time later they were completely astounded. They saw students flying in formation and doing aerobatics and landings never dreamed of by their counterparts elsewhere. As a result, Gosport was renamed the School of Special Flying. Smith-Barry wrote a booklet entitled Notes on Flying Training and his methods were summed up in just three sentences: "The object has not been to prevent flyers from getting into difficulties or dangers, but to show them how to get out of them satisfactorily, and having done so, to make them go and repeat the process alone. If the pupil considers this dangerous, let him find some other employment, as whatever risks he is asked to run here, he will have to run a hundred

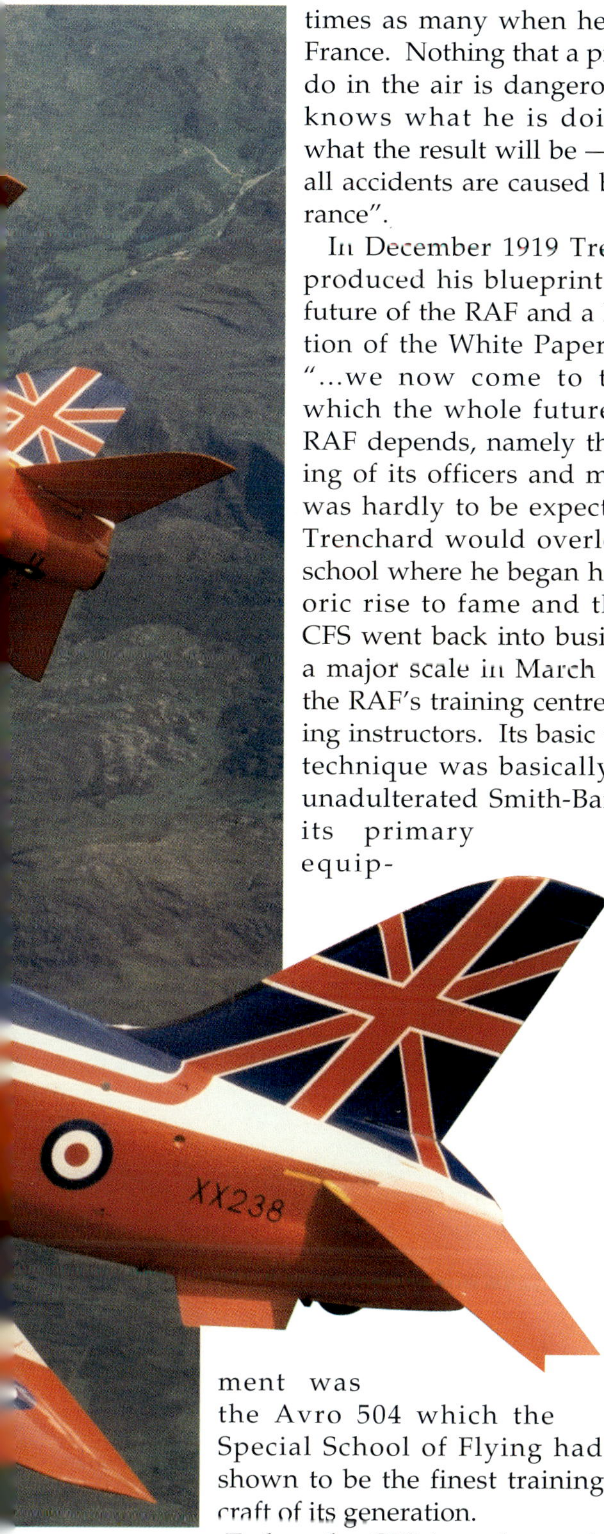

times as many when he gets to France. Nothing that a pilot may do in the air is dangerous if he knows what he is doing and what the result will be — almost all accidents are caused by ignorance".

In December 1919 Trenchard produced his blueprint for the future of the RAF and a key section of the White Paper stated: "...we now come to that on which the whole future of the RAF depends, namely the training of its officers and men". It was hardly to be expected that Trenchard would overlook the school where he began his meteoric rise to fame and thus the CFS went back into business on a major scale in March 1920 as the RAF's training centre for flying instructors. Its basic training technique was basically sheer, unadulterated Smith-Barry and its primary equipment was the Avro 504 which the Special School of Flying had shown to be the finest training aircraft of its generation.

Today, the CFS is no longer based at Upavon. After moving to RAF Little Rissington, in Gloucestershire, where it spent several years, the school moved to RAF Leeming, near Northallerton, in North Yorkshire in 1977 after a brief spell at Cranwell. In 1984 it moved again, this time to RAF Scampton, Lincolnshire, former famous V-Bomber base, vacating Leeming to make room for the RAF Tornado F.3 squadrons. At Scampton the CFS HQ, previously with Jet Provosts and now with Bulldogs and Tucanos, was joined by the Red Arrows team but other elements of the school still remain based elsewhere, alongside other units for ease of maintenance. RAF Valley accommodates the CFS's Hawk T.1A while the Gazelles HT.3 of the Helicopter Flight are based at RAF Shawbury.

Since 1927 the CFS has had to maintain an Examining Wing whose job is to fly out to wherever the RAF and its friends operate to check that training techniques and instructors are kept to the high standards which the School itself pioneered. These standards are aptly summed up in a Charter drafted by Air Chief Marshal Sir Ralph Cochrane:
"The tradition of organised flying instruction, which was born at Gosport during the first war, has grown with the passage of time, and is now a major factor influencing RAF efficiency in peace and war."

The Central Flying School is the guardian of that tradition.

M.B.

COMMANDANTS OF THE CENTRAL FLYING SCHOOL

Captain	G.M. Paine, CB, MVO, RN	1912-15
Lt Col	D. Le Pitcher	1915-16
Lt Col	C.J. Burke, DSO	1916
Lt Col	A.C.H. Maclean, CBE	1916-17
Lt Col	A.J.L. Scott, MC	1917-18
Lt Col	P.H.L. Playfair, MC	1919
Wg Cdr	C.D. Breese, AFC	1919-20
Wg Cdr	N.D.K. MacKewen, CMG, DSO	1920-22
Wd Cdr	E.A.D. Masterman, CMG, CBE, AFC	1922-23
Gp Capt	F.V. Holt, CMG, DSO	1923-25
Gp Capt	W.R. Freeman, DSO, MC	1925-27
Gp Capt	C.S. Burnett, CB, CBE, DSO	1927-29
Gp Capt	J.E.A. Baldwin, CBE, DSO	1929-32
Gp Capt	P.C. Maltby, DSO, AFC	1932-35
Gp Capt	H.G. Smart, CBE, DFC, AFC	1935-36
Gp Capt	J.M. Robb, DSO, DFC	1936-39
Gp Capt	H.H. Down, AFC	1939-42
Gp Capt	A.J. Holmes, AFC	1942
Air Cdre	C.S. Oddie, DFC, AFC	1942-44
Air Cdre	C. McC Vincent, CB, DFC, AFC	1944-46
Gp Capt	E.A.C. Britton, DFC	1946
Gp Capt	W.L.M. MacDonald, CB, CBE, DFC	1946-48
Gp Capt	G.D. Stephenson, CBE	1948-50
Gp Capt	G.T. Jarman, DSO, DFC	1950-51
Air Cdre	A.D. Selway, CB, DFC	1951-54
Air Cdre	C.J.C. Paul, CB, DFC	1954-56
Air Cdre	N.C. Hyde, CBE	1956-58
Air Cdre	J.N.H. Whitworth, CB, DSO, DFC	1958-61
Air Cdre	H.P. Connolly, CB, DFC, AFC, AFM	1961-63
Air Cdre	H.A.C. Bird-Wilson, CBE, DSO, DFC, AFC	1963-65
Air Cdre	F.L. Dodd, DSO, DFC, AFC	1965-68
Air Cdre	I.G. Broom, DSO, DFC, AFC	1968-70
Air Cdre	F.S. Hazlewood, CB, CBE, AFC	1970-72
Air Cdre	R.H. Crompton, OBE, BA	1972-74
Air Cdre	J. DeM Severne, MVO, OBE, AFC, MBIM	1974-76
Air Cdre	J.M.D. Sutton	1976-77
Air Cdre	A.W. Fraser, ADC	1977-79
Air Cdre	D. Allison	1979-83
Air Cdre	R. Kemball, CBE, ADC	1983-85
Air Cdre	A.B. Blackley, CBE, AFC, BSc	1985-87
Air Cdre	D.E. Leppard	1987-89
Air Cdre	K.B. Latton, BA, MRAeS	1989-91
Air Cdre	G.L. McRobbie	1991-93
Air Cdre	S.N. Bostock, MSc, FIMgt	1993-

PETER MOBBS

Chapter Six: PERSPECTIVE THROUGH PEOPLE

LEE JONES

I joined the RAF late in 1946 on one of the first "all-through" courses – that is ITW (square bashing), EFTS (Tiger Moths) and SFTS (Harvards) – which constituted an 18-month stay at the one Flying Training School (FTS), Nº 6 at Tern Hill, which had an illustrious predecessor in Guy Gibson (1936-7). There we played rugger, boxed, boozed and graduated in 1949. While I was at OC TU, Spitfire OCU closed down and thus I was posted onto Mosquitos (night fighters) – great stuff, though highly dangerous. Onto NF.11s, NF.14 & Vampire 10 and Venom in 1951. PAI course, IRE course and switched to Meteor day fighters in 1952. Got interested in formation aerobatics! In those days the blue-eyed boys were Nº 54 Squadron from Odiham and Nº 74 at Horsham St Faith. But just about every fighter squadron had a Friday afternoon team. Five years in 2 TAF Sabres and Hunters and back to OCU at Chivenor as Flt Cdr on Hunters. Led the station team during 1958-59 on four-ship Hunters.

Roger Topp had made the Black Arrows (named by the French, incidentally) the best team from 1957 to '58 (with the big 22-ship loop at Farnborough) and Pete Latham took over in 1959-60 and continued the process. I joined (in the bar) at Chivenor as Number 18 doing thirty to forty shows a year – Europe Nato bases and flower shows, then promoted to Flt Cdr. Superb formatic aerobatic aircraft with a 16-minute display including the 18-ship loop, split to two nine-ships, synchro for five minutes, then second nine-split to five by four for a while then we all joined up for two breaking loops renumbered and splitting off from each side – nine downwind right and nine downwind left. Smoking on finals, very impressive!

In 1961, 92 Sqn Blue Diamonds took over but I got posted to Selection Duties at Hornchurch/Biggin Hill. In those days many postings were 'arranged' in the bar and I was hard at it trying to get onto the Lightning fighter development squadron, when I was approached by a legendary chap, Air Marshal Sir Richard Atcherley, KBE CB AFC* (fondly known as Batchy Atcherley), who was retiring and joining Folland Aircraft Co. and he thought I'd like to know that it was 90% certain that the RAF would select the Gnat as its advanced trainer and that he felt I ought to form a team on this new aircraft. So it was decided! A few months later I was posted to CFS and was the first neddie to undergo the CFS course on the Gnat. Then up to Valley (4 FTS) as an honorary temporary acting B2 in early 1963.

The C-in-C was Sir Gus Walker (one-armed Bomber Command chap – splendid fellow) who, when broached on the all important business of forming a team, as opposed to dull old teaching of Bloggses, said "Get on with it". So I did.

I spent that year doing solo aerobatics around the home shows and by spring of 1964 got on with the selection process up at Valley. Batchy had called me and said that it had been agreed to have the team painted yellow in memory of wartime FTS colours – I was not best pleased – but as I was detached to Dunsfold for a week to oversee the essential markings and test fly the new smoke emission system I decided to make the best of it. In truth, against a blue sky the lime yellow little aircraft looked great. Against the standard UK grey you couldn't see them too well!

Selection was difficult. I could have formed three teams from the QFIs at Valley. In the end I went for compatibility and Bill Edwards (the CI) agreed and off we went. The RAF Gnat Aerobatic Team (official name) was formed at RAF Valley to work up a combined show for Farnborough '64 with the Sparrowfarts (The Red Pelicans) who were the official RAF team for that year.

I had taken lots of advice from Roger Topp and Batchy on how best to operate a small team – the days of 18- and 22-ship teams were over! We were allowed five with two reserves. I objected, and requested nine but was overruled. We had 10 beautiful brand new yellow Gnats but the staff girls at FTC thought we needed a 50% reserve! To make my point, we lined up all ten at Farnborough – cocooned five of them, and used the same five 100% serviceable aircraft throughout the week. Their Airships were suitably impressed. The difference being, that (learned from Treble One) I requested, and got, my own servicing team as opposed to centralised servicing, which is great for bombers and yanks. With my own 'chiefy' and 20 splendid mechanics we always had nine out of 10 serviceable. And that applied during 1966 with Chiefy Hutson as well as 1964.

We did 16 shows, all in UK, in 1964 plus seven daily combined shows at Farnborough. It was enough. We had arrived. I was informed by the SASO in September of that year that I was to move from Valley onto CFS staff at Little Rissington and there to form the RAF Team for 1965.

On Treble One we used the radio call-sign 'Blackjack'. So, naturally, I used the call-sign 'Yellowjack' with Valley team. And it stuck. 'Birdy' (Air Commodore H.A.C. Bird-Wilson, CBE, DSO, DFC, AFC, the Commandant at CFS) hated it and kept giving me veiled threats if I didn't change it. So we did – to 'Daffodil Patrol'. More threats, so back to 'Yellowjack'.

The Gnat was delightful but sensitive, and much more difficult for formation aerobatics than the Hunter – on the other hand by using 10° flap and dropping the slipper tanks, we had a perfect display aircaft. It 'looked' so fast and could be pulled in to stay close to crowd centre, while never exceeding 300-310 knots. (The 'Sparrowfarts' never got over the fact that our show was much tighter than their Jet Provosts).

'Birdy' told me to come down to CFS for a visit in October, 1964. He told me that C-in-C had approved the formation of a Gnat team at CFS – to be the RAF Team – and that I was to form and lead it, and to move down to Little Rissington pronto. So I did.

The selection was hilarious! I had to go to see the new C-in-C, who was fortunately absent during my short visit to HQ FTC. The problem was that I was suffering from an old rugger back injury (restricting me to 6-g) which literally doubled me up. I was OK sitting down! So when I was ushered in to discuss Neddies with this Wg Cdr Postings chap (Education branch – didn't like aeroplanes or girls) he couldn't believe his eyes. "You're the leader?" he exclaimed. "Good God! Well let's get on with it – who do you want?" There followed a conversation that I wish I had taped. You remember the war stories – "F/L Penrose DSO, DFC – Eton-Cambridge and 60 operations".

Well what can you do with "F/L Nice-Borstall – The Merchant Navy – The Sparrowfarts". Then again "But you only have one Cranwell Boy – and he's already been passed over twice!"

"Yes Sir, but some of them – like most of them – are not awfully terribly good at – dare I say it – flying, for instance".

In the end he gave me precisely who I wanted, but only seven of us. He wouldn't budge on Ben Lewis and Officer Hoare (later to lead) simply because seven was the limit! SASO then told me that 'Birdy' was insisting on repainting our lovely Gnats in RED. (Probably to avoid the name 'Yellowjacks'!) I said "Fine, Sir, but please, please do not name the team the 'Red Pelicans'. "No, certainly not – this is the RAF Team. You must select a suitable title which the C-in-C must approve – what do you think?"

"Well, 'Red' if it must be and 'Arrows' to remember Treble One", I replied.

"OK", he said. "I'll send a list down through channels and you can formally select a name – but I take it, if the C-in-C agrees, you are happy with 'Red Arrows'?"

Air Marshal Sir Richard Atcherley, KBE CB AFC*

"Yes Sir," I said, and so it was.

I brought down from Valley N° 4 Gerry Ranscombe and N° 5 Pete Hay and Henry Prince N° 7. The other Yellowjacks I couldn't get due to postings, promotion, etc. This allowed me to slot in Brian Nice (ex-Pelicans) at N° 2 and Ray Hanna, ex-Strubby Meteor team, at N° 3. Bill Loverseed (staff CFS Gnat QFI) was the obvious choice as N° 6, behind me, and ready to slip into the lead should I go u/s, and also, already in mind, was the forming of N° 6 and 7 as the Synchro Pair – Loverseed and Prince. A little later I got 'Birdy' to agree to N° 8, Eric Tilsley, ex-Pelican. No real change from the 1964 Yellowjack format except to design the show to include the Synchro Pair. This we did by trying out many and various items, e.g. formation 4-point roll incredibly difficult, but Bill L and Henry P achieved it on 5 out of 6 goes. So we ditched it.

Mirror stuff – yes, but had been done before, so no!

Meanwhile we had our Air Attache spies out and quickly assessed the 'Frecce' tricks as the main opposition in Europe. We were much tighter but they had coloured smoke, and nine aircraft. There were several problems.

On the flying side we had twelve weeks before Paris! Otherwise no sweat! On the ground there were two main problems. The Air Secs people had told me that they were not going to promote me on the General List, but that I would be promoted on the Supplementary List if I elected not to retire at my 38/16 point in December, 1965. Thus I led as a Flt Lt, and Birdy insisted on appointing a Sqn Ldr as Team Manager. I

Air Vice-Marshal H. Bird-Wilson, CBE DSO DFC AFC photographed in 1970 when serving as Officer Commanding N° 23 Group

disagreed. It was my team. I formed it, and you lead from the front a-la-Treble One – not a-la-Pelicans.

The first chap left after a few days – they promoted him – it was easier than the hassle that me and my crew of pirates would have caused. Enter Dick Storer, an old mate and quite the best possible choice. "You run the show, Lee. I'll handle the administration and take the brickbats". It worked like a charm.

The second problem was (strangely, perhaps) one of loyalty to a unit. These were all exceptional pilots and QFIs in their own right – for example, some of them believed that we had all been nominated and that we would now sit down and decide on who leads and who goes where!

The ex-Pelicans needed Type Rating on the Gnat. As 'Staff CFS' previously, their loyalty was to 'C' Flight of CFS, and they felt we should all come under the 'Gnat Squadron' at Little Rissington.

One painful Friday afternoon in the first two weeks, I stuck it to them forcefully. "We are the RAF Team. Your loyalty is to me – as founder and leader and you will accept that by Monday morning or I will dismiss the dissidents and start again".

By Monday we were a 100% team! And we did it my way.

So apart from working on the Synchro (I designed Russian Roulette by standing out on the runway while N° 6 and 7 screeched across me time after time till they were perfect) the team just put in three or four practices a day before clearance from C-in-C. The Press Day followed by the first show at Clermont Ferrand. Success. I cannot leave the first year without describing two outstanding items – the 'Twinkle Roll' and 'Chateauroux'.

We saw the 'Thunderbirds' at Paris perform a superb individual roll in their four F-100 Super Sabres. We wished we could do it. But our sensitive longitudinal and rate of roll precluded this. We discussed it.

Bill Loverseed broke his sometime taciturn introspection to say "Why not pull fuse 13?" This electrified those, who, unlike Bill, did not have such fantastic inner knowledge of the Gnat.

Someone who shall be nameless went out to the line and pulled all the Fuse 13s. We now had a 400°/sec-plus rate of roll! We tried it (carefully) and then in Arrow all together. It really was a show-stopper. We showed it to 'Birdy'. We were based at Fairford, so flew over to Little Rissington and there he was, watching. We did it. He called us. "Do it again". We did. And again. And again. After six times he said "Come and see me". You couldn't fool 'Birdy'! "How is it done?"

"Well, Sir, it's skill you see, and, er...."

"Don't bullshit me LJ – how is it done?"

"I pulled Fuse 13, Sir". "You did what?"

Telephone rang in the nick of time – busy, busy.

"OK, LJ, be it on your head – get on with it – it looks terrific".

What a Commandant!

Later on some snide sod must have reported it and the Boscombe Down 'girls' got tetchy because no-one had asked them to form a committee and take a year to try it out. So I was hauled in before 'Butcher' Dewhurst, Station Commander Little Rissington, and explained that although it hadn't happened on 105 other Gnats in four years service, all our fuses weren't working, "It's the G-forces, Sir, you understand". He didn't! We had to put them back – but again the genius of Bill — "Why don't we put 'em back but blow them first?" So we did. Happy Days!

We only got caught again at Biggin Hill by bloody BBC TV, and wouldn't you know who just happened to be watching. The C-in-C was never overly keen on the young leader. For one thing he never could understand how we managed a team of nine on many occasions when he had ruled 'Max Seven'. Well 'Birdy' had approved N° 8 (officially a spare) Eric Tilsley and no-one ever did discover the originator of the detachment orders to Ben Lewis of Valley to come and fly 'Red Nine' from time to time. A congratulatory telegram (copy C-in-C) from a very high place obviated the otherwise painful interview.

'Chateauroux'. By a splendid stroke of fortune, we staged through this USAF Transport Base early in the season. Col Pope, the Cdr, was an ex-'Thunderbird' chap and insisted on his 'right' while we were there, to order extra shows, and even had us take him and all his Execs to fly back seat with us. We were given freedom of his base, and did we ever use it. Dick Storer had to field several awkward questions as to why, when we were doing a show at Grimsby, we staged through 'Chateauroux'. We forged great bonds with them and eventually 'Birdy' invited all the USAF top brass from 'Chab' to a formal dinner and pub crawl, etc. Great stuff.

Away in darkest Australia, a Vampire team led by, would you believe, yet another Jones, had come to a sudden stop in perfect formation during a too low miscalculated barrel roll. Eight QFIs deceased. To a small Air Force, eight QFIs is like 20% of the total force, so they were only too keen to grab ex-RAF chaps, and their offer together with the Air Secs gloomy prophesy of another year or so with the Arrows and then unlimited ground tours made my decision to go at 38/16.

In the RAAF I made an instant hit with my assessment of their CFS team as 'Friday afternoon standard'. No sense of humour! They didn't ask me to join! So I did 2000 hours on Vamps and Macchis in four years. Flew three balloon attempts on the world record of 1800 miles (I got across but didn't exceed the previous record by 10%). Became a civilian CFI and then returned to civilisation in 1972. Took ATPL on several occasions (well, twice) and having got it, went out by invitation to be King Hussein's chief neddie at his civil/military flying school. Five years there. Then bought a briefcase and became a consultant for a while, then went to Venezuela as chief pilot for a company. Falklands war brought that to a sudden stop, and I finished up in Nigeria for the last ten years as CI of their Air Force 301 FTS.

Have now accrued about 12,000 hours, and keeping

MICHAEL STROUD

Forerunners of the Red Arrows, The Yellowjacks in their all-yellow Gnats

a real good thing to the end. I have just finished three years of test flying and designing a splendid primary trainer for the Nigerians to replace their old Bulldogs. They have just ordered 60 examples.

I suppose everyone is given one chance or time to achieve fame/notoriety or whatever. I saw, in 1961, a coming opportunity. I have always deplored our amateur attitude in the RAF to display flying, while the Skyblazer 'Blue Angels', 'Patrouille de France', etc were leaving us for dead. I determined to form a full-time professional RAF Team if I could. When the time came I refused to let petty people or things get in my way. I founded and led the Red Arrows. Top that! Thirty years on and they are still the best team in the world. I must have done something right.

Everywhere I go the name Red Arrows is synonymous with excellence. Rarely has there been such good value for money. If our present batch of poor quality politicians, apparently cloned to boring ineptitude, dare to suggest otherwise, I am sure the public reaction will be decisive – and I will be in there with something to say.

Lee Jones

RAY HANNA

The name of RAY HANNA AFC has been linked with the Red Arrows for many years, and justifiably so, as Ray could be described as one of the 'Founding Fathers' of the Royal Air Force Aerobatic Team. Ray was born in New Zealand and has an interest in aviation which dates back to his early childhood as he recalls: "I used to persuade my parents to take me out to Mangere Airport which was just a small grass field at the time, and I'd just hang around watching the planes". He later joined the Air Training Corps, and eventually joined the Royal New Zealand Air Force's basic flying training scheme, which was similar to the RAF Flying Scholarship. He learned to fly Tiger Moths, ostensibly to become the nucleus of what would have been the New Zealand equivalent of the Royal Auxiliary Air Force. However, Ray's impatience led him to apply to the Air Ministry in London, and he received a suitably encouraging reply.

He worked his way to England on a boat, scrubbing decks, although he later took responsibility for the ship's account book-keeping, leaving him with spare time to enjoy his trip from New Zealand. He was sent to the RAF aircrew selection centre at Hornchurch and was accepted for training, beginning at Feltwell on Prentices and Harvards. He progressed onto Meteors at Driffield in 1951, often operating from Carnaby, and his first operational posting was to N° 79 Squadron at Gutersloh, flying Meteors on reconnaissance missions. He later found himself at Benson, flying various aircraft types with the overseas ferry wing which was based there, until his twelve-year commission ended and he returned to New Zealand. It took just one year for Ray to realise that he wanted to return to the RAF, and after re-applying, he arrived at the Central Flying School, where he was trained as an instructor.

After moving to the College of Air Warfare, Ray flew with the resident Meteor display team which (after converting onto Jet Provosts) became the Macaws; "we bumped into Lee Jones, the leader of the Yellowjacks team from time to time. Previously I'd known Lee when I was in Germany, as he was a pilot attack instructor at Sylt, a base we visited twice each year for armament practice. Lee and I were old friends, and when it became known that the Yellowjacks were to become the Red Arrows, I was asked if I'd like to join them, and naturally I jumped at the idea. Prior to this time I had led a four-ship Hunter team at Benson in 1957-59, and I'd flown with the Meteor team, so I had plenty of aerobatic experience".

The Red Arrows first formed at RAF Fairford, later moving to Kemble "We flew our first nine-aircraft formation in 1966, and there was talk of disbanding the team during the following year, because of budgetary restrictions, but fortunately this didn't happen, and we worked through a difficult period with only seven aircraft that year. We only had one minor incident while I was leader, and this was in Cyprus during 1966 when we were displaying to the Army at a cliffside site. There were some high tension cables which were well hidden and we hadn't been briefed, and unfortunately, as the two solo men split from the main formation, numbers six and seven flew directly at the crowd, and in so doing they encountered these cables, and one aircraft struck them. It didn't do much damage, the pitot head was bent, the cable ran over the canopy and along the fin leading edge, and the two solos flew back to Akrotiri, and when we arrived back at Akrotiri we found that nobody was talking to us on the radio. What had happened was that the solo had cut off power to the south side of the island.

Ray Hanna in the cockpit of his Gnat just prior to take-off from Kemble for a display on April 13, 1968

VICTOR PISANI

VICTOR PISANI

"From 1965 through to 1968 there was continuous development of formations, and manoeuvres, and over this period the team built its show, which continues to be developed until the present day. The Gnat was a delight to fly. People talk about finger-light controls, and it's the only aeroplane I've ever flown that is truly finger-light, particularly on the aileron. If anything it was too sensitive for good, steady formation flying. It had a very low wing loading which resulted in lots of bumping around in turbulence. I've since flown with the team in the Hawk, and I do feel that the Hawk is a better formation station-keeping aeroplane.

"While I was with the team, we displayed all over Europe, and we went to Jordan at the invitation of King Hussein. Perhaps the most memorable displays in those days were when we were in Italy, and in particular I remember the friendship and kindness shown to us by the Frecce Tricolori, a great team. My proudest moment was when the team was at its best in 1968. They were superb, and that show season was superb. On one occasion we displayed at the Biggin Hill show, and we were scheduled to display on arrival. The weather was awful, and the RAF had installed a basic radar there, but there was no GCA at that time, and we were handed-over to the temporary radar, while we descended in Diamond Nine formation, with gear up, a bit of flap down, and we broke cloud at about 200 feet, right on the runway centreline, and we entered into a flat display immediately, flying the complete show even though the cloud base was only a couple of hundred feet. That was something that really stands out in my memory. The 1968 Farnborough show was also memorable, and I think we flew our best performances at that event".

After completing his five-year period with the Red Arrows, Ray was posted to a ground tour at Brampton, although in his spare time he flew Rollason Beta racers as a member of the Tiger Club. He wanted to fly an aircraft with a much better performance, and he was put into contact with Adrian Swire, who had just bought a Spitfire. Ray's long association with Spitfire MH434 began, and he displayed the aircraft at shows all around the UK. He left the RAF and began commercial flying with Lloyd International at Stansted, later joining Cathay Pacific. He now flies a privately-owned Boeing 707 diplomatic aircraft based in Switzerland. Of course, he is also well-known for his connections with the Old Flying Machine Company, run by his son Mark, from Duxford. Their collection of World War Two vintage aircraft continues to expand, and now includes a Lockheed T-33 and a Phantom FGR2!

Ray continues to demonstrate the Spitfire at air shows, and admits that the classic Supermarine design is one of his favourites, despite having flown more than a hundred different types. He also has a high regard for the Hunter and the Swift and, of course, the diminutive Gnat which he displayed so brilliantly, during the 1960's.

VICTOR PISANI

R.B. 'DICKIE' DUCKETT

AIR COMMODORE RB 'DICKIE' DUCKETT's RAF flying career began at Cranwell, where he undertook initial flying training on the Chipmunk before progressing to the Jet Provost which had just been introduced at the RAF College. He graduated with his wings in 1963 and transferred to Valley, where he joined the second Gnat course. After completing his advanced flying training, he then moved to Chivenor, where he continued his training on Hunters prior to joining the Lightning Operational Conversion Unit at Coltishall. Air Commodore Duckett continues; "from there I went to 19 Squadron at Leconfield where I spent just under a year, and then the whole squadron was posted to Gutersloh in Germany during September 1965. I spent two years there. I joined the Royal Air Force for two main reasons. Firstly, my father was in the RAF and was an instructor at Cranwell, and while I'd been at school I was in the Combined Cadet Force and I'd done some flying which I'd really enjoyed.

"While I was on the Gnat course at Valley in 1963, Flight Lieutenant Lee Jones was my instructor. He of course, was the man who effectively started the Red Arrows by forming the Yellowjacks team. He was thinking about forming such a team when he was my instructor, and now and again, he would arrange to meet with one or two other instructors over Wales somewhere to do the odd loop and roll. I would be in the back seat and just sit and watch with a certain amount of amazement and a little bit of trepidation as we didn't really know what was going on. My next connection with the Red Arrows was when they came out to Germany on a couple of occasions in 1966 and 1967 by which time they had gone from their original seven aircraft to nine Gnats, and two of the team members were guys whom I knew. I reckoned that if they could do it, I could do it too, so I applied to join the team. At that time I hadn't really done any formation aerobatics although I had been a member of the 19 Squadron four-ship demonstration team, and we'd done a few displays around Germany, although that only involved turns, wing-overs and the odd formation change.

"I left 19 Squadron in September 1967 and I was provisionally selected as the Red Arrows weren't formally established at that time. All the people on the team were Qualified Flying Instructors although they spent almost all their time doing Red Arrows-type flying. So I had to become a QFI and I went to the CFS at Little Rissington, completing the instructor's course at the end of January 1968, and I joined the Red Arrows the next day. I did my first display with the team about seven weeks later, so it was a fairly steep learning curve. The team were at Kemble at that time, in fact the CFS Gnat detachment was there, so I did the final bit of my course there, which enabled me to get to know the team members. We started off with small formations, and I found things quite difficult. Some of the senior team members were quite concerned about my lack of experience. I was only 25 and I'd only done one tour, indeed I'd got less than a thousand hours total flying. They were a little encouraged when they heard that I'd come top of my QFI course, but they weren't too impressed at my first attempts at a formation loop.

"The Gnat had very light and sensitive controls, so it was very easy to over-control, particularly in pitch when the g came on as you came out of the loop, and I remember pulling out of my first loop and building up a series of 'yugs' as we called them, coming right out of position. It's worth emphasising that there was a big difference in policy at that time as to what positions new team members assumed on the team. In those days, all the new members went into outside positions unless they were particularly experienced. When I joined, there were three other new guys who had joined the previous September. Because I was last in, I became number nine, even though I flew on the right-hand side which is traditionally an even-numbered side. The theory was that the inside positions needed very steady and experienced pilots to provide a firm base for the outer aircraft. When you're further away from the centre of the formation, you have to make bigger

control movements during manoeuvres, and good power anticipation. It was felt that young and enthusiastic chaps would be better suited to the outside positions, and if they did get out of position, it wouldn't affect the rest of the formation. The inner slots had to be rock steady. Nowadays, the policy is reversed, and the new guys go to the Two and Three positions. I don't know why the change was made, but either system seems to work, and maybe the more stable Hawk was a major factor. I flew in 1968-70 a total of 274 displays as a Red Arrows team member and in 1970 I was Synchro Two which was one of the highlights of my time with the team. In those days the rules were much easier than they are now and we were officially cleared down to 35 feet, and at that kind of height it becomes rather academic and you fly with reference to the ground rather than any kind of altimeter. It was all fun, both off and on duty.

"The only really major accident I should mention was when Jerry Bowler flew into a wood just behind a hangar at Kemble during a practice display. He was joining-up with the two synchros, attempting to do some pairs manoeuvres and was re-joining away from the display line. For some reason he just nicked the top of the woods with his wingtip and was killed instantly. This happened quite late in the winter training season, so we had to get another pilot in pretty quickly, so we took in a CFS Gnat instructor, a chap who was on exchange from the Royal Australian Air Force, and that was the first and possibly last time that the Red Arrows had a non-RAF team pilot.

"We had a pretty good time off-duty, even during the winter season, I lived in the Mess at Little Rissington, and there were lots of nice local pubs in the area, and during the display season we went to whatever functions were arranged at the show site, or we'd arrange our own event at our operating base if it was away from the show site. In 1969 when we went to Paris, we were allowed to take wives and girlfriends, so we had an enjoyable time in Paris when we weren't flying.

"During my first tour with the Red Arrows, I don't recall being involved in the introduction of any major new manoeuvres. We did try some formation shapes, but eventually we decided that they weren't 'guaranteeable' so we stuck with the formations we actually flew. When I was the Synchro in 1970 we invented the Boomerang manoeuvre which required us to approach from behind the crowd at 45 degrees towards each other, crossing at datum, and then flying up into a loop, rolling off the top back towards the crowd, and then crossing again at datum before leaving at 45 degrees to the crowd line again.

"The Gnat is probably my favourite aeroplane. I've flown lots of types such as the Hunter, Lightning, and Harrier, but from pure flying aspect, the Gnat was the most fun to fly. It was so precise and responsive. In a way this was a slight disadvantage when it came to formation flying as it was very sensitive. On a bumpy weather day it really was hard work. The power response was very quick too, and you could go from idle to full power very quickly, quicker than the Hawk can today. One disadvantage was that the Gnat didn't have separate airbrakes to flick in and out to control your speed in formation changes. The airbrake was attached to the undercarriage and it was fairly slow moving. It was also very short on fuel. We operated about 95% of the time without the underwing tanks so we relied on internal fuel, and one tank had been isolated to carry diesel oil for smoke generation. So we were pretty limited in range, no more than about 300 miles, and for a low level transit and return, our maximum display radius was about 35 miles.

"I can remember that we were once asked to do a display at 40 miles radius, which required us to operate out of Manston, and we had to tow the Gnats out to the end of the runway to give us an extra few minutes of fuel. It was certainly a critical factor. The Gnat also had a very narrow track undercarriage which could be a real handful when you're in a crosswind. I remember landing in a display in France which we had to curtail because of a thunderstorm, and the runway was pretty well flooded with a 20 knot crosswind. I streamed my braking chute, but the crosswind got it, and I went sideways along the runway until I finally came to a halt. In 1968 we did a display at Brighton, and we operated from Thorney Island. We ran in to break over Thorney Island in Nine Arrow formation and the procedure was that we didn't stream the brake chute unless the leader asked for it. I was first to land, I touched down, and it became clear that I was getting virtually no braking effect on the runway which was much wetter than we'd been led to believe. I streamed the chute, and it came out but didn't deploy properly, so I went into the barrier. I knew there would be nine people coming up behind me very rapidly, and the next chap came streaming past me as I'd taken out the barrier which was under my wheels. He went over the barrier, continued along the runway and turned-off. The next chap managed to turn-off before he reached me, and by this time I'd managed to tell them on the radio what had happened, and they started overshooting, but it was a pretty hairy business sitting there helpless, wondering whether another eight aircraft would come charging into me.

"We were lucky to go overseas quite a lot, although we never went that far afield but we did go to Germany, France, the Netherlands, Italy, Cyprus, Malta and Scandinavia, even Finland, when we were based at Helsinki. We put underwing tanks on for our transit to Finland, and it was decided to leave them on while we were over there, so we had done some training with empty tanks on to get the feel of the aeroplane which handles differently with tanks attached. About an hour before our display we heard that the Hercules had burst a tyre on landing, blocking the runway at the display airfield which was about 100 miles away. We certainly didn't have enough internal fuel to go up there, display and come back, so we worked-out that we could put fuel in the underwing tanks, use it on the transit up there and we would then have empty tanks when we began the display. It went fine although my aircraft felt a little odd, and when we split off to do a Synchro opposition loop, I realised that there was some fuel left in my right-hand tank, as my right wing dropped quite violently when I began the 5g pull-up. We all learned a lesson about making unscheduled changes.

Sqn Ldr Duckett (2nd left on aircraft) with his 1976 team

"We would often change between full, rolling and flat shows depending upon the weather conditions, and it was pretty rare for displays to be cancelled entirely. I think the worst one was when we were operating out of Manston to do a display at Southend. The weather at the two places was quite different, with a weather front going through Manston, giving a very strong crosswind way over our limits, and forecast to get even worse. Unfortunately the weather at Southend was pretty good, and the people there found it very difficult to understand why we couldn't make it. We could fly in pretty bad weather, and I remember one display when we couldn't even reverse the formation as we didn't have enough cloud base height to do that. Flying in poor conditions was mainly a problem for the leader unless the conditions were very bumpy, when the team members would have a hard time keeping a steady position within a sort of three-foot area.

"I left the team in 1970, when the RAF reminded me that I was a relatively inexperienced QFI, and they suggested that I should actually do some instructing. I persuaded them to let me go to Coltishall as a Lightning instructor, and I did my first QFI tour on an operational aircraft type, which is quite unusual. I was posted in 1974 to a Staff course at Bracknell in anticipation of a move to Strike Command on a ground tour. While I was at Bracknell it was suggested that I should consider being Red Arrows Team Leader for the 1975-6 season and I was delighted to be selected. So I didn't go to my ground job, I went back to Little Rissington. I was lucky to have experienced people around me who were never short of good advice. We were rather limited in 1975 as economy measures were in force. The team's existence was being questioned and some overseas venues were cancelled, so we flew maybe thirty shows less than normal. 1976 was much better and it was the best summer anyone can remember, and we did 109 displays that year, giving me a total of 185 displays as Leader. That year, the countryside went completely brown, the whole place looked like a desert which made navigating very interesting as even the lakes and rivers had shrunk, which changed their shape. I only got off-track once, when we ran-in to display at Manchester, arriving a half-mile right of datum, but after about three manoeuvres we were back in place although my navigating officer never let me forget it.

"In 1976 nearly half of our displays were done away from airfields, mostly over seaside resorts. It was a positive effort to take us away from airfields where the crowds were, by definition, already interested in aeroplanes. The year essentially ended with Farnborough which was blessed with good weather for a change. The final display was done on October 1st at the Dunlop Masters Golf Tournament near Chepstow which was pretty appropriate for my final display, as I'd managed to win the RAF Golf Championships that year. After we ended the display my navigator told me what heading to fly, to head back to Kemble, and off I went.

After a minute or so I looked around for the other team members and I couldn't see anyone. I started to smell a rat and I realised what had happened, that they had decided to make their own way back to base. So I went to endurance speed, flying as slowly and carefully as I could until I was at minimum fuel. I did a long straight-in approach to land, hoping that they wouldn't see me land, but they did of course, and they were waiting for me with a bottle of champagne, which was a nice gesture. I then handed-over to Frank Hoare who commented to me that I'd had such great weather for two years, I'd probably used it all up, and it turned out to be the case as his two summers were nothing like as sunny as mine!

"I was lucky enough to subsequently command N° 1 Squadron, and flying the Harrier was a demanding experience. I then commanded RAF Benson where I was Deputy Captain of the Queens Flight, and also Station Commander at RAF Stanley for four months in 1985. After a Staff tour within the MoD I went to the Royal College of Defence Studies. I was promoted to Air Commodore, and after some time in RAF Germany, London, and back at Cranwell, I arrived in Scotland in September 1993, where I expect to stay for a couple of years. Certainly, my time with the Red Arrows was very enjoyable, and probably the highlight of my flying career."

BRITISH AEROSPACE, via MICHAEL STROUD

BRIAN HOSKINS

GROUP CAPTAIN BRIAN HOSKINS enjoyed a particularly interesting and enjoyable time with the Royal Air Force Aerobatic Team, overseeing the team's transition from the much-loved Folland Gnat to the (then) new British Aerospace Hawk. From the British Embassy in Santiago, Brian recalls his Royal Air Force background; "I had been working in a London office for some three years after leaving school, and I had realised that it wasn't the career I really wanted. Joining the armed forces seemed to be the right answer for me, and although I hadn't even been in an aeroplane, a career as a pilot seemed quite appealing. The Red Arrows were first formed while I was undergoing pilot training and I saw them display at several air shows".

After completing pilot training, Brian joined N° 20 Squadron in 1966, flying Hunters from RAF Tengah in Singapore. He then trained as a Jet Provost Qualified Flying Instructor, and in 1969 he was posted to RAF Manby in Lincolnshire, joining the School of Refresher Flying where he became part of the Macaws aerobatic team (the name was derived from RAF Manby, and the resident College of Air Warfare), flying Jet Provosts, leading the team in 1970 and 1971; "after flying in this small aerobatic team, applying to join the Red Arrows seemed to be a logical thing to do".

After leaving Manby, Brian moved to Wittering, where he joined N° 45 and 58 Squadrons as a Hunter pilot and instructor until 1974 when he first joined the Red Arrows at Kemble during the last month of that year's display season. "As I had been flying in the RAF for some ten years, I knew many of the team members and had also met them on the display circuit whilst flying with the Macaws. I flew with the Red Arrows in 1975 and 1976 as number seven and then number six. I was very lucky to spend my first tour with the team in the synchro pair".

Brian continues; "For me, the most enjoyable aspect of being a member of the team was undoubtedly the flying. There were no really low points to the job, although one has to say that the RAF hierarchy didn't always understand what we were trying to achieve, and they occasionally made life a little difficult. Being away from one's family for most weekends of the summer also added more pressure. Flying fast jets on a squadron will inevitably involve the odd minor incident, but while I was with the Red Arrows, we had only one major accident while I was leading the team in 1981. Steve Johnson hit the mast of a yacht with his aircraft during a display at Brighton. The yacht didn't have any sails up and would have been extremely difficult for a member of the synchro pair to see until the very last moment. Unfortunately, the pulley shackle on top of the fibreglass mast acted like a wire cheese-cutter and took about two feet from the wing, leaving the aileron flapping ineffectively. Steve ejected from the aircraft safely.

"Off-duty life with the team was very similar to that on any other squadron, except we had many more organised functions to attend. Flying and living together as a team for a year enabled us to get to know each other very well: this led to many good times but occasionally caused some friction. As we also worked most weekends, those of us with school-age children often went for weeks at a time without spending time together as a family. I led the team for the last year of Gnat operations and for the first two years with the Hawk, so I was very much involved in evaluating the Hawk's capabilities and evolving a well-tested formation aerobatic sequence that would display the aircraft's capabilities to best advantage. This wasn't difficult because the Hawk is a delightful aircraft to fly, but we had to modify

Brian Hoskins, seated right, during the hand-over ceremony of the first Red Arrows Hawk

the use of the throttle and airbrake during aerobatic manoeuvres, and during any speed changes. The major display sequence changes were the introduction of a five/four split, and the caterpillar.

"Although I enjoyed flying all aircraft types, I think the Gnat was my favourite. It wasn't difficult to fly in formation and for a jet, the instant response to change in power setting and very effective airbrake, enabled the team to make very rapid and safe formation changes. The only difficulty with the Gnat was that even with full tanks, you always took-off short of fuel. The team's radius of action and reserve for diversion were extremely limited. I didn't instruct on the Gnat so I can't really comment on its suitability as a trainer, but I thoroughly enjoyed my own training on the aircraft, and I believe it provided excellent transition from the Jet Provost to front-line aircraft.

"As I spent five years with the Red Arrows, I obviously visited many other countries. We only undertook one major overseas tour during these years and that was to the Gulf States and Jordan. Many of the overseas displays were at sites quite different to those we experienced in the UK. The most enjoyable for me were those in valleys or on top of hills and ridges, as they allowed us to use the contours and give another dimension to the show. One of my favourite sites was Auf dem Dumpel in Germany, although I also enjoyed displaying over the lakes at Constance and Geneva. The Hawk's greatly increased range provided many memorable incidents; one that comes to mind is having sat at Luton for several hours, waiting for the weather in Denmark to clear. We eventually took-off, went direct to Aalborg, let down through cloud as a nine-ship and crossed the threshold at the moment that we were meant to start our display. The cloud base was still low but we were able to perform the majority of our flat display, much to the surprise and delight of the large and wet crowd. For similar reasons we also displayed at the Hockenheim Grand Prix out of Geneva. It's worth noting that the Hawk could leave Kemble, fly high level to Geneva and do a full display before landing, whereas the Gnat couldn't get to Geneva high level without refuelling unless slipper tanks were fitted, something the team rarely did.

"Contact with the public was a major part of the job. Most of the encounters were straightforward but people were usually interested in how difficult and how safe it was to fly with the team. The only really amusing comment I remember, which may be slightly apocryphal, was an elderly lady who assumed that there were no people in the aircraft, just robots controlled from the ground! The weather was the main cause of displays being cancelled. One year, for reasons unknown, the French authorities cancelled a display at Evreux with only 24 hours to go. Fortunately the Ministry of Defence and RAF Germany were able to make quick decisions, and we were able to go to Auf dem Dumpel instead. The display sequence was rarely altered but on the odd occasion when we were an aircraft short or when a pilot was unwell, we had to give an eight-ship display. For example, although Steve Johnson was fit and well after ejecting at Brighton, we did give an eight-ship display at Biggin Hill the same afternoon. It's impossible to choose a favourite display, as I enjoyed them all, but there were some favourite sites as I've mentioned. Sidmouth with its glorious red cliffs was memorable, and both Fowey and Dartmouth were particular favourites. Occasionally when we displayed against all odds, despite weather or aircraft unserviceabilities, the displays remain very clear in my memory.

"In the latter years of my time with the Red Arrows, all of the display sites had to be surveyed and cleared from a safety point of view, however we were still expected to display at a wide variety of locations. I left the team at the end of the 1981 display season. In those days, towards the end of the leader's last year, the team would always try to play some kind of practical joke on him. In my case, it was being briefed that after a Jersey display we would reform from the spaghetti manoeuvre and do a flypast at Alderney. I set-off in the right direction, hearing all the right sorts of radio calls, expecting the team to join me. My successor, who was in the back seat, kept reporting aircraft approaching or crossing ahead of us, to ensure that my eyes were looking in every direction except where the other members of the team should have been! Fortunately for me, but not the rest of the team, one of them made a radio call that I wasn't expecting, indicating that he was about to land at Jersey. A quick look around me proved that I'd fallen for their plan! I rushed back to Jersey to be greeted with a bottle of champagne.

"After leaving the team I went to Brawdy as OC Flying, with Hunters and Hawks, and then after a quick tour with the Ministry of Defence, I went to RAF Akrotiri where I flew everything that visited the station, and thoroughly enjoyed my first experience of helicopter flying. I will always believe that my tours with the Red Arrows were the pinnacle of my flying career although being Station Commander at Akrotiri was the pinnacle of my RAF career.

"There's no doubt in my mind that the Red Arrows achieved all that was required of them in terms of publicity, public relations and recruiting. However their role was far wider than just that. In most of our overseas visits we were clearly representing our country and our service. The fact that we were flying an aircraft built in Britain meant that we were representing all that was good in British industry. Having been overseas for the past three years, I've had little contact with the Red Arrows, but I suspect that the display, the day-to-day life and the team members will not have changed significantly. I'm convinced that each leader has brought his own style to the flying and management of the team and as in every other part of RAF life, I believe that this is a real strength, rather than a weakness of our system."

JOHN MYERS

FR AVIATION

JOHN MYERS has gone to war – only this time he's on the wrong side! Soon after his three year tour (1981-83) with the Red Arrows, Myers left the RAF and joined FR Aviation at Bournemouth and his primary job now is to provide the 'enemy' for the Royal Navy and Royal Air Force.

Did being a Red Arrow help him to adjust to civilian life?

"My tour with the Red Arrows helped me immensely to succeed in life as a civilian. The one thing it does for you is to take you out of the RAF. For three years you're not in the RAF at all; you are on a stage, you're a performer and you view it that way. You meet a tremendous cross-section of people of different backgrounds and nationalities and this gives you an insight into what goes on in civilian life. In a 'normal' RAF existence you live a sheltered life, the military is quite separate from the civilian world so being a Red Arrow gave me an ideal opportunity to find out how the other half lives. It was a great advantage for me not only to find out about civilian life but particularly about civilian aviation as we worked very closely with civilian authorities (CAA) and air traffic control".

For many years Squadron Commanders had warned applicants for the Red Arrows that the chances were that promotion within the RAF would subsequently be difficult. John Myers confirms that he had been warned that by joining the Red Arrows he would have been reducing his promotion prospects but feels that the situation has now been rectified judging by the number of promotions over the past five years. Yet during John's time as a Red Arrow many more members left the RAF after their tour than do today. John explains that "at that time when we transferred to the Hawk we had an older team. The members were very experienced people, they had to be with a brand new aircraft coming into service. I've noticed however over the last few years that the actual average age of the team has reduced dramatically and I think that has made the difference. Also, of course, people are being promoted at a younger age. If there had been more promotions after a Red Arrows tour maybe more would have stayed on.

"I was, in fact, promoted after my tour so it's not the reason for my leaving; mine was entirely family driven. One is taking quite a gamble leaving the RAF, one goes from total security to the great unknown. In the services, you'll never be rich but you'll never be poor. However, at least you know that you are an expert in your particular field and that is why almost all who leave end up in aviation-related jobs".

John went straight back into aviation after leaving the RAF. Although he had been offered three airline jobs, he also had a call inviting him to fly Hawker Hunters at Yeovilton. His life as an 'enemy' had started.

The Hunters are equipped with underwing threat-simulator pods intended to provide the fleet with specific electronic threat such as an air-to-surface missile of the 'Kitchen' and 'Kelt' type fired from a 'Backfire' or 'Blinder' bomber. A Falcon 20 business jet, converted for miltary use, flown by FR Aviation crews, provides the threat platform and is able to reproduce the attack radar signature of virtually any airborne threat radar. During the attack the ship will see and hear the reproduction of the attack aircraft's radar in search, acquisition and locked-on fire mode. At the appropriate time the Hawker Hunters are launched at the ship and the ship will then see and hear the simulation of the missile. Once the Hunters have flown over the ship they can rejoin the Falcon for a second or third attack; much cheaper than firing real missiles. "Anyway, the real thing might make holes in the ships," John explained with a grin.

At FR Aviation John has over thirty aircraft under his command. "We're not only responsible to the Royal Navy for training ships coming into service, but we complete their radio, radar and weapons systems calibration as well. We also tow targets for them to shoot at, either with guns or missiles. We are also very specific in our briefing to gun crews, we PULL the target; we don't PUSH it! We then carry out threat simulation runs in order to allow them to check out their Electronic Support Measures and Electronic Counter Measure equipment, we then jam their radars so that they can learn to actually see through our jamming. We then put the whole package together and we have what is called a 'Thursday War' – Every Thursday we go to war. This exercise is carried out under the control of the Flag Officer Sea Training at Portland. He has a group of ships under his command that actually come through a set training programme and we are involved every week in training them. So that before they go into a specific area of hostile operations we will have taken them through situations that are very representative of the real thing.

"I am the Project Director of a new contract with the RAF. The full contract is not due to start until June, 1995; however, we do have an interim service available now. The service to the RAF will be very similar to that provided to the RN. It is a civilian replacement for the 360 Squadron Canberras who are the electronic aggressor squadron at the moment. We will have a facility at Teeside Airport with six aircraft and two aircraft based here in addition to the fleet that we currently have. Our fleet can also carry out ancillary jobs such as passenger flying, freight and surveillance for the Ministry of Defence. We can also fly VIP charter flights for business and commercial customers. In addition to the twenty-two Falcons, one of which is based in the South of France carrying out similar military operations with the French Navy, we also have two Cessna 441 Conquests which can tow targets and can be used as silent target aircraft. They can also provide an airport radio calibration facility. We also have four surveillance aircraft as we are responsible to the Ministry of Agriculture, Fisheries and Foods (MAFF) for the surveillance of UK waters up to 200 miles from shore".

Undoubtedly all this is very new for a country that has always had these services provided by its armed forces. Yet in an era of reduced Defence expenditure, the Armed Forces of many nations are increasingly seeking cost-effective, reliable and responsive civilian organisations to perform vital tasks in the military support area. Amongst its many services, FR Aviation offers a total Air Defence Training package which can be flexibly mixed, programmed and flown in accordance with varied requirements, from a single aircraft to exercise a single system to a large, yet safely integrated formation, to satisfy the training needs of a major land, sea or air Commander.

John's feelings are that, 'contractorisation', as the Government refers to it, is here to stay and it's going to increase. We are the cheap effective option; it's pointless hanging electronic pods on a Tornado and have it fly against other Tornados, that is a very, very expensive asset and it's not doing the job it was designed to do. The Falcon is just a normal business jet designed to military specifications which can do the job very efficiently, cheaply and effectively. We provide a team of specialist pilots and electronic warfare operators with many years of experience in the successful design, planning and execution of often complex training exercises to meet exacting requirements".

John's new job may be exciting and exacting yet memories of the Red Arrow tour still stand out like a beacon. Going back in time to those days, John well remembers the flag-waving overseas tours. "I remember them as being tours of very large markets. One in particular that we thought we would never break into

was the Middle East where in 1981 we ended up not only selling Hawks to the United Arab Emirates, but also a good deal of British products and technology as well. Another market that is traditionally very difficult to break into is the United States – ask any businessman. Yet with BAe and McDonnell Douglas we helped to market the VTX-TS (Goshawk) to the US Navy. They looked at the RAF Central Flying School (CFS) system, which is the oldest flying school serving the oldest air force in the world and were impressed by the excellence of this school, coupled with the efficiency of the Hawk as a trainer aircraft and this combination convinced the US Navy to take the Goshawk (a Hawk redesigned for carrier operations)".

A Red Arrows tour is as exciting as it is tiring but at the end of it all is it really all it's made out to be? John comments: "There is a lot of glamour in being an Arrow, but there are minuses as well. Being a Red Arrow doesn't just take you out of the mainstream Air Force for three years,it deprives you of your family for three consecutive summers. I looked in my logbook recently and found that we had flown three displays in one day in three different countries and, at the end of a three-day period, I think we had completed eight displays in five different countries. In fact, what I found most difficult was not really the flying but the continuous nature of the job. In winter, although you're based at Scampton, you find that you're flying the equivalent of four displays a day – practice displays. Be it either a half formation or full formation, it's still a display. Then off to Cyprus for the work-up and there again it's three displays a day until the summer season begins again, so it's hard work throughout the year".

I asked John whether he thinks that the Arrows' displays have changed much during the ten years since he left the team and his reply was: "The basics are and will remain the same. There's not much new that you can do that is safe and predictable and I think these are the two operative words. Primarily the display has got to be guaranteed and safe; you must be able to fly each manoeuvre to perfection, which is, of course, the purpose of the winter season. We would construct and regularly rehearse new manoeuvres. Often they would look simple and safe on paper and in theory they should work. However, when flying them for the first time, the results could be both surprising and occasionally very frightening".

After ten years as a civilian, John Myers considers himself to be one of the lucky ones. Many of his former team mates are flying passenger jets and therefore doing the thing they love; John is flying jets too but he is still in an operational environment and his 'squadron' is organised very much on military lines. "We take the best elements of military operations and civil operations and put them together; that way I believe we achieve the best possible solution". Apart from the fact that now he's on the 'wrong side', life is not much different from life in the RAF – and he's enjoying every minute of it.

The majority of the RAF's fleet of VC10s are being converted into tankers by FR Aviation at Bournemouth

FR AVIATION

ERIC STEENSON

ERIC STEENSON (4th from the left) joined the Royal Air Force in March 1966 as a Cranwell cadet, graduating as a Pilot Officer in August 1968. After flying Jet Provosts at Cranwell, he moved to Valley where he flew the Gnat and Hunter, eventually joining the Lightning fighter force with N° 111 Squadron at Wattisham. He then joined the Vulcan-bomber force, transferring to N° 35 Squadron in Cyprus in 1973, and during the following year he was in Cyprus during the Turkish invasion as he recalls; "it was quite an interesting time to be in Cyprus, I remember being woken up one morning when they blew-up the Communist party headquarters in Limassol, about two hundred yards from where we were living. I always wanted to join the RAF, it was a boyhood dream, although my family had no RAF connections. I joined a Combined Cadet Force while I was at school in Bristol, and I started a little bit of Air Experience Flying. I then won an RAF Scholarship which provided me with a Private Pilots Licence at the age of seventeen, indeed I only got my driving licence some fifteen months later".

Eric continues "I suppose the biggest influence on my flying interest was my best friend's father, who was the chief test pilot for what was then Bristol Siddeley, developing the Pegasus engine for the Harrier and the Olympus engine for Concorde, and he also flew their Communications 125 and I used to be given trips during the school holidays to various manufacturing sites in Europe. I suppose everyone was aware of the Red Arrows. They came to Cranwell to give a display when I was training there, and gave us quite a show, including one particular incident which is not suitable for publication! The team also came to Valley during the winter when the weather wasn't too good at their home base at Kemble. While I was doing my Gnat training at Valley I flew in Terry Kingsley's Red Arrows Gnat back seat a couple of times, listening to him swearing and cursing. I'm six foot three so I shouldn't have even been flying the Gnat, but I cheated in my medical. It was uncomfortable sitting in the front during training, and it was even worse in the back seat, trying to keep my feet out of Terry's way on the rudder pedals. From that early experience in 1968 I was well aware of the team's existence.

"When I returned from Cyprus in 1975 I was posted to the Central Flying School at Little Rissington for my instructor's course. The team was based just down the road at Kemble, and some of the Red Arrows pilots lived in the mess at Rissington, so I met quite a few people from the team, including one or two who are sadly no longer with us. I had a general interest in air shows and display flying, and that attracted me to the team even more. Prior to joining The Red Arrows I didn't really have much formation flying experience. Earlier guys often had the chance to have flown with Jet Provost teams like the Poachers and Macaws, whereas I had relatively little experience, apart from one flight with the Rothmans Aerobatic Team. I did a great deal of solo aerobatics, and at one stage I was a military representative on the British Aerobatic Association committee, helping them to organise various competitions and events, and in later years I organised the British National Championships on a couple of occasions. After the sad death of Neil Williams, I was given the opportunity to develop the Cranfield A1, a single seat aerobatic trainer, meant for full competition, but sadly it was built too stable and too heavy. It was given to me on almost permanent loan in 1979 and for three years I entered it in a number of competitions, attending airshows all around the country. I started bumping into Red Arrows team members all around the country and I got to know them pretty well".

Eric continues; "by the time I was approaching thirty-four, the powers that be were beginning to insist that I should go and work in an office somewhere. I was about to give them my choice which was to be a Squadron Commander at Cranwell when I was lounging on the grass at Mildenhall watching the air show, when a colleague came up to me and we started talking. He told me that Ray Thilthorpe was about to retire as Red Arrows Team Manager, and he suggested that I might consider taking over. Although it would be a ground tour, it would include lots of flying, and I figured that this wouldn't be such a bad idea. The next day John Blackwell sat down with me and we chatted about it, so just a few days later I received a call asking me if I'd like the job. Of course I said 'you bet', and off I went to Valley to do a conversion course onto the Hawk.

"I was very fortunate in that I was used to doing basic formation flying after being a Jet Provost instructor at Finningley, so I came to the job with a reasonable flying pedigree, and with lots of air show experience. The team was still at Kemble in 1972 but I only saw the winter there, and my first administrative task was to supervise the move to Scampton. Having started my RAF career at Cranwell, Lincolnshire wasn't a place which I was particularly attracted to, and the thought of moving to Scampton was pretty horrible, but the decision had been made and they are still there to this day.

"In 1983 the Red Arrows went to the USA for the second time, participating in the bicentennial of manned flight at Andrews Air Force Base. The whole tour was well-documented as I was instrumental in arranging for a television programme about the trip. Rolls Royce sent a cameraman with us and we put a film together, which we sold to the BBC. We went to Finland and Sweden in 1974 too, and of course we went to Cyprus, so these were some of the highlights. One of the real low points was Chris Hurst crashing on the first display practice in 1984, while we were in Cyprus. Having been commentator through 1973 and having watched many of the winter practices, it was easy for me to stand on top of the control tower and know exactly what was going to happen, watching the accident develop, and knowing that the guy was going to hit the ground. It was a low point for about a minute or so luckily, as by the time I got inside the tower I heard the rescue vehicles reporting that Chris was alive, which was absolutely amazing and a great relief. We had one or two other incidents, but nothing serious, and it was a very enjoyable job.

"Perhaps the biggest frustration was not being up in the air doing the job. I did some filming with Arthur Gibson and one or two other guys, and I flew virtually the whole display sequence for him to do his film work, sitting on the outside or at the back of the formation, and that was one of the great parts of the job. Life off-duty was a real pain sometimes. Her Majesty doesn't provide the best of expenses, but apart from being away from home too much in the summer, it was pretty good, and it was my job as Manager to make things as comfortable as possible, trying to get the best hotels we could afford and so on. The show organisers could never understand our position. They catered for pilots who did maybe ten shows a year, always at weekends, and each show was a big party. They didn't have to do shows during the week, and it wasn't their full-time job, and they were just out to party. I think that this is why we got an unfair reputation for being prima donnas, as I'd demand certain standards of accommodation while other pilots were happy to crash-out on camp beds and so on. Of course that wasn't good enough for a full-time team. Similarly, a pilot who just takes an aeroplane for static display, well maybe he likes living on hamburgers one weekend each month, but when you're on the road five or six days every week, the last thing you need is another hamburger, and it was always a challenge to get the team good accommodation, food and so on.

"I also lay claim for being the first Manager to organise proper transport for the Manager and cameraman. My predecessors had to beg, borrow or steal transport to get to the display sites, and I felt that it was vital that I was on the ground as safety officer, ready to warn the leader of obstructions, flocks of birds, or anything else that he couldn't see from the air. I was still qualified on the Bulldog, and the University Air Squadrons were tasked to supply Bulldogs when required. That applied for the UK but in Europe a Puma was tasked to transport us to each display site when necessary. For sites that we could not reach with fixed-wing aircraft, RAF Shawbury was tasked to supply a Gazelle, although on a few occasions the Army or even the Navy provided a helicopter. I remember the synchro pair persuading the Navy to dunk me in the harbour at Dartmouth after the show! I became quite proficient with the Gazelle, and I enjoyed flying the different aircraft types.

"Very occasionally I'd put our transportation into the hands of an air show organiser, but in those instances you never knew what you'd get. I remember one German site where they just lost interest in us after we'd displayed. I jumped up and down complaining and some flying club member put us in the back of an aeroplane to take us back to Wildenrath or wherever, and it was obvious that he'd never seen a big concrete runway before, and he slammed the aircraft down onto the ground, we were lucky not to end-up with spinal injuries! Pete Lees ejected at Sidmouth in 1984 in the middle of a display just before the Vixen Break. The seven aircraft pulled up and Pete broke out of the formation at the top of the loop with an engine fire. I was listening to this on my hand-held radio, and we had about 30,000 people listening to my commentary and it was also going-out over the local radio network. Suddenly there was Pete coming down under his parachute, and his jet disappearing into the sea. I appealed for anyone with pictures to let me have them, and someone stuck a microphone under my nose to ask me what had happened. Fortunately I'd been on a joint services public relations course, so I was trained by the rather daunting Kate Adie on how to cope in these kinds of situations. The first that the Chief of the Air Staff heard about the accident was what he heard on the local radio news, hearing my interview.

"Undoubtedly the most interesting display venues were Washington, in Texas, and a place in Finland where we got very close to the Russian border and saw a MiG on display. It was great to visit the Patrouille de France and the Frecce Tricolori on the way to and from Cyprus. During the US tour we flew at the Naval Academy at Annapolis, and it was interesting to see the Blue Angels display at the same event. We also visited the Blue Angels at their base at Pensacola where we were hosted by the local Mayor, and we were invited to a local Bar. One of the wives made a wisecrack about buying a used car from the Mayor, purely as a joke, and it turned-out that he was a used-car salesman and had provided all the cars we were driving around in. Back in the UK, I think Dartmouth was probably my favourite show venue.

"I left the team in December 1984. We had four divorces within the team that year, so I didn't leave at a particularly happy time, but I handed-over to Henry Ploczek who is a great guy, and a good friend of mine. He was no doubt the oldest Manager the team had, and one of the best administrators, and certainly one of the most capable pilots having flown in Lightning and Hunter display teams. I left the RAF when I left the Red Arrows and moved into civilian industry working in conference and video production. I co-presented a Farnborough show on the BBC and I went back into civil aviation and now fly as a captain on Boeing 737's with British Midland, based at Heathrow.

"To be honest, I don't think the time with the Red Arrows was the highlight of my RAF career, although I enjoyed all of my RAF jobs, perhaps with the exception of my time with Lightnings as too many of my friends were killed at that time. I guess it'll be interesting to see how long the team survives, but the RAF needs to recruit high calibre people, and the RAF needs to let the taxpayer know that they're being properly defended by capable pilots. The team is also a great public relations machine for British industry and the Red Arrows show off the skills of British manufacturers, which is really tremendous. My son is fourteen and he wants an RAF career, so I guess I'll start going to air shows again, but I think I'll only go if I can put him in an aeroplane, fly in during the morning and fly out in the evening. I don't know how the general public do it really, it just shows how very enthusiastic they are! I hope that the powers-that-be will keep the team going. Good luck to them! I hope very much that they survive and continue flying into the future."

ARTHUR GIBSON

Arthur Gibson, arguably the greatest of all aviation photographers, considered himself to be a dedicated amateur. He was trained as a graphic designer and it was only an inherent love for flying that steered him towards a career that would culminate in his being made an honorary member of the Red Arrows.

Born in 1926 Arthur trained as a graphic designer at the Willesden and Bolt Court Schools of Art in London between 1940-1944. In 1944 he joined the RAFVR and was trained as a Spitfire pilot; he was demobilised four years later and embarked on a career that should, by rights, have centred on freelance design. Yet as a consultant designer, he became increasingly involved in the advertising and promotion of British aircraft in association firstly with Vickers, then British Aircraft Corporation and subsequently British Aerospace. It was, naturally, an aircraft which helped to lay the foundations for his success. The aircraft was the famous Viscount and it was thanks to this airliner that Arthur was introduced to aviation photography, although up to this moment in time he considered himself to be a proficient amateur photographer, still-photography became something more than a hobby to meet requirements that arose in his design work. But it was as a film cameraman that he undertook his first air-to-air assignment and not as designer when he took to the air in the bomb aimers position of a Valetta trainer to prove the advantages of the first anamorphic cine lens.

In 1967 Gibson needed a photograph of Concorde with the Red Arrows. He was introduced to the then Red Arrows leader Ray Hanna and as a result he took his first air-to-air photographs of the team in action. His friendship with Hanna was to become a lasting one; his association with the Red Arrows was to last a quarter of a century. So enthused was Gibson with the team that he kicked off almost immediately with a privately financed documentary on the Red Arrows that had the distinction of being selected for the Royal Command Performance of 1968 and which was snapped up by Paramount for world-wide cinema release. When the Red Arrows switched from Gnats to Hawks Arthur Gibson filmed and produced another award winning Red Arrows spectacular that was extensively shown on television throughout the world. In the official programme to launch the first showing of this film in December 1980 it was stated that "like the original film, it does not attempt to present a coherent pictorial account of the Red Arrows display programme..., the aim is solely to give an impression of what it is like to fly with an outstanding jet aerobatic team and to convey at least a fraction of the speed, precision and teamwork..."

Gibson's love of adventure led to him being asked by two former Red Arrow pilots, Terry Kingsley and Peter Evans, to join them as the third member of their crew in the London to Australia air race. Their aircraft, a Marchetti SF260, was severely penalised by the race handicapping and that, together with appalling weather over the Mediterranean, robbed them of virtually all chance of winning a major award. With nothing to lose they decided to go to the aid of Sheila Scott who was grounded in Indonesia by faulty radio and navigation aids. Their attempt to escort her to Australia ended with a dramatic emergency landing on Flores Island on Christmas Day, when for 24 hours they were reported missing.

During a career that spanned over forty years Arthur Gibson photographed every kind of aircraft from tiny single-seat sporting bi-planes to Concorde and jumbo jets, from historic veterans like the Battle of Britain Spitfire to today's most advanced supersonic warplanes. In a magazine interview he once admitted that the period after a shoot until the films were developed "can be the biggest strain on your nerves – after all, you can't ring up the RAF or BAC and say: "Sorry chaps those pictures were no good - let's do it all again tomorrow".

Photographing the Red Arrows is no easy task either. When he was asked what difficulties he had encountered he said "...for instance, when I first flew with the Red Arrows, I didn't allow for the fact that some of the manoeuvres imposed something like four or five times the force of gravity on the pilots - and, of course, on the photographer. It becomes virtually impossible even to lift your camera - so you have to learn to anticipate what is going to happen and get the camera to your eye beforehand, ready to capture the split second shot you need".

In an interview with Photography magazine Arthur gave a hint at what made him such a successful photographer. "The big advantage that I possess is that, as a designer, I know precisely what final effect I need to

ARTHUR GIBSON

"I have never been afraid. I have too healthy a regard for my own skin to take unnecessary risks - so I make sure that I fly only with totally professional pilots with the same attitude!"

achieve with a picture. Most full-time photographers often have to guess at what their client wants. I'm lucky in being, in a sense, client as well as cameraman. What I aim at is capturing something of the individual character of a particular aircraft and something of the feeling of flight. My photographs are atmosphere pictures. The techniques needed to photograph a formation of aircraft differ from those that can be used when only one aircraft is the subject. If you are photographing an airliner you want to give a sense of smoothness, ease and comfort - a feeling of serenity. With military aircraft on the other hand, you are trying to capture an impression of power, speed and manoeuvrability".

Competing in two long and dramatic air races would undoubtedly harden the most intrepid aviator, yet flying over 150 sorties with an aerobatic team might conceivably provoke some moments of fear. When asked about this Gibson replied:

"I have never been afraid. I have too healthy a regard for my own skin to take unnecessary risks - so I make sure that I fly only with totally professional pilots with the same attitude!

" Some of the Red Arrows' manoeuvres look risky to spectators at an air display, I know, but few people realise how carefully they are planned and how intensively they are practised. I run bigger risks crossing Fleet Street to buy cigars. The truth is that I love flying and I love photographing aircraft in the air. And I suppose that has more to do with whatever success I have achieved as an aviation photographer than any other factor."

ARTHUR GIBSON

Arthur Gibson retired from advertising in 1988 and became the leading light in the organisation of the annual Fighter Meet for vintage warplanes at North Weald. His last sortie with the Red Arrows was on their famous trip to the Soviet Union in 1990. He was also a member of two expeditions which found the remains of the lost Doolittle bombers in China and of American B17 bombers in Rumania.

ARTHUR GIBSON

Arthur Gibson was still in his prime when he died, aged 65, in January 1992. He was a larger-than-life character who was always modest of his achievements. He has bequeathed to posterity an immense legacy of exceptional aviation photographs and books that will be the target of researchers for many years to come.

Throughout his working life Gibson had a gift for communicating his enthusiasm and inspiring loyalty among his associates. He had no supporter more loyal than his charming wife Eira, who he married during his early freelance days. Although he was very proud of his two daughters, Arthur did not fit the description of a 'family man'; he was in fact a restless workaholic. Once, when he agreed to take a rare holiday, he asked Eira where she would like to go. Rashly she replied - "Anywhere as long as there's some sand for the children." She found herself making an eventful car journey through the Sahara!!

It all started one afternoon at...

HENDON

Hawker Fury I, K1945 of N° 25 Sqn, flown by the Commander of "B" Flight during the memorable displays of 1933-35, featuring tied-together aerobatics
Colour Art: Richard J. Caruana

Members of the general public who attend airshows believe that aerobatic flying is performed for the sole benefit of providing entertainment; nothing could be farther from the truth, as aerobatic training has always been an essential element in the making of a fighter pilot. Such exercise gives the pilot confidence in himself and in his flying machine, and performed within a team or squadron it inspires confidence in the leader and in all the other members of the group. These reasons remain as valid today as they were during the early stages of manned flight.

Back in the days of the open cockpit, aerobatics already formed an essential part in the curriculum of air fighting. The pilot's own life and his success in combat depended entirely on such skill. Between the end of World War One and the mid-thirties no military pilot in the world could boast about an edge in speed or fire-power; manoeuvrability and personal qualities won the day. Within the Royal Air Force (RAF) teaching these essential tasks was the sole purpose of the Central Flying School (CFS).

To trace the origins of public display flying one has to go back to pre-1914-18 war days. Hendon had its own spectacles even then where early types of biplanes and monoplanes flew wingtip to wingtip round its pylons. Daring pilots gave exhibitions of aerobatics which included looping, then regarded as a marvellous stunt. Shortly before the outbreak of war no fewer than 60,000 spectators went to Hendon to see the start and finish of the Aerial Derby of 1914, a remarkable crowd for those days.

Excellent local transport services facilitated the assembly of large crowds at Hendon, and this must have been one of the main factors which swung the Air Ministry's influence in favour of the staging of a Royal Air Force Pageant at this base just after the end of the war; the idea began to materialise in 1920. Numerous aerodromes were busy with rehearsals for this inaugural pageant. It is no wonder that at the first Hendon air display the CFS were featured with five Sopwith Snipes. These single-seat scouts put up a spirited display which attained a remarkably high standard. A full programme of formation aerobatics was performed, including loops and rolls in perfect unison and some of the finest inverted flying which had been seen up to that time.

Bristol Fighters, then still mainstay equipment of most RAF squadrons, simulated aerial combat against two other Snipes. Also at that inaugural event an inanimate character was introduced which was afterwards to become famous at a whole succession of future displays. This was a dummy figure, nicknamed 'Major Sandbags', which descended by parachute from a kite balloon as soon as this balloon had been set on fire by attacking aeroplanes.

Notwithstanding the enormous success which crowned this first effort, there were many lessons to be learned. The programme for the following year, for example, was better timed and a greater effort was made to secure novelties in the shape of special items.

The pageant of 1922 was marred by bad weather. Yet, though conditions were extremely unfavourable with heavy and almost continuous rain, the organisers had the satisfaction of carrying through a fine programme without having to abandon a single item, a fact which won unstinted praise from everyone.

In 1923 the main event was provided by SE5As of the Royal Aircraft Establishment (RAE). These five aircraft were led by Flt Lt PWS Bulman (later to become Chief Test Pilot at Hawkers) who put on an impressive display of formation aerobatics, including inverted flying. Highlight of the display was a surprising (and hair-raising) spin of all five in formation. By that time participation in the Hendon Pageant began to be considered as the mark of a unit's standard and RAF squadrons vied for a chance to perform. That year saw N° 56 Squadron in their shiny silver Snipes marked for the occasion with the characteristic unit red and white checks on fuselage sides and above the top wings. An item was also introduced which was to become a standard feature in each year's programme, the "set-piece" which that year included the destruction of a bridge.

The pageant's popularity had grown to such proportions that newspapers made as much of a feature of the traffic problem as they did of the event itself. The careful organisation of crowd and traffic control, which remains as essential at today's airshows as then, was learned the hard way but was tackled most efficiently. Official attitude towards the Hendon Pageant also changed as one year followed another. The first few displays were framed rather like a glorified air circus. The object was now to use the potentialities of the RAF to give the public a good flying display.

Such immense popularity and enormous attendances which they attracted soon began to impart to them an almost national significance. It was not long before it was decided to refer officially to this great event as 'The Display'. This was followed by an official edict which discouraged any idea that the display was to be regarded as a purely popular spectacle, contrived merely for the annual amusement of the general public.

The display now became very correct, very military in its precision. The set-piece for 1924, for example, was an attack by air on an armed merchant cruiser. This dummy vessel itself was a most ingenious masterpiece, a tribute to the stage craftsmanship of the mechanical department of the RAF.

By the time of the N° 17 Squadron's participation in the 1925 Hendon display (which had only been reformed the previous year on Snipes) the unit was fully constituted and put up a superb show with these aircraft marked with their new double black zig-zag on fuselage sides and above the top wing. The Gamecock, however, was the most predominant aircraft that year, together with superbly piloted Grebes and Siskins.

By the following year the RAF was flying nine-ship formations in three sections of three. N° 25 Squadron's Gloster Grebes were the stars of the 1926 edition.

N° 41's turn at showing its prowess during the Hendon Display came in 1927. The Northolt-based unit was in the phase of exchanging its Armstrong Whitworth Siskins III to the improved IIIa at that time. Carrying the unit's red bar on fuselage and upper wing, these Siskins created a sensation by performing an aerial ballet, their display being accompanied by music! Also during that year's pageant the CFS introduced its Genet Moth teams. Under his command Flight Lieutenant D'Arcy Greig led a section of five which introduced a number of novel items including the outside half-loop (or bunt) and re-introduced the formation spin. Among the members of the CFS formations were a number of names who were to become famous years later — Boothman, Stainforth, Atcherley, Chick, Boyle, Waghorn, Johnson, Pike, Constantine, Broadhurst and Embry.

RAF principal representative in March 1928 was N° 19 Squadron flying the Siskin IIIa from Duxford. The unit had already performed at Hendon on the Grebes. That year, however, the unit appeared in the silver

Gloster Grebe, J7585 flown by the Commander of N° 19 Sqn, as it appeared in 1925
Colour Art: Richard J. Caruana

Siskins with the characteristic blue and white checks on fuselage sides and above the top wing. A taste of things to come was provided by a huge monoplane which was referred to by the contemporary press as the 'Inflexible'. This great, dark-painted machine rumbled over the crowd heralding the multi-engined night bombers of the immediate pre-WWII era.

Another Duxford unit, N° 29, already well known in display circles due to its home-base open days flying Snipes and Grebes, appeared at Hendon for the first time in March 1929 on the newly-acquired Siskins IIIa. These were freshly painted with the unit's three red 'X's with a horizontal red bar above and below in the usual fuselage and wing positions. Also on the Siskin IIIa was another participant, N° 56 Squadron. However, that year's limelight was stolen by a pair of Grebes of the Aeroplane & Armament Experimental Establishment from Martlesham Heath which gave a synchronised display trailing smoke to good effect.

On to 1930 and the appearance on the scene of one of the RAF's most famous units, N° 43, a squadron which had already become famous for its daring displays throughout Britain. Resplendent in the black and white markings on silver wings and fuselage sides, the 'Fighting Cocks' flew three flights of three Siskins each. The novelty consisted in that in each flight, each aircraft was linked to the other with easily breakable cords. Tied together in this manner, the nine aircraft took off, performed their usual routine and landed with cords intact. During that year's Pageant the RAF proudly gave the Bristol Bulldog Mk II its public debut. N° 3 Squadron, which was the first to receive Bulldogs in May of 1929, had just re-equipped on the Mk IIs. A magnificent spectacle was provided by the appearance of the ill-fated rigid airship R101 which serenely cruised above the crowd against a clear summer sky.

N° 43 Squadron had converted to the superb Hawker Fury by the time of its reappearance at Hendon in 1931. Flying out from the unit's base at Tangmere, the squadron's black/white checks were proudly displayed on the new mounts and at least one aircraft, K1930, carried a black/white chequerboard on the entire fin. Another well-known RAF unit to perform during the 1931 display was N° 54 Squadron which enjoyed an excellent reputation as an aerobatic unit. It had only been reformed at Hornchurch on Siskins the year before but re-equipped with Bulldogs IIa in April 1930. For the 1931 season, the Bulldogs carried a yellow stripe on the fuselage and top wing, a marking which proved unpopular and was later changed to a red bar with white diagonal stripes. That year's CFS contribution consisted of five Gipsy Moths with distinctive red markings on the upper surfaces of their wings to enable the spectators to identify the aircraft while flying inverted — which was almost throughout the display.

In case one might think that replica aircraft are something which airshows have taken on as a recent innovation, it would be interesting to note that a number of replica aeroplanes were presented that year at Hendon. One of these was a Blériot Monoplane, similar to the one Louis Blériot had flown across the Channel in 1909. Such a public display also provided an ideal launch pad for new products and ideas, such as the appearance of the Cierva Autogiro at the 1931 Display, the first attempt at producing a creditable short take-off and landing machine.

Motorless gliders were the novelty of 1932. CFS contributed to that year's Hendon Display with a five-ship formation of Tiger Moths, painted with distinctive red markings similar to the previous year's Gipsy Moths. Bulldogs from Martlesham gave their first public display executing a perfect 'Prince of Wales Feathers' using smoke to great effect — the leader rolled while the wingmen half-rolled to either side.

The growing importance of wireless communication between aircraft in flight and ground control became an essential feature of these displays. Already illustrated to the public at previous displays, this exchange of messages reached a dramatic culmination when at one of these events, His Majesty King George V, seated at a table in the Royal Enclosure, spoke into a microphone a sequence of orders which were instantly executed by a

Armstrong Whitworth Siskin IIIa, J8664, of N° 29 Sqn, as it appeared for the 1929 display at Hendon
Colour Art: Richard J. Caruana

Bristol Bulldog, J9576, of "A" Flight, N° 3 Sqn
Colour Art: Richard J. Caruana

number of fighters thousands of feet above. Loudspeakers all over the aerodrome conveyed these messages to the public.

Starting in 1933 N° 25 Squadron took part in the Hendon Pageant for three consecutive years. The squadron had converted from Siskins to the elegant Hawker Fury I in February of the previous year. These superb aircraft enabled this unit to become one of the main exponents of formation aerobatic flying. At the 1933 display the squadron thrilled the crowds with a nine-ship formation take-off. All aircraft were tied together until well airborne when they deliberately split into three flights, each flight's three-ship formation remaining tied together throughout the rest of the display ending with a tied-up formation landing. However, this was another year when most flying was marred by "wretched weather, with heavy rain, wind and low cloud".

N° 25's exciting display was repeated with great success the following year. An interesting feature of that year's Display was a flypast by flying boats over the aerodrome that afternoon. These machines included such types as the Southampton and Singapore. Another 'heavy' on public display for the first time was the Heyford night bomber.

It is also noteworthy to record that during 1934 another "Hendon Display" was organised across the Atlantic, when N° 1 Squadron's Furies were the guests of honour at Canada's first Air Force Day on July 14, an event which was dubbed as 'Canada's Hendon'. Tangmere's 'C' Flight consisting of five Furies Mk I put up an exceptional display. They were on a tour of Canada and had already performed in London, Kitchener, Hamilton, St Catherines and RCAF Camp Borden.

1935 is recorded as the most memorable of the Hendon Pageants not only for the number of aircraft and units from within all branches of the RAF but also for the daring displays that were presented. Hawkinge's N° 25 Squadron again put up a spirited display of tied-together formation aerobatics in their nimble Furies, including new items such as changes in the formation during loops. N° 43, now also on Furies, performed an immaculate sequence. A particularly important visitor was the DeHavilland Comet 'Grosvenor House', winner of the England to Australia race.

A novel feature of 1936 was the appearance of many historical aircraft of early days, reconstructed so that they could play their part in the display. In addition, the public were able to secure a glimpse of a fast new fighter, the Supermarine Spitfire prototype.

The final Hendon Pageant was organised in 1937. An innovation at that year's pageant was N° 1 Squadron's introduction of a fourth aircraft in the 'box'. The aircraft flew far enough below the leader to avoid his slipstream. N° 25 Squadron was back, now on the Hawker Fury II, performing a low level attack on the setpiece. By now the RAF was going through an accelerated remodernisation programme as war clouds began to gather all over Europe. Both factors contributed to the swansong of Hendon's golden age. The new monoplanes, in particular, required a completely novel approach to air combat tactics.

A decision to discontinue these airshows was taken soon after the 1937 display. Preoccupation with the rearmament programme was the main reason which made the authorities consider it advisable to suspend the Royal Air Force Displays. However, it is interesting to notice how subtle was the official reason handed down to the public, no doubt in an effort to avoid any cause for alarm. The following is reproduced from a contemporary publication:

"One striking fact is that the speed and performance of the modern flying machine have made it increasingly difficult to stage any aerial display which can be seen effectually by any great gathering of people assembled on any particular spot. Anyone, for example, trying to stage with Hurricane fighters an item to be seen by people surrounding an aerodrome is confronted by the fact that these machines move through the air at so great a speed that they may be over the flying ground one minute and several miles away the next. It is much the same with the latest high-speed bombers. They, too, are here one moment and gone the next".

One seriously wonders how the Red Arrows manage today!

R.J.C.

E.J.v.KONINGSVELD